Just when we thought "job done," Europe is o
Ukraine, Brexit, divisions within the EU, confuse
the climate crisis, and the rise of neo-fascist and po
of anyone Other. And once again, our editors, Th
have risen to the challenge with this addition to the Cultural Complex series. What
is unique about this book is its utter realism and laser-like psychosocial focus on
the important things happening in the troubled continent.

Professor Andrew Samuels, author of *The Political Psyche*

Cultural Complexes and Europe's Many Souls

This timely and important new volume examines the impacts of Brexit and the war in Ukraine through the lens of the cultural complex model, in an exploration of the underlying dynamic relationships within and between countries.

There have been seismic changes in Europe in recent years, with the onset of Brexit and the Russian–Ukraine war, and pre-existing cultural complexes have erupted in fragmenting divisions and war, creating an atmosphere closest to that of the ominous animosities of the Cold War after World War II and impacting the psyche on both an archetypal and cultural level. In this volume, contributors provide early attempts to make sense of the current situation and to think about it in terms of activated cultural complexes, specifically in Britain and Eastern Europe, and perhaps across the globe.

This will be an important read for Jungian analysts interested in the underlying dynamic fueling Brexit and the Ukraine–Russia war, as well as those interested in Jungian studies, analysis and political activism, and international affairs from a Jungian perspective.

Jörg Rasche, MD, is a child psychiatrist and Jungian analyst, working in private practice in Berlin. He served for many years as president of the German Jungian Association (DGAP) and was vice president of the International Association of Analytical Psychology (IAAP) and president of the German Association for Sandplay Therapy (DGST). Also a trained musician, he has published many papers and some books on mythology, music, sandplay therapy, and analytical psychology, as well as serving on the board of various Jungian journals.

Thomas Singer, MD, is a psychiatrist and Jungian psychoanalyst who trained at Yale Medical School, Dartmouth Medical School, and the C. G. Jung Institute of San Francisco. He is the author of many books and articles that include a series of books on cultural complexes that have focused on Australia, Latin America, Europe, the United States, and Far East Asian countries, in addition to another series of books featuring Ancient Greece, Modern Psyche. He serves on the board of ARAS (Archive for Research into Archetypal Symbolism) and has served as co-editor of *ARAS Connections* for many years.

Cultural Complexes and Europe's Many Souls

Jungian Perspectives on Brexit and the War in Ukraine

Series Editor Thomas Singer

Edited by Jörg Rasche and Thomas Singer

Routledge
Taylor & Francis Group
LONDON AND NEW YORK

Designed cover image: © Jörg Rasche. Photographer: Leonid Fishman

First published 2025
by Routledge
4 Park Square, Milton Park, Abingdon, Oxon OX14 4RN

and by Routledge
605 Third Avenue, New York, NY 10158

Routledge is an imprint of the Taylor & Francis Group, an informa business

© 2025 selection and editorial matter, Thomas Singer and Jörg Rasche; individual chapters, the contributors

British Library Cataloguing-in-Publication Data
A catalogue record for this book is available from the British Library

Library of Congress Cataloging-in-Publication Data
Names: Singer, Thomas, editor. | Rasche, Jörg, editor.
Title: Complexes and Europe's many souls : Jungian perspectives on Brexit and the war in Ukraine / edited by Thomas Singer and Jörg Rasche.
Other titles: Jungian perspectives on Brexit and the war in Ukraine
Description: Abingdon, Oxon ; New York, NY : Routledge, 2024. | Series: The cultural complex series | Includes bibliographical references and index.
Identifiers: LCCN 2024014931 (print) | LCCN 2024014932 (ebook) | ISBN 9781032695112 (hardback) | ISBN 9781032695082 (paperback) | ISBN 9781032695143 (ebook)
Subjects: LCSH: European Union—Great Britain—Psychological aspects. | Russo-Ukrainian War, 2014—Psychological aspects. | Great Britain—Relations—21st century. | Europe—Relations—21st century. | International relations—Psychological aspects.
Classification: LCC D2025 .C66 2024 (print) | LCC D2025 (ebook) | DDC 327.4—dc23/eng/20240415
LC record available at https://lccn.loc.gov/2024014931
LC ebook record available at https://lccn.loc.gov/2024014932

ISBN: 978-1-032-69511-2 (hbk)
ISBN: 978-1-032-69508-2 (pbk)
ISBN: 978-1-032-69514-3 (ebk)

DOI: 10.4324/9781032695143

Typeset in Times New Roman
by Apex CoVantage, LLC

Contents

Cover image: A Hodegetria Ikon

A *Hodegetria* is an iconographic depiction of the Virgin Mary holding the Child Jesus at her side while pointing to him as the source of salvation for humankind. The Virgin's head usually inclines toward the child, who raises his hand in a blessing gesture. This type of ikon is sometimes called *Our Lady of the Way*.

This ikon was the travel ikon of a Russian-Ukrainian woman. During World War II, she was forced by the Nazis to work in Germany. The ikon was, for her, her only remaining possession from her lost homeland. She never returned to Stalin's Russia after the war. Rather, she remained in Germany.

My father was a young medical doctor in the German Army during World War II. In September 1943, he was severely wounded near Zaporizhzhia, Ukraine. He was sent back to Germany for recovery. Six months later, he was sent to the front in France where he was captured and held in a French prisoner-of-war camp until the end of the war. He was able to return to Germany at the end of the war in 1945, where he opened his practice as a general practitioner in Wurzburg. He, too, was traumatized by the Nazis and, after the war, he became an ardent pacifist. No War Again! In Wurzburg, he became the doctor of the Russian woman who, on her deathbed, gave him this ikon in gratitude.

Jörg Rasche, Berlin, 2023

Editors

Dr. Jörg Rasche, MD, lives in Berlin, Germany, and is a practicing Jungian analyst for children and adults. He trained as an analyst at the C. G. Jung Institute in Berlin and as a sandplay therapist in Zürich with Dora Kalff. He teaches at the Jung Institutes in Berlin and Zürich and in many countries. Dr. Rasche served for many years as president of DGAP (German Association for Analytical Psychology) and he is a former vice president of the IAAP (International Association of Analytical Psychology). He has published about psychoanalysis, sandplay, music and psyche, and the history of Jungian analysis. In 2016, he co-edited, with Tom Singer, *Europe's Many Souls: Exploring Cultural Complexes and Identities* (Spring Journal Books). Jörg Rasche is also a trained musician. For his work for reconciliation between the German and Polish peoples, Dr. Rasche was honored in 2012 with the Golden Cross of Merit by the president of Poland. His recent publications include *Franziskus und der Sultan* (ISBN:978-3-95612-035-0); in Italian, *Francesco e il sultano. Un'imaginazione attiva* (ISBN: 978-88-7487-470-5); *Menetekel. Der Ökozid und das Unbewusste. Was die Klimakrise mit uns macht* (ISBN 978-3-8260-7782-1); and *Spinozas Freund und die Substanz der Freiheit: Roman* (ISBN 978-3-8260-8315-0).

Thomas Singer, MD, is a psychiatrist and Jungian analyst in private practice in San Francisco. He is the editor of a series of books that explore cultural complexes in different parts of the world, including *The Cultural Complex*, Australia (*Placing Psyche*), Latin America (*Cultural Complexes of Latin America: Voices of the South*), Europe (*Europe's Many Souls*), North America (*Cultural Complexes and the Soul of America*), and East Asia (*Cultural Complexes in China, Japan, Korea, and Taiwan*). In addition, he has edited *Psyche and the City, The Vision Thing,* co-edited the Ancient Greece, Modern Psyche series, and co-authored *A Fan's Guide to Baseball Fever.* Dr. Singer currently serves as the president of National ARAS, which explores symbolic imagery from around the world.

Contributors

Jules Cashford studied philosophy at St. Andrews University and was a supervisor in literature at Cambridge on a Carnegie Fellowship. She is a member of the Association of Jungian Analysts. Her books include *The Moon: Symbol of Transformation*; *The Mysteries of Osiris*; a translation of *The Homeric Hymns*; a novel, *The Crane Dance*; and (co-authored) *The Myth of the Goddess: Evolution of an Image*. She has made two films on the Early Netherlandish painter Jan van Eyck and three films on *Gaia*: *Gaia in Ancient Greece*, *The Eleusinian Mysteries*, and *The Return of Gaia in Our Time*.

Dmitry Kotenko is an analytical psychologist. Dmitry's primary research interest concerns the dynamic life of Russian cultural complexes, the archetypes of life and death, and the variety of shapes they have taken in recent history. His research interests also include the healing of collective trauma and the effects new media have on privacy and human behavior. He lives and works in Moscow.

Ann Kutek is an analytical psychologist working in London. A graduate of the Universities of Oxford and Edinburgh, she moved into the analytic sphere in the late 1970s, becoming a family therapist, student of group processes, and Jungian analyst during a twenty-year career as a manager in local government. A spell followed as first clinical director of an early scheme offering psychological support to employees in the commercial and third sectors. Hers is an international perspective with a commitment to diversity drawn from travel on four continents, the study of history, and collaboration with analytical colleagues across Europe and beyond. She is a translator of analytical texts and contributor to Routledge books and other publications.

Natalia Pavlikova is a Jungian analyst practicing in Moscow. She is a clinical psychologist and graduate of the Psychology Department of Moscow State University. Following graduation, she worked at the Scientific Center for Mental Health and at the Clinic for Medical Nutrition as a medical psychologist. She received additional training in psychodrama and Eriksonian hypnosis. Natalia was certified as a Jungian analyst in 2010. She works with adults and has been in private practice for more than twenty years. Natalia served as vice president for the Russian Society of Analytical Psychology (2012–2015) and as president until 2023. Throughout her professional career, Natalia has developed connections between international colleagues and professional societies of different countries. She lectures on Jungian typology and psychosomatics at the Moscow Association of Analytical Psychology. In 2022, she assembled a group of psychologists to work with combatants, their families, and civilians who have been traumatized by war.

Viktoriya Roslik was born and currently lives in Kyiv, Ukraine. She is married with two adult children. Victoria received the status of Jungian analyst in 2022 and is also a sandplay psychotherapist with twenty-two years of experience working with adults and children. She has been a frequent presenter of educational programs for working with children and also conducts dream groups. She is currently secretary of the Ukrainian Jungian Association.

Gert Sauer is a psychotherapist and Jungian psychoanalyst who likes to wonder about the miracles of the human, animal, and cosmic psyche. He harbors the sometimes-crazy notion that there are issues in individual and collective crises that can be understood by persistent, careful attention. Desperately fighting with his own and others' blindness, Gert Sauer works and teaches in Freiburg, Germany, as well serving as a senior analyst and supervisor at the Institute for Analytical Psychology in Stuttgart. He has been married for fifty years to Rodtraud, with whom he has three children and five grandchildren. Gert and Rodtraud support the development of analytical psychology in Eastern Europe in the hopes of increasing Western understanding of Eastern Europe and Eastern understanding of Western Europe.

Elena Volodina lives and works in Moscow, Russia, where she maintains a practice as a Jungian analyst and supervisor. She is a member of the International Association of Analytical Psychology (IAAP) and the Russian Society of Analytical Psychology (RSAP). From 2016 to 2022, she was a member of the Ethics Committee of IAAP.

Dmytro Zaleskyi, a psychiatrist and Jungian analyst, graduated from Kyiv Medical Institute and worked at Kyiv City Psychoneurological Hospital and then at the Union Research Center of Radiation Medicine. He has held the positions of paramedic, neuropathologist, and psychotherapist. Not only is he the first president of the IAAP Development Group in Ukraine, but also, in 2010, he became the first individual IAAP member in Ukraine. In 2015–2016, he was mobilized to serve in the Armed Forces of Ukraine as the chief of the medical service of a battalion. As a member of the First Voluntary Mobile Hospital organization, he conducts tactical medical training for service personal in the Armed Forces of Ukraine in addition to working in private practice and as a volunteer.

Luigi Zoja, past president of the IAAP, is a Jungian clinical analyst trained in Zürich. He has had a practice in a clinic in Zürich and then private practices in Milan, New York, and, at present, again in Milan. He has also served as a visiting professor at the Beijing Normal University and at the University of Macao (China). His writings have been translated into fifteen languages. The books in English include *Drugs, Addiction and Initiation* (Sigo, 1989; Daimon, 2000); *Growth and Guilt: Psychology and the Limits of Development* (Routledge, 1995); *The Father: Historical, Psychological and Cultural Perspectives* (Routledge, 2001; 2002 Gradiva Award); *Cultivating the Soul* (Free Association, 2005); and *Ethics and Analysis* (A&M Texas University Press, 2007; 2008 Gradiva Award); *Violence in History, Culture and the Psyche* (Spring Journal Books, 2009); and *Paranoia. The Madness That Makes History* (Routledge, 2017).

Acknowledgments

This is not a usual book. It is more of a confession to life in a time of crisis and urgency. In the years of its preparation, we, the editors and our contributors, felt the deep disturbance of an unhinged world all around us and inside us. Sometimes we fell into states of hopelessness about the world situation and were unable to work on this project at all. Under such stress, the mind can become sluggish, as if mired in sludge. The emotions become raw, sometimes numbed, sometimes heightened. But we were uplifted again and again by friends and colleagues who created networks of mutual support. We express our deepest gratitude to colleagues in our C. G. Jung Institutes and in our professional associations: the International Association of Analytical Psychology (IAAP), the International Society for Sandplay Therapy (ISST), and the group for Analysis and Activism. We are grateful to colleagues who are managing projects such as the Social Dreaming Matrix, or online circles such as the Trialog between Ukraine, Russian, and German Jungians managed by Stefan Alder in Potsdam or With Jungian Ukrainians, led by Catherine Cox in England.

Jörg wants to add his personal thanks to David Steindl-Rast OSB of Grateful Living (grateful.org); his wife, Beate; his children; and the healing gift of being in his garden. Tom wants to thank his wife, Jane, and the healing gift of being in her garden; his children; and Allison Tuzo of ARAS. Both want to thank the contributing authors, each of whom has been more than generous in their individual contributions and who, collectively, managed to stay with this project when there was little room to think or feel clearly. We also want to thank the Routledge team and especially Katie Randall, who nursed the book as it took shape through its many iterations. Finally and foremost, we want to thank LeeAnn Pickrell, whose unfailingly kind presence, unshakable stamina, and excellence in editing actually brought this work into being.

Jörg Rasche and Tom Singer

Preface

Thomas Singer, San Francisco

In 2016, Jörg Rasche and I coedited a book about European cultural complexes entitled *Europe's Many Souls*.[1] We followed Jörg's lead in framing the book based on his experiences of Europe over decades. Jörg was born in 1950, but he had intimate knowledge of the nightmare of World War II, the post-war divisions of Europe symbolized by the Berlin Wall, and the attempts at healing between Germany and its neighbors after WWII. He knew in his bones the massive destruction of that war followed by the miraculous rebuilding of post-WWII Europe and the deep hopes for further renewal that emerged after the fall of the Soviet Union. It is worth noting that Jörg was personally honored for his work on reconciliation between the Polish and German people when the Polish president presented him with the Polish Golden Cross of Merit.

As we were working on the book, Jörg was guided by this spirit of hopefulness and ongoing renewal following catastrophe. Our book was modeled on the notion that the individuation of Europe was happening in front of our eyes. Individual nations were more fully realizing their own unique identities while at the same time joining in a new, collaborative European Union. We were getting multiple glimpses of these individuation processes unfolding in Europe through the eyes of our contributing authors. It seemed as though soul-making encounters with their individual cultural complexes were ongoing in the varied countries at the same time: many individuating nation-states contributing to one individuating European whole. The dedication of our book celebrated this idea of the many and the one coming together, with an emphasis on diversity as essential to unity:

> Cultural diversity is a precious heritage that we should treasure and protect. The soul loves variety and the human psyche needs the freedom to imagine, to play, and to create. When globalization and homogenization join forces with militaristic thinking and its unceasing expansionist politics, the soul in all its variations is endangered. This book is dedicated to *Europe's Many Souls*.[2]

Retrospectively, it was as if we were celebrating the birth of the spirit of an individuating continent. Within a few short years, however, Brexit in Great Britain and the Russian invasion of Ukraine have shattered this new spirit into conflict and chaos. It has given way to the most serious "regression" since WWII. In personal terms, this was a brutal shock to Jörg who had devoted his considerable psychoanalytic, philanthropic, and cultured energies to the development of a European world in which countries maintained their individual identities while belonging to a larger, integrating whole.

If individuation signals something about an individual or group psyche that has both differentiated out its different parts while cultivating a relatedness and wholeness among its different parts, that vision of individuation has failed us again—as it did many young Americans, including myself, in the hopefulness of a "cultural revolution" during the Vietnam era of the mid-1960s–1975 in which we imagined a world at peace, with the end of racism at home and war abroad. Clearly that version of individuation eluded us then and now, and a European version has eluded us now.

In short, there have been seismic changes in Europe since the publication of the first volume of *Europe's Many Souls* in 2016. With the onset of Brexit and the Russian–Ukraine war, pre-existing cultural complexes have erupted in fragmenting divisions and assault, creating an atmosphere closest to that of World War II and the ominous animosities of the following Cold War. This is quite different from the spirit of integration and individuation that marked the conditions under which we prepared the first edition of *Europe's Many Souls*. Now we are confronted with harsh shadow aspects as occurs within every individuation process. Nevertheless, we continue to believe that the cultural complex model offers one way to understand and bring to greater consciousness underlying dynamic and polarizing relationships within and between countries.

In an effort to bring some beginning understanding of the current unraveling in Europe through the perspective of the cultural complex theory, this volume has been assembled in the very midst of an ongoing war between Russia and Ukraine, with major involvement from many other European and non-European countries. We are in the *fog of war*, as Robert McNamara said in this book about the Vietnam War: "What 'the fog of war' means is, war is so complex it's beyond the ability of the human mind to comprehend all the variables."[3] Of course, one of the characteristics of the "fog of war" is that it can present itself as being crystal clear in its causes and purposes, its perpetrators and victims, its good guys and bad guys. The causes and purposes of the war in Ukraine can indeed seem clear enough to most of us in the West.

But we are, in fact, for the most part in the fog of war in terms of understanding the multiple layers of this complex breakdown of European society. This is not only true about the course and outcome of the war in Ukraine itself, but also about knowing with any certainty which cultural complexes have been activated and how they are affecting conflicting forces and populations. Like everyone else, the contributors to this volume are in the "fog of war," and, even when not at war, it is difficult to see one's own cultural complexes clearly. Therefore, these chapters should be received in the generous spirit of knowing that these are early attempts to make sense of dramatically shifting and unpredictable forces—military, political, economic, and psychological. The cultural complexes that add considerable fuel to the motivations and conduct of the war by the combatants and global participants are only just beginning to reveal themselves. These essays, then, are preliminary attempts to make sense of the cultural complexes that are contributing to the hostilities.

Among the major shifting forces contributing to the war between Ukraine and Russia are the roles of other European countries, the United States, China, North Korea, Iran, and, in fact, the whole world. Even as we are writing this introduction, the profoundly divisive cultural complexes that are paralyzing most political processes in the United States are threatening to splinter the previously wholehearted US support of the Ukrainian war effort. Fully exploring the subject of shifting international alliances and complexes contributing to the war in Ukraine is well beyond the scope of this volume. But I do want to say something about what this war means to the United States and those European countries that have strongly allied themselves with Ukraine.

Prior to the outbreak of the war in Ukraine, we had been witnessing a dramatic shift toward authoritarianism around the world. An increasing number of prophecies about the eclipse of the age of democracy have been uttered in recent times. and there are those in China, Russia, the United States, and other countries who have taken the position that more authoritarian regimes are the future of the world in terms of the capacity to make efficient decisions and oversee an orderly society— not to mention to consolidate the drive for power and domination of one group over others. It certainly has seemed as though the democratic societies of the world have been in retreat and decline. The fierce resistance of the Ukrainian people to what most experts thought would be a rapid invasion and conquest of their country by Russia surprised the world. It fired and united the imagination of Western nations laboring under debilitating, dystopian, and polarizing moods. Suddenly, the forces of democracy were experiencing the most unexpected reawakening of a unifying spirit from a most unexpected place. For many around the world, Ukraine became symbolic overnight of the front line in a global struggle between democracy and authoritarianism, a struggle that seems to be going on everywhere. Just as our fears were peaking that the democratic experiment was being swept away by authoritarian leaderships, Ukraine improbably rekindled a belief that democracy was worth fighting for and could stand up to the rising tide of authoritarianism.

Most of my fellow Americans were buoyed by the surprisingly successful defense by the Ukrainian people against the blitzkrieg of the Russian army. It was as if a refreshing democratic wind blew strong and clear from the East. At the same time, my good friend and coeditor of this volume, Jörg Rasche, although totally in support of the Ukrainian people, saw the American commitment of increasing military armaments as an expression of a basic American cultural complex: the military industrial complex's unstoppable will to domination. Jörg's concern was not an uncommon view of Europeans who see America's will to power through NATO as being equally dangerous, if not more so, than Russia's. Cultural complexes take many forms. From this perspective, NATO is viewed as being a pawn and extension of United States imperialism and the voracious appetites of capitalism and consumerism. From Jörg's perspective, the United States, driven by its own cultural complexes, is complicit in furthering violence in its own embrace of militarization and warmongering.

These are political positions, but they also represent deep-seated cultural complexes fueled by powerful emotions, fixed ideas, and self-selecting memories—thus, the *fog of war*.

Notes

1 Jörg Rasche and Thomas Singer, *Europe's Many Souls* (New Orleans: Spring Journal Books, 2016). To be republished in 2024 by Routledge under the title *Cultural Complexes and Europe's Many Souls, Vol. 1*.
2 Rasche and Singer, *Europe's Many Souls*, p. vii.
3 James G. Blight and Janet M. Lang, *The Fog of War: Lessons from the Life of Robert J. McNamara* (Lanham, MD: Rowman & Littlefield, 2005), p. 207.

Preface

Jörg Rasche, Berlin

One way to think about division and war in Europe is in terms of activated cultural complexes—in Russia, in Ukraine, in Germany, in Britain, in all of the Western world and perhaps the whole world, as the world now seems to be aflame everywhere, especially, most recently, in Israel and Gaza. Taking a direct look at our activated cultural complexes is as profoundly challenging as gazing in horror at one's own house going up in flames. Just as it is impossible to keep a rational mind when your house is on fire, it is equally impossible to stand by silently when friends and colleagues are suffering, violently silenced as in Russia, or even killed by anonymous rockets, or drones, or by brutal killers such as Yevgeny Prigozhin's Wagner Group or Putin's butchers in Ukraine. In our Jungian approach to such human bloodbaths, we do not espouse an ideal of absolute neutrality but find it essential to acknowledge an emotional sympathy, even identity, with victims of atrocities—however rapidly the brutal perpetrators change face. We cannot just observe "objectively" what we and the world are suffering. We try to understand and, perhaps at our best, we witness with empathy.

In a way, this book is a witness to our European house going up in flames. The chapters in this book describe the burning house from quite different perspectives, at times even diametrically opposed perspectives. Surely, war is high season for activated cultural complexes, and cultural complexes are the arena of outsized emotions and atrocious behaviors. The combatants on all sides live and die in the energy fields of these complexes. For instance, the apparent passivity and collective anesthesia of most of the Russian people who support Putin's war policies by a 70 percent margin can be seen as the product of decades of intensive propaganda and manipulation layered on top of the historic legacy of Stalinist and Tsarist terror. At the same time, most in the West have sided with the Ukrainians, more than a million of whom have left their homes and country to take shelter from the war in Western Europe. Most of the weapons for defending Ukrainian territory have been contributed by NATO states. But there are ambivalent feelings in Europe, too, because of the obvious economic and military interests of the United States. Europe does not want to become the battlefield for a third world war. And there is a growing concern about ecological destruction. Everybody is part of the ongoing events in which the collective fate of humanity is at stake.

In this second volume of *Cultural Complexes and Europe's Many Souls*, we bring together several different chapters, each of which should be thought of as early attempts by colleagues with quite different perspectives to make sense out of what is almost impossible to fathom. Living inside activated cultural complexes, on whichever side one finds oneself, is like trying "to see through a glass darkly" (1 Corinthians 13:12). As the authors of these chapters are gazing through a dense fog, each reader must thread their way through varying and conflicted narratives to see which fits best with their own impressions gleaned from newspapers and digital media, and maybe from friends in Ukraine or Russia. It might even be worth trying to keep an open enough mind (the "good enough mind"?) to see how narratives that diverge or conflict with what we are most comfortable with might have their own truth worth considering.

We must always keep in mind that all of this is so highly charged and there is so much suffering, death, and destruction on the ground that it should come as no surprise if our own unconscious cultural complexes get triggered and lead us to unexpected deep emotions and convictions that result in black-and-white thinking or the inability to reflect at all. At the end of reading through these different perspectives, it is quite possible to conclude that all of the narratives are both true enough and even false enough. A cultural complex can behave like a highly sensitive trigger on our group psychic body. To be touched by a cultural complex may feel like an electric shock that is deeply upsetting, causing something akin to a mix of vertigo and a seizure.

Some of the contributors to this book don't speak with each other anymore. It is impossible to talk to each other with a gun at your head. This contributes to a profoundly divided, almost schizophrenic atmosphere between European countries. All of the parties in the conflict claim to be on the right side of morality and history. Our Ukrainian colleagues are defending their territorial, cultural, and existential integrity; our Russian colleagues are identified with and trying to understand what it means to be a Russian in today's world.

This book, then, is about Europe's house ablaze. It burns with destructive passions and divisions. This book is not a dialogue, so there is little crossing over from the trenches of one side to the other. That crossing over, that dialogue, must start in us, the readers. We are not bystanders, but active witnesses. The state of Europe's "Many Souls" is at stake in this book. In that sense, this book is a defense of European values regarding the integrity of individuals and the rights of all women, children, and men. This defense includes the longings of both Ukrainians and Russians for a restoration of their traumatized countries, of their traumatized bodies and souls. These lines are written in October 2023 at the outset of even more horror in Palestine and Israel. Dare we even hope for an ending to the atrocities and the beginnings of a process of peace?

Introduction

Thomas Singer and Jörg Rasche

A Theory of Cultural Complexes, by Thomas Singer

The first major crack in the long-standing but somehow stable Cold War structure of Russia and the United States as the two competing world powers was the fall of the Berlin Wall in 1989. Not long after the fall of the Berlin Wall, Jörg had a dream about this massive shift in the structure of the competing superpowers and its potential dangers as well as opportunities. *In the dream, he found himself walking on a glacier that was melting and causing torrents of water to carry away trees, rocks, and anything else that got in its way.* As we know all too well now, the consequences of the thaw in Europe after the fall of the Berlin Wall have not all been positive, as Jörg's dream anticipated. His dream of the melting glacier and the raging waters brings to mind Jung's essay about Nazi Germany in his 1936 "Wotan."[1]

Archetypes are like riverbeds that dry up when the water deserts them, but can flood again at any time. Like an old watercourse along which the water of life has flowed for centuries, an archetype digs a deep channel for itself. The longer it has flowed in this channel, the more likely it is that sooner or later the water will return to its old bed. The life of the individual as a member of society, and particularly as part of the state, may be regulated like a canal, but the life of a nation is a great rushing river that is utterly beyond human control, flowing on unchecked, without guidance, unconscious of where it is going—until it is stopped by an obstacle stronger than itself. Political events move from one impasse to the next, like a torrent caught in gullies, creeks, and marshes. All human control comes to an end when the individual is caught up in a mass movement. Then the archetypes begin to function, as happens also in the lives of individuals when they are confronted with situations that cannot be dealt with in any of the familiar ways.[2]

We remain in awe of Jung's prophetic vision and his formulation of what happens to the collective psyche and nations when they experience an onrush from the archetypal layer of the unconscious. What Jung was not fully aware of in 1936 was the power and influence of the new, modern mass media as they were being so *perfectly* manipulated for the first time in history by Goebbels. The high tide of constellated archetypes in the collective unconsciousness not only provokes the media but also can be triggered by the media.

DOI: 10.4324/9781032695143-1

But, over the years, we have become increasingly aware that an exclusively archetypal perspective on events between nations can itself become dangerously misleading by generating deep, even irreparable misunderstandings. The failure to speak clearly to, and fully recognize, the immediate and specific economic, historic, and social causes of upheaval in nations can have its own disastrous consequences. Jung's "Wotan" is a perfect case in point. Wotan didn't just seize Germany. Germany was ripe for a possession because of the terrible aftermath of World War I, the Great Depression, burdensome war reparations, the humiliation of the German people, and profound shifts in economic and political forces. All of these practical and psychological factors contributed to the ripeness of a people and a nation to be thrown into fear, disorder, chaos, and a deep yearning for simple answers and clear structures. For the past two decades, we have been trying to tease out and give legs to a notion of the cultural complex in which we might better understand what happens to the psyche of a people when unconscious forces stimulated by social, economic, religious, and other disruptive forces reawaken old conflicts and wounds that then give way to the breakthrough of destructive archetypal possessions.

Clearly, what Jung wrote in 1936 resonates with our current crisis between Russia and the West. The ancient, archetypal riverbed of rivalrous conflicts is once again overflowing with a rushing torrent that threatens to flood the world. This is happening at the archetypal level of the psyche. But it is also happening at the cultural level of the psyche where contemporary forces—religious, economic, political—are shaping the form in which the archetypal contents are expressing themselves. We think of this cultural level of the psyche as existing in the mid-belly or mid-region of the collective psyche—existing part way between the deep collective unconscious and the personal unconscious in a realm that Joseph Henderson called the "cultural unconscious."

Archetypes and Cultural Complexes

Our old Jungian theory of archetypal possession unleashing destructive forces is good on its own terms. But it has gotten stale in its application when everything unpleasant, whether it be in the individual or the group, is explained away by the "shadow." Once we begin to use the "shadow" to explain every destructive force in the psyche, we stop thinking. We stop asking essential questions that have to do with the specificity of forces at work in a particular place, to a particular people, at a particular time. We need to concern ourselves with basic questions of history, economics, sociology, anthropology, and religious studies to get a sense of what is happening in the world and what is happening in the collective psyche. At the same time, none of these specific disciplines addresses the question of how these various forces take shape and live in the psyche of individuals and groups.

In order to answer questions about where economic and other cultural forces live inside of people, we need to consider the reality of the psyche. The kinds of opinions and emotional reactions that people have to events both close to and far away from home usually have bits and pieces of history, economics, sociology, and so on, in them—but their life in the psyche of the individual or the collective is not organized according to these disciplines. In fact, what order these ideas and feelings have in the psyche can be inchoate, rapidly shifting and yet paradoxically long-standing, and often quite immune and impermeable to the reason that traditional disciplines of thought would impose on them.

Our central thesis is that all of these various forces take shape in what we are calling *cultural complexes*. This is how they live in the psyche. We believe a theory of cultural complexes helps us understand how people think and feel about many of the major events and forces that shape their lives. In that sense, this is not sociology, which is descriptive of how these things look from the outside—not how they live inside. We have said before that the study of cultural complexes is more like an inner sociology with a bit of history, psychology, anthropology, economics, mythology, sociology, and even poetry thrown into the stew, everything except perhaps mathematics and physics. Therefore, this is not a book about history, although there is lots of historical information. It is not a book about mythology or religion, but there is a lot of them, too. It is not about economics or anthropology or poetry, but there is a lot of them as well. It is about how all of these things form a living reality of ideas, beliefs, memories, feelings, images, and behavior in the psyche. This living reality does not provide a particularly coherent narrative or linear sequencing of facts and events. At the same time, it shapes what it means to be a European, to be a citizen of a particular country or city or region of Europe. It contributes to the many souls of Europe. If we want to understand something about that, cultural complexes are one way of approaching this most elusive subject. Another way of saying this is that complexes exist in the psyche, and history exists in the mind. In this study, we are interested in the many cultural complexes in the psyches of Europe.

What Are the Characteristics of a Cultural Complex?

This book is the seventh in the Routledge series on cultural complexes. Previous volumes have been about Australia, Latin America, the United States, Southeast Asia, a first volume on Europe, and an original volume on the notion of cultural complexes around the world. In a sense, each of these books, including this most recent one on Europe, is an exercise in exploring what a cultural complex is.

Early on, when Sam Kimbles and I were thinking through basic aspects of the cultural complex notion, I felt it important that we define the characteristics of a cultural complex in simple language that would be easy to understand and apply in a variety of settings for those who found this particular perspective useful. In addition, I thought it was important that we keep our language consistent with what had gone before in our tradition. Because Joe Henderson defined a *cultural unconscious*, it made sense to talk about cultural complexes rather than group complexes, for instance. As a result, I have developed, along with my esteemed colleague Chauncey Irvine, a set of characteristics that allows us to define and recognize a cultural complex. We have made the language of cultural complexes consistent with the theories of analytical psychology that have gone before. Over the past two decades, in the books that I have put together, the following characteristics have emerged time and again in the ninety separate chapters contained in these volumes about cultural complexes in various parts of the world:

- Cultural complexes are autonomous. They have a life of their own in the psyche that is separate from the everyday ego of an individual or group. Sometimes they are dormant. Sometimes they become active in the psyche and take hold of one's thoughts, feelings, memories, images, and behavior.
- Cultural complexes are repetitive. The ongoing life of a cultural complex goes on uninterrupted in the psyche of an individual or group, sometimes for generations and even millennia. When they are activated, they are surprisingly unchanged, in the sense that they are recurring, repetitive, and expressive of the same emotional and ideological content over and over again.
- Cultural complexes collect experiences and memories that validate their own point of view. Once a cultural complex has established itself, it has a remarkable capacity—like a virus replicating—not only to repeat itself but also to make sure that whatever happens in the world fits into its pre-existing point of view. Cultural complexes are extremely resistant to facts. Everything that happens in the world is understood through their point of view. In this context, for example, one might think of climate change deniers as caught in a cultural complex. Cultural complexes collect experiences and self-affirming memories.
- The thoughts of cultural complexes tend to be simplistic and black and white. Although they form the core cognitive content of a cultural complex, the thoughts themselves are not complex. They are unchanging and without subtlety. They are rigid and impervious to modification. Indeed, they seem to be impermeable to any outside influence.
- Cultural complexes have strong affects or emotions by which one can recognize their presence. Knee-jerk affectivity or emotional reactivity is a sure sign that one has stepped on a cultural complex.
- Not all cultural complexes are destructive; not all cultural complexes are ego-dystonic to the cultural identity of a group or individual. Indeed, some cultural complexes can form the core of a healthy cultural identity.

Another parallel set of criteria that I have developed as a way of identifying a cultural complex involves a series of questions about the various types of mental activity that are recruited when a cultural complex is triggered. A good way to think about a particular cultural complex is to ask the following questions:

- What feelings go along with this complex?
- What images tend to appear with this complex?
- What memories come to mind when this complex is activated?
- What behaviors are triggered by a particular complex?
- What stereotypical thoughts recur with a particular complex?

When you read the various chapters of this book, you will discover that the individual authors do not necessarily describe a cultural complex by listing these characteristics. Careful reading of each chapter, however, will reveal the presence of most of these characteristics. I am convinced that we will be able to identify what we are calling cultural complexes in the neurophysiological laboratories of the future. Areas of the brain associated with memory, affect, image, thought, and behavior will "light up" and be linked when a trigger word activates a cultural complex.

Cultural Complexes: Psychopathological or Normative?

In the course of working on this series of books over the past two decades, I have found myself becoming more and more focused on cultural complexes that cause problems in a society or cultural complexes as being the psychopathological land-mines of a culture. Certainly, the cultural complexes that catch our attention are the ones that cause disturbances in society. For instance, in the Australian volume, *Placing Psyche*, considerable attention was given to the various ways indigenous people have been treated by the non-indigenous immigrants to Australia over time. It is not a pretty picture; social attitudes toward the Aboriginal people are clearly in the realm of entrenched cultural complexes that we can say are psychopatho-logical. The same can be said of antisemitism and anti-Islamism in Europe and the West. And the same can be said of entrenched attitudes to Black and Brown people in many parts of the world. These are expressions of deep-seated, long-standing cultural complexes that are causing enormous problems today. But it is a mistake—and one that I have fallen into often in my work—to think of cultural complexes only as psychopathological. They can also be normative in the same way that Jung characterized the ego as a complex. Another way of saying this is that one can define a cultural complex with all the characteristics that I have outlined previously, and it does not mean that the cultural complex is necessarily destructive or that it goes against the grain of what is best about a culture.

Cultural Complex, Identity, and Soul

Related to the issue of cultural complexes as normative or psychopathological is the issue of the relationship between cultural complex, cultural identity, and the soul of a culture. In *The Cultural Complex*, I wrote the following:

Cultural complexes are not the same as cultural identity or what has sometimes been called "national character," although there are times when cultural complexes, cultural identity and national character can seem impossibly intertwined. For instance, those groups emerging out of long periods of oppression through political and economic struggle must define new identities for themselves which are often based on long submerged traditions. This struggle for a new, group identity can get all mixed up with underlying potent cultural complexes which have accrued historical experience and memory over centuries of trauma and lie slumbering in the cultural unconscious, waiting to be awakened by the trigger of a new trauma. In the fierce and legitimate protest for group identity freed up from the shackles of oppression, it is very easy for groups and individuals within the group to get caught up in cultural complexes. And, for some people, their complexes—cultural and personal—are their identity. But, for many others, there is a healthy cultural identity (or "cultural ego") that can clearly be seen as separate from the more negative and contaminating aspects of cultural complexes.[3]

It is not always clear if one is talking about a cultural complex, cultural identity, or even the soul of a country as they can all shade into one another, particularly as one gets closer to normative along a spectrum of psychopathological to normative. The more psychopathological a cultural complex appears to be, the less likely it is to get confused with cultural identity. Furthermore, a people's sense of their soul can often be forged out of their struggle with their cultural complexes and search for a national identity. Thus, soul, complex, and identity seem to grow out of one another and into one another. They can also cause great harm to one another.

Structure of the Book, by Thomas Singer and Jörg Rasche

We have divided this book about European Cultural Complexes, specifically about the war in Ukraine and Brexit, into three separate parts: (1) Pre-existing Cultural Complexes in Great Britain, Germany, and Russia; (2) Cultural Complexes Emerging in the Context of a Europe Divided and at War; and (3) Complexes and Archetypes.

Part 1: Pre-existing Cultural Complexes in Great Britain, Germany, and Russia

Chapter 1, Jules Cashford: Britain: Autonomy and Insularity in an Island People

Jules Cashford's chapter was shifted from the first edition of *Europe's Many Souls* (2016) to this new volume. It is a brilliant analysis of fundamental aspects of a core cultural complex of Great Britain. By examining the historic origins of a world empire in an island people, unappeased shadows of its heroic past and colonial expanse, phantom pain after the loss of empire, and the struggle for a cultural identity under drastically changed conditions, Jules Cashford lays bare a clear look at a foundational cultural complex that contributed to Brexit.

*Chapter 2, Gert Sauer: About Two Cultural Complexes: The German
Complex of Superiority and the Russian Complex of Feeling
Encircled by Hungry Barbarians*

Gert Sauer's chapter, also migrating from Volume 1, draws a picture of mutually reinforcing, complementary cultural complexes in the German and Russian psyches. Six years before Putin's invasion of Ukraine, Sauer described the Russian cultural complex of feeling "encircled by hungry barbarians" that finds its reciprocal pairing in the German cultural complex of superiority. It is hypothesized that both complexes, although different in origin, history, and content, grow out of the need to compensate for deeper inferiority or guilt complexes.

Chapter 3, Luigi Zoja: Russia, a "Therapy" for the West?

Luigi Zoja takes us on an unexpected excursion into what we can think of as a cultural complex fantasy in which the timelessness and spaciousness of an aspect of the Russian inner and outer landscape serves as a compensation for the relentless timebound march of the "productivity compulsion" that consumes the Western imagination and psyche. Zoja's untimely, counterintuitive drift is certainly not the first thing we think of when we contemplate the Russian invasion of Ukraine. It also takes us to another level of the psyche that is neglected at our own risk: the postmodern Western relationship to space and time and materiality that is devouring us. In Zoja's words:

> The Westerner is short-winded and suffocates inside the boundaries of place and time, which are intertwined. . . . The magic of the infinite for which we postmodern Westerners have felt acute regret as long as we have lived in a world in which everything is measurable, materializable, and finite, appears to manifest itself above all in the Russian landscape, in the irreversible sadness that every Russian epiphany leaves in our ears and in our eyes. . . . This yearning for Russian immensity also tells us how immense our shortcomings are.

Chapter 4, Elena Volodina: The Mysterious Russian Soul

Another refugee from Volume 1, "The Mysterious Russian Soul" explores the unparalleled Russian cultural heritage known as the Great Russian Literature. All the characters of the great Russian novels live within the national unconscious and represent collective aspects of autonomous emotionally charged complexes, which can, under the right circumstances, constellate and take over a person completely. By becoming conscious of these complexes, the national character becomes conscious of itself and its suffering collective soul.

Part 2: Cultural Complexes Emerging in the Context of a Europe Divided and at War

Chapter 5, Ann Kutek: A Tale of Two Referenda: Convulsions in the Post-Brexit United Kingdom and in Ukraine

At either extremity of Europe, historic passions have broken through again in the last decade to see a renewed cycle of harm exacted from its peoples as well as from the planetary environment. Even a cursory historic perspective into both situations suggests the hypothesis that striking commonalities and parallel patterns can be discerned from each situation, the post-Brexit United Kingdom and invaded Ukraine. The chapter examines some of the psychosocial features of the fault lines exposed and the damage caused in each situation

Chapter 6, Dmytro Zaleskyi: The War of Symbols

This chapter begins with reflections about the traumatizing effects of an acute and ongoing war. It inquires about the moment when people, under wartime conditions, find a way of returning to an active existence and a sense of life. In the background of the acute war are the repetitive traumas of the "bloodlands" as well as the democratic development in Ukraine after its independence.[4] In contrast to this is a "mass amnesia" in Russia. Two different ethical systems are described, which exist in parallel, in Ukraine and Russia.

Chapter 7, Dmitry Kotenko: Transcorruption: Russian Boundlessness and Shadow Aspects of European Civilization

This chapter examines the phenomenon of *transcorruption*, a term that encompasses not only Russian corruption processes but also the occurrence of transnational collaboration by Western nations in collusion with Russia that are aimed at concealing illegally acquired funds. The author analyzes the multifaceted relationships between Russia and the West, asserting that Russia can be viewed as a shadow reflection of the West. With a particular emphasis on the two cultural complexes of boundlessness and lawlessness within the interwoven fabric of the Russian collective psyche, the author describes the underlying factors that contribute to their emergence and profound influence at both individual and collective levels.

Chapter 8, Viktoriya Roslik: Perseus: A Myth for Our Times

The chapter by Viktoriya Roslik offers an archetypal perspective on the hero both in Greek mythology and in Ukraine today. Complementary to Zaleskyi's view, she focuses on an original Ukrainian symbolism and historical narrative, namely the Zaporozhian Cossacks. Heroism, the activated archetype of a positive warrior, helps the fighting people. Attached to the chapter is a letter exchange with coeditor Jörg Rasche about the ambivalence of archetypes that are never only positive or negative.

Chapter 9, Natalia Pavlikova: Inside the Russian Complex

This chapter looks at elements of the inner psyche in Russia today. It raises questions such as: Is it possible to remain a citizen of Russia and not obey the orders of the country's leadership? It explores the roots of cultural and ethnic identity in the former USSR and how the collapse of the former Soviet Union led to an individualistic way of surviving and a kind of re-archaization of the society. What is happening now in Ukraine has its roots in the processes that were frozen in the 1990s. Pavlikova opens a perspective for us on the dramatic dilemma of a Russian society that has lost its guiding center and has fallen into an abyss. Pavlikova does not name the current state of Russia as dictatorship or a kleptocratic horde. But we can sense a deep uncertainty in her mood, just as one senses a profound dystopian mood in so-called democracies such as Netanyahu's Israel or the deeply divided state of American democracy.

Part 3: Complexes and Archetypes

Chapter 10, Thomas Singer: Archetypal Defenses of the Group
Spirit in Russia and Ukraine: The Axes of Destruction

In this chapter, Singer explores, through a collage of images, an archetypal frame for understanding the crisis in Eastern Europe. Archetypal forces, cultural complexes, and personal lives get caught up in the maelstrom of activated defenses on both sides of the conflict, which wreak havoc and destruction on civilized society. Symbolic imagery is one way to evoke the deep psychic forces that unleash highly charged emotional energies. The chapter explores how these demonic forces might be transformed into the daemonic energy of creative transformation.

Chapter 11, Jörg Rasche: War in Europe

The short spring for *Europe's Many Souls* began in 1989 with the end of the Cold War but has now ended in a terrible way. The Maidan revolution in 2014 was the signal for an emerging democracy in Ukraine, but Russia has unveiled a brutal face that we overlooked for years with our Western blue-eyed romanticism. Gorbachev's peaceful revolution now seems to have been too easy. Most of us were not aware that the basic conflicts and traumas of two world wars and the lies of the last century were not wiped out overnight, either in the West or in the East. We were not aware of the still-persisting groundswell of totalitarian mentality and attitudes in Stalin's, and now Putin's, empire. Most of us did not come to realize soon enough what the shadow sides of the melting mental permafrost of the Cold War would bring. We did not anticipate the negative effects of the winner attitude of the capitalist powers in the worldwide liberal economy and of the loser attitude of those who did not thrive in that environment. The shadows of the cultural complexes of capitalist democracies and totalitarian communism were not done with one another. And we overlooked the suffering of those people and states who were the victims of the new transformations. We didn't observe what Solzhenitsyn or Vaclav Havel so often emphasized, based on their experiences in the totalitarian state: that freedom cannot be kept and preserved without responsibility. Freedom means responsibility and maintaining an awareness of one's enemies and a readiness to defend peace.

Notes

1 C. G. Jung, "Wotan" (1936), in *The Collected Works of C. G. Jung*, vol. 10, eds. and trans. Gerhard Adler and R. F. C. Hull (Princeton, NJ: Princeton University Press, 1968).
2 Jung, CW 10, § 395.
3 Thomas Singer and Samuel L. Kimbles, *The Cultural Complex: Contemporary Jungian Perspectives on Psyche and Society* (London: Routledge, 2004), p. 5.
4 *Bloodlands: Europe between Hitler and Stalin* is a 2010 book by Yale historian Timothy D. Snyder. It is about mass murders committed during World War II in territories controlled by Nazi Germany and the Soviet Union.

Part 1

Pre-existing Cultural Complexes in Great Britain, Germany, and Russia

Chapter 1

Britain

Autonomy and Insularity in an Island People

Jules Cashford

Anyone trying to discuss a cultural complex must be presumed to be speaking, to some degree at least, out of that very cultural complex they are trying to discuss: "Only the psyche can know the psyche," Jung warns.[1] So the question shifts as to what, in each case, is chosen to serve as a perspective upon the value judgments that an individual of a particular culture will be implicitly making, not least in the selection of evidence, asking, first, why would I (or anyone else) select and call this "evidence," which is to say, "what are the criteria?" And second, how do my (or anyone else's) criteria reflect my or their fundamental paradigm, and further, on reflection, would I call this paradigm predominantly collective or individual (bearing in mind that these terms themselves have acquired values, which themselves reflect . . ., and so on)? Because we can never entirely break free from circularity, it seems important to set out the sources and influences that will be serving as my best attempt toward a more objective point of view than I could reach without them, though of course they are ultimately no more objective than any others since they are my own choice.

Nonetheless, when Jung said that Philemon taught him the "objectivity of the psyche," he—or they—were implying that the closer we are to the collective unconscious (and the further away from the ego), the more likely we are to receive images with no designs on us, except perhaps the deepest correction to the orientation of a worldview.[2] This would be an orientation that is either out of balance and in need of compensation, or simply the creative disorientation of the process of continual evolutionary change. "In the collective unconscious of the individual, history prepares itself," Jung says.[3] Since poetry is also an expression of the collective unconscious, as are all forms of art and mythology, I will be turning to them initially as potential sources of wisdom, invoking Shelley's claim that "poets are the unacknowledged legislators of the world."[4] For some checks and balances on what constitutes "evidence" at this particular time, I will be calling on witnesses from a variety of newspapers, letters, and articles, as well as contemporary discussions on television.

DOI: 10.4324/9781032695143-3

The Archetypal Core

The idea of a cultural level of the psyche, or a *cultural unconscious*, existing between the personal and collective unconscious, allows us to talk of cultural complexes in the same way that we talk of individual complexes, so that we can talk of the pathology and psychopathology of a group or nation, asking where strengths or imbalances may tend to appear. Tom Singer has defined cultural complexes as "emotionally charged aggregates of ideas and images that tend to cluster around an archetypal core and are shared by individuals within an identified collective."[5] Because cultural complexes have archetypal cores, as do personal complexes, they "express typically human attitudes and are rooted in primordial ideas about what is meaningful, making them very hard to resist, reflect upon and discriminate."[6]

When we speak of the "cultural unconscious," or the "cultural level of the collective unconscious," it is clear that we are speaking descriptively, but, when we use the language of *cultural complexes*, we need to distinguish whether we are talking descriptively (that is, pointing to what we see as a fact) or normatively (that is, making a value judgment, whether explicit or implicit), even though the context usually makes it clear. Turning to etymology as holding the earliest meanings of words—the mythic and poetic impulses of their original formulations—the word *complex* comes from the Latin *com*, meaning "together," and *plex*, meaning "to plait, braid, twine, weave, twist," also "embrace, entwine," and so a way of describing a number of things woven together, a relation of disparate elements, an aggregate. The term *complex*, however, is more often used in Jungian psychology in a pejorative tone to refer to a "knot" in the unconscious, where elements are intertwined that do not in themselves belong together, which, if brought into consciousness, may be usefully separated. By the same token, consciousness may itself assist the releasing of the complex into consciousness by trying to recognize and then discriminate between the elements of which it is composed. For we know that "what is unconscious is projected, that's the rule," Jung says, with a warning that "projections change the world into a replica of one's unknown face."[7]

I shall use the word *complex* normatively, with an implicit value judgment that it is something we would do better without, such that bringing it into consciousness offers some chance of understanding it, shaping it, and, in extreme cases, controlling it. Just as we can talk of *mythological* conditioning and *individual* conditioning, we can also talk of the *cultural* conditioning that lies between them when we absorb attitudes and ideas belonging to our culture before we can personally evaluate them as individuals.[8] The term *conditioning* suggests how difficult it is to become aware of them. A cultural complex is, in this sense, like a reflex action, an automatic response of the unconscious that ultimately impairs our ability to act morally. It may be tracked as a split-off aspect of ourselves, which does not reflect or promote the values of the whole psyche.

Let us begin, then, with considering an archetypal core that might lie at the heart of a British cultural complex.

The Mythic Image of an Island

The Irish poet W. B. Yeats asks: "Have not all races had their first unity from mythology that marries them to rock and hill?"[9] This question invites us to consider that the first mythology of Britain is of an island—"this precious stone set in the silver sea"—in Shakespeare's captivating image (referring, in his play *Richard II*, to England alone, but extended here to include the whole island).[10] Since, for Jung, "the whole of mythology could be taken as a projection of the collective unconscious," it follows that the archetypal core would find expression as a mythic image.[11]

Perhaps, then, we could initially explore the idea that the mythic image of Britain as an island is the original image of which Yeats speaks, symbolic or evocative of the particular state of mind out of which a race defines itself and nations come into being. Bounded by a sea, at once beautiful, enthralling, and dangerous, the island is enclosed and protected, yet at the same time constantly exposed to the fascinating

Figure 1.1 Beachy Head from the Land, East Sussex, England (Photo by David Iliff. License: CC-BY-SA 3.0)

but unpredictable element that encompasses it—all that is unknown, nonhuman—the islanders standing, as it were, on the shore looking outward, watching the restless waves continually disappearing over the edge into *the beyond*. Does this not provoke a yearning to transcend boundaries, the distant horizon of sky and sea inspiring impossible journeys across uncharted waters? And, over many millennia of human habitation, we can understand this as cultivating a spirit of exploration, restless in its turn—open to imaginings, both in body and mind: "Much have I travelled in the realms of gold,/And many goodly states and kingdoms seen," writes John Keats in his poem "On First Looking into Chapman's Homer."[12]

However, an island (a word deriving from the Latin *insula*, island, and *insulanus*, islander) moves through the Latin *insulatus*, "made into an island", to Italian, *isolato*, to French, *isolé*, which comes into English in the eighteenth century as *isolated* and *insular*. The sea cuts the land off from other nations—"as a moat defensive to a house"—preventing that natural mingling and exchange of ideas that provides each culture with a mutually enriching perspective on their own and other peoples' virtues and vices, foibles and follies.[13] In earlier centuries, an island was mostly on its own, lacking, therefore, the ease of a genial eye from another culture, smiling at its idiosyncrasies and offering a foil to parry any unbridled pursuit of its own priorities.

Yet, for many thousands of years, strangers were first glimpsed as indecipherable sails on the horizon, boats bearing friend or foe, with no way of knowing, until they reached the shore, which one it was. Though islands are initially easier to defend against invaders, they are also harder to leave: In the "olden days," there was, in an assault, nowhere else to go. The cry "The Vikings are coming" once echoed around the coasts for 200 years, from the ninth to eleventh centuries, followed by the Normans in 1066—the only date anyone remembers according to the indispensable spoof on history *1066 and All That*.[14] After that, invasions ceased, and there has not been one since. England—taking its name from the *Land of the Angles*—had been unified in the tenth century, as a result of earlier invasions by the Germanic tribes of the Angles, the Saxons, and the Jutes who, in the fifth and sixth centuries, had invaded from northwestern Europe. Earlier, in 43 CE, the Romans had crossed the channel and landed on the shores of Kent, defeating the Celtic army on the River Medway, and leaving 400 years later, with the collapse of their empire, in 410 CE. Britain took its name from the Roman province of *Britannia*. The native tribes whom Julius Caesar called the Celts had earlier come from Central Europe in the Iron Age, c. 1250 BCE, and before them the late Neolithic Beaker culture from Western Europe—who built Stonehenge—and no one knows where the first known settlers in the Upper Paleolithic period came from; perhaps they were "already here."

Britons typically think of themselves as an *island race*—a television program on anything British invariably begins with white waves smashing down upon a rocky shore—and, especially in times of war, the island becomes the bedrock of its primary mythology, the touchstone to which thought returns. Fear of invasion has always been a motivating force, uniting the differing and often dissenting kingdoms of the island into one *United Kingdom*, which becomes far less united once the danger is over. Hence the archetypal potency of Churchill's response to the imminent threat of invasion on June 4, 1940, after the evacuation of British troops from Dunkirk, when, calling on "Our Island Home," he turned the reality of the island into a symbol of the native spirit:

> We shall defend our island, whatever the cost may be. We shall fight on the beaches, we shall fight on the landing grounds, we shall fight in the fields and in the streets, we shall fight in the hills; we shall never surrender.[15]

(Significantly, imagining the fighters throughout the land itself, pushed back, step by step, from the shores to the hills, he used only seven words that did not come from Old English: *fight*, for instance, instead of the French *battle*).

In times of peace, however, the self-sufficiency of "the Island character" may be seen not only as a source of strength and pride, but also—less apparently perhaps to the islanders themselves—as a source of vulnerability and weakness. *Insularity* has inevitably acquired the pejorative meaning of being cut off from other people and different points of view, inclining, in turn, to a national character that is over-preoccupied with its own country and ideas and so self-enclosed, resulting in a certain narrowness of feeling, predisposing it to arrogance, prejudice, and triviality. D. H. Lawrence's short story "The Man Who Loved Islands" parodies this attitude: The man loves islands just because they are desolate and keep people out, but people come, nonetheless, and he moves to ever smaller, less peopled islands until he ends up alone on just one small bit of rock.[16]

The Elizabethan English poet John Donne (1572–1631), doubtless aware of the temptations inherent in his island race, warns of the dangers:

> No man is an island,
> Entire of itself,
> Every man is a piece of the continent,
> A part of the main.
> If a clod be washed away by the sea,
> Europe is the less.
> As well as if a promontory were.
> As well as if a manor of thy friend's
> Or of thine own were:
> Any man's death diminishes me,
> Because I am involved in mankind.
> And therefore never send to know for whom the bell tolls;
> It tolls for thee.[17]

Archetype and Complex

In the language of analytical psychology, *the island* would be the archetypal core from which all other images flow. The archetype in itself is, as it were, morally neutral, simply an instinctive predisposition to feel and act in a certain way, with potentiality for both creation and destruction, gain and loss. Once the archetype issues into images—the way it comes into our consciousness—the moral dimension enters in through the way we relate to them, for which we are responsible. And, as Jung says, we are also responsible for trying to bring all the images of the archetype into consciousness: "Man's task . . . is to become conscious of the contents that press upward from the unconscious. . . . It may even be assumed that just as the unconscious affects us, so the increase in our consciousness affects the unconscious."[18]

We would look, then, for a country's *cultural complex* (using the term descriptively here as the complex of attitudes and values bound together as common to a culture and loosely shared within a culture) as a consequence of the inevitable tensions within this primary image. For all countries, as all persons, incarnate as parts of a whole, are located in a distinct place on Earth, at a particular time in the Earth's history, composed of a specific tribe or tribes, born to particular parents. It follows that every incarnation—of person and culture alike—has its own unique virtues, as well as its own specific predispositions or tendencies to imbalance that obscure or distort the original archetypal wholeness. When a *tendency* to imbalance, typical of a particular culture, takes form as a thought or an action shared and endorsed, or at least not prevented, by a culture, then we may speak of a cultural complex in the pejorative sense—that is, a way of thinking and acting that ultimately lessens and wounds a culture (and its relationship with other cultures), preventing the full range of archetypal expression and working for the part alone—the culture alone—not the whole, the universal values of the human race, inherent in the archetypal language of myth.

Yet we might also see this *partiality*, and the deviations to which it gives rise, as itself archetypal. This is not only because some imbalance is inherent and inevitable, but also because, paradoxically, the struggle to rectify it presupposes and discloses a more inclusive consciousness beyond it, continually offering the chance of attempting to find or create a harmony between what we might call metaphorically, on the model of the individual, the culture's "ego" and the culture's "Self."

The Unifying Image of a Culture

In the same passage in his *Autobiographies*, Yeats continues:

> Nations, races, and individual men are unified by an image, or a bundle of related images, symbolical or evocative of the state of mind which is, of all states of mind not impossible, the most difficult to that race or nation; because only the greatest obstacle that can be contemplated without despair rouses the will to full intensity.[19]

The particular combination of isolation and adventure inherent in an island race makes for a mythology that has freedom or liberty and autonomy as its primary values—the freedom to rule oneself, to be independent, to make one's own decisions, to speak freely, make one's own discoveries, forge one's own destiny. *Freedom* (Old English, *freodom*) and *liberty* (Latin, *libertas*) are both words originating in the idea of being "freed *from*," that is, derivative from another's law, still carrying the memory of enslavement, just as, in Roman times, the freed slave had to wear an undyed cap (*pileus*) as a sign of his liberty; the goddess *Libertas*, figured on the coins of Antoninus Pius in 148 CE, held this cap in her right hand.[20] *Autonomy* (Greek, *autos*, "self," and *nomos*, "law") is, by contrast, self-generated—ontologically prior to freedom, but only legally possible once freed from another's dominance. It means, first, having one's own law, and, second—and more ambiguously—being a law unto oneself.

The cultural habit of freedom and autonomy may perhaps plausibly be suggested as a unifying image that would rouse any nation's and individual's will to discovery and achievement—and that image of freedom is most likely to have encouraged in Britons an independence of spirit—in invention and discovery and particularly in language and literature—which has fostered a culture of tolerance and freedom of speech. But, in so far as these values have remained embedded in the cultural unconscious, they would have, as it were, "come with the territory"—where independence and insularity may be unconsciously yoked together—in which case the values are likely to be assumed—again unconsciously—to be a right for Britons alone. We should ask: Has the right to freedom, which an "island mind" values so supremely for itself, been similarly extended to other nations—whose own right to freedom is no less—whether living on continents or islands, whatever race, color, or creed, whether on land or sea? And the answer has to be, emphatically, No. Where the assumption of inherent superiority has prevailed—as in the existence and practice of the British Empire—it has proved to be a great obstacle to the culture's moral progress—precisely in the refusal to grant that same autonomy and freedom to other nations.

For freedom, as Professor Stefano Carta has written in an online discussion, is "an ethical dimension. It must be a *syzygy* of mine/yours freedom at the same time. Without limits it turns into a grandiose abuse."[21] (*Syzgy* is originally an astronomic term from the Greek *suzukos*, meaning "yoked together," adapted by Jung as a symbol of a sacred marriage of opposites.) The right to govern oneself by one's own law should surely be universal, an inherent dimension of the human birthright. As Donne says, "Any man's death diminishes me, because I am involved in mankind."[22] When a culture takes this right away—a right that it knows to be essential for its own humanity yet denies to others—we are in the presence of a cultural complex (highly pejorative).

Then we have to ask: Why has that simple question been so rarely asked in the past, and, following on from that to the present, why is the British memory of colonialism frequently so selective? Why is "The British Empire: Explain and Discuss" not a subject on every school curriculum, and at an age before specialization takes place? (In my school, the empire was—movingly—presented as an "opportunity for service.") And, lest this degenerate into yet another British preoccupation with itself, what can be learned for the understanding of cultural complexes as a whole?

But how does such a complex get away with it? How can it not be held up to moral scrutiny by more than just a few, initially lone, voices?

Tracking a Cultural Complex

Cultural complexes, like personal complexes, arise early and imperceptibly and, for the most part, together. The child instinctively absorbs the values of the family, which inevitably, to a greater or lesser extent, involve the family's relation to its culture and religion, often further yoked together. As the earliest expression of an archetypal image, we would also expect them to be carrying a vision and a value assumed to be essential to survival—both for the tribe, for the family, and for the individual as a member of that tribe—itself bound up with what is conceived to be "the good life."

Shakespeare expresses this complexity of values in his play *Richard II*, where the beguiling images and rhythms of his poetry suggest how, as with all conditioning, we fall in love with something before we are able to understand it. To take one example to stand for all the similar instances we overlook: Many, if not most, schoolchildren, have had to learn by heart John of Gaunt's dying words to the reprobate King Richard, in which the character's expression of his love for England has become not just a primary text but also a symbol for an Island Home:

> This royal throne of kings, this scepter'd isle,
> This earth of majesty, this seat of Mars,
> This other Eden, demi-paradise,
> This fortress built by Nature for herself
> Against infection and the hand of war,
> This happy breed of men, this little world,
> This precious stone set in the silver sea,
> Which serves it in the office of a wall,
> Or as a moat defensive to a house,
> Against the envy of less happier lands,
> This blessed plot, this earth, this realm, this England.[23]

This "scepter'd isle," with its initial fusion of Nature and Culture, suggests that archetypal sovereignty is projected onto both *island* and *kings* alike. The island itself later becomes the nurse and womb to kings, just as though, as in ancient times, land and king were one. But, as John of Gaunt's speech continues, the astonishing beauty of the poetry obscures the arrogance inherent in the assumption that "conquering others" is a sign of England's greatness:

> This nurse, this teeming womb of royal kings,
> Fear'd by their breed and famous by their birth,
> Renowned for their deeds as far from home,
> For Christian service and true chivalry,

As is the sepulchre in stubborn Jewry,
This land of such dear souls, this dear, dear land,
Dear for her reputation through the world,
Is now leased out, I die pronouncing it,
Like to a tenement or pelting farm:
England, bound in with the triumphant sea
Whose rocky shore beats back the envious siege
Of watery Neptune, is now bound in with shame,
With inky blots and rotten parchment bonds:
That England, that was wont to conquer others,
Hath made a shameful conquest of itself.[24]

The primary power of archetypal projection onto the particular place we live on Earth, which we call *home*, is common to all cultures, as the terms *motherland, fatherland*, and *homeland* show. But, in this speech, we can see the potential danger in that union of natural love and cultural survival, which, if they are not consciously distinguished from each other, allows *Culture*—the *relative* way a society chooses to live in that home—to be archetypally empowered by *Nature*—the *absolute* personal instinctive passion for one's home. So the *absolute* drives the *relative*, as though *Culture* had no need of the patient, enduring processes of human moral effort and deliberation to bring the archetypal "images of instinct" into consciousness in order to shape a destiny that could be called good. In this case, *Nature* (albeit the *Nature* that Culture calls natural) ends up as a justification for the all-too-human demand that we rule by our conscious will alone. Jung writes in various ways, capturing the paradox, that there is a tragic conflict between Nature and Culture, and we want Culture to win, but we don't want Nature to lose.[25] But Culture loses if we allow our innocent love of our natural home to justify our unconscious desires for our own superiority and gain—"wont to conquer others." Looking further into the symbolism—disclosing the deeper layers of the psyche—in the second passage, the "triumphant" sea takes on the warlike nature of England's self-appointed cultural hero, John of Gaunt, yet is itself beaten back, "Whose rocky shore beats back the envious siege of watery Neptune," and indeed, ultimately, in a final victory of Culture over Nature, the island becomes the envy of the sea god himself.

The disparate threads of religion, politics, and war, together with love of the Island Home, are here so tightly interwoven that the speech (typically quoted without its context) could stand as a symbol for all the many indefinable ways in which the "layers" of mythological, cultural, family, and individual life merge imperceptibly into each other and so are almost impossible to isolate and consider in separation from one another. This also suggests that we might expect to find a cultural complex most deeply embedded in those members of a culture whose personal complexes are least known to them. That is to say, the points at which we, as individuals, are least conscious of, and are most vulnerable to, our own personal complexes are likely to be where we are least critical of the assumptions we ourselves hold—and especially those that are widely shared within the culture. Equally, a culture's complexes may blind individuals to their own personal complexes, not least by offering an easy way out of not looking at them since they are common to the majority and subtly reinforced in a shared language. This imperceptibly lowers the standard of morality, which then, in turn, feeds back into the collective that implicitly condoned them in the first place: "Where's the *avant-garde* when the procession/runs continuously in a closed circle?" Dannie Abse, the Welsh/Jewish poet, asks.[26]

Understandably, personal and collective complexes become, at the beginning of a journey, difficult to distinguish. Further, beneath the subtle call to conformity and, in times of trouble, *patriotism* (with its Latin root of *pater*, "father") may lie a deeper and more sinister kind of oppositional thinking that appears to leave no alternative—"with us or against us." The gravitational force of the collective paradigm cannot be underestimated for those who try to follow their own course and make the complexes conscious, as Tom Singer describes in his essay on Barack Obama running for election, "Playing the Race Card: A Cultural Complex in Action."[27] In a similar way, the speed with which, at the beginning of the Falklands conflict, the people of Argentina became, in the "patriotic" press, "Argie Bargies" was terrifying—depersonalization of "the other" being always the first weapon of collectivity.

So it makes sense that, in Joseph Campbell's definition of the stages of the heroic path—*Separation, Initiation, Return*—would-be seekers have to begin by moving, or, more likely, wrenching, themselves away from the group and calling into question all the habits, customs, and beliefs of their culture, *all* tangled together—the whole of what Jung calls "the collective."[28] It would seem that only an initiation into universal human values allows those trying to free themselves from the collective to gain a perspective upon the interwoven values of the particular culture they have inherited, discriminating among them in order to forge their own unique personal relationship to each one. So only the returning hero with his bundle on his back, as in the final picture of the Zen ox-herding sequence, can see through his culture's complexes, having first seen through his own, which is why he has to go back into the world he had to leave to understand himself and his culture.[29] Becoming conscious, then, begins in loss—the loss of a culture, a family, a nation, the loss of a simple instinctive containment and allegiance—and, in turn, the culture's loss of the seeker—which is why Jung calls individuation a tragic process and one for which we have eventually to make reparation, each in our own particular way.[30]

For, as Wolfram von Eschenbach's story of Parzival reveals, how else can he distinguish between manners and morals, which are given to him together—undifferentiated—not least the image of the divine handed down by family and society? Parzival's turning point comes when he refuses to put God on his shield, declaring that he will trust only what he personally knows—his love for his wife. Only when he learns compassion from his "heathen" brother and asks the Question of Compassion of the wounded Grail King—"What ails thee?"—can he become the Grail King himself and bring his own unique values into his society. In the terms we are using here, Parzival transforms his culture by bringing the culture's complex into consciousness.[31]

History and Myth

Although psychology is not history, philosophy, anthropology, mythology, archaeology, or any of the other disciplines that it cannot know as well as experts, it enters into all of them and may know them differently.[32] Its justification is to hold them up to the light, like Hamlet's mirror, "held up, as 'twere, to nature, to show virtue her own feature, scorn her own image, and the very age and body of the time its form and pressure."[33] The idea of history we have as children—that it is a record of the past, telling the story of what did or did not happen—has to be "put away," along with all the other "childish things" of which St. Paul divested himself when he became a man (1 Corinthians 13:11). Even to say history is intermingled with myth implies that there is an objective template which we can call history, and some will say, more radically, that history is simply the myth we take literally and project as real, after which it hardens into fact. But we use the term *history*, nonetheless, believing in some kinds of evidence more than others, while reserving the greater subjectivity for *myth* in its colloquial sense, meaning "invented" or "untrue," though proponents of *myth*, in the sense of archetypal story, prefer to claim that it is "more true," arising from the objective dimension of the psyche.

We could settle for a shared language without too many ambiguities, however, by conceding that all cultures remember some aspects of their history mythologically, and this sometimes falsifies it and sometimes brings it closer to an archetypal core. But psyche can draw attention to the way in which a culture *remembers* what it takes to be its history, by asking what mythic structures might underlie a particular kind of interpretation and, if so, following them as images that could lead through the layers of a cultural unconscious to a more inclusive orientation—one that anticipates undercurrents of energy tending to swing toward a certain type of story, one that expresses its archetypal core. In particular, how a culture relates to the way others who have participated in a shared history remember it, and how it thinks about what it remembers as history, would disclose how conscious a culture has become.

The criteria would be similar to those of individuals who have come to terms with their shadow and their complexes—to be shown in, for instance, openheartedness, willingness to make mistakes and admit to them, resilience to conflict, absence of envy and will to power, capacity to feel remorse for the harm caused to others, to forgive, and primarily, perhaps, the capacity for compassion.[34] If we may draw a metaphor of comparison with an individual, we would be asking whether the culture's ego is in harmony with the culture's Self. There are, of course, many ways of understanding, or symbolizing, this relationship. It may come down simply to "a confession of a common humanity," as Jung defined the catharsis that was a condition of individuation.[35]

In Britain, this enterprise is complicated from the outset by the problematic question of whether what we call *Britain* or, still more problematically, the *United Kingdom* belongs itself more to myth (both colloquial and archetypal kinds of myth) than to history—that is, here, the question of whether its identity is closer to a symbol than an empirical fact—which affects the further question of who is doing the remembering at any one time. It would be difficult to find any "Briton" who did not have (at least) two allegiances: one to the country as a whole—Britain or the United Kingdom—and one, the deeper one, to their own particular "kingdom"— what we might call the England, Scotland, Wales, and Ireland of the Imagination (as well as, more recently, those originating beyond Britain who also perhaps have the Imagination of their own "kingdom," the country they have "come from"). Each of these kingdoms has its own unique identity and life story, its own sources of inspiration—England, the larger, predominantly Anglo-Saxon, with Scotland, Wales, and Ireland predominantly the inheritors of the Celts. They all have distinctive myths of origin, rituals, music, folk customs, national dress, patron saints complete with flags—and so also their own version of the past, their own language, and their own love of the beauty of their own countryside. Since these kingdoms have shared a frequently warring history, both with each other and with invaders from outside, they all remember their history in their own way. Yet one of the defining characteristics of all four kingdoms is the way they take pride and inspiration from their own unique literature.

The Welsh poet R. S. Thomas writes of Wales and apprehending the blood that made the skies and colored the rivers.[36] The Scottish poet Robert Burns writes: "Wherever I wander, wherever I rove/The hills of the Highlands for ever I love."[37] The English poet William Blake's "Jerusalem" begins with "And did those feet in ancient time/Walk upon England's mountains green" and ends with "Till we have built Jerusalem/In England's green and pleasant land."[38] And, more poignantly, Rupert Brooke's poem "The Soldier": "If I should die, think only this of me/That there's some corner of a foreign field/That is forever England."[39] From Ireland, W. B. Yeats's poem "The Lake Isle of Innisfree" begins

> I will arise and go now, and go to Innisfree
> And a small cabin build there of clay and wattles made;
> Nine bean rows will I have there, and a hive for the honey bee,
> And live alone in the bee-loud glade."[40]

Not one of these poets would call himself British first.

The richness of the literary imagination of all the kingdoms is essential to an understanding of the importance of their role in political life. There have always been two distinct strands of "British consciousness"—the *political* and the *poetic*, sometimes known as the *heroic* and the *mystical*, which have been mythically overlaid on historical figures such as Alfred (who fought the Romans and burnt the cakes) and Arthur (King of the Round Table and Avalon), to the extent that no one knows how exactly to place them in history. However, the strength of the "poetic" has enabled it to serve as an (albeit usually unwelcome) critique of political rule and, at its best, to propose the values by which the country should be governed—ideas of tolerance, free speech, and fair play, for instance, and the self-deprecating humor, so sharply contrasted to the political theory and practice of empire, which nonetheless persisted untroubled by criticism from individual Britons for over 300 years.

So, while we might talk of an England of the Imagination, and an Ireland, Scotland, or Wales of the Imagination, it would be harder to think of a Britain of the Imagination, except in times of war and threat of invasion, when the archetypal image of the island takes over. In one way, this is intelligible in the light of the relatively short period of the union. Not until 1603, when James VI of Scotland also became James I of England, after Queen Elizabeth I died without an heir, was there an overriding reason to bring them together. Just over 100 years later, in 1707, in the Treaty of Union, a new Kingdom of Great Britain came into being as a political union of the Kingdom of England, which since 1284 had included Wales, and the Kingdom of Scotland, to which was added Ireland in 1800 to create the United Kingdom of Great Britain and Ireland. In 1922, Ireland was divided into north and south when the Irish Free State finally achieved its own hard-won independence from English rule. The systems of law, education, and forms of religion, however, remained separate.

This suggests that the idea of a United Kingdom is more of a political entity, more an idea, than a heart-felt allegiance to a shared home, as though the different "nations" are yoked together less by indigenous feeling than by the geography—and mythic image—of an island and the common face with which to relate to the rest of the world. It is easier for "England" to experience the island as a whole, and the kingdom as united, partly because, for not always admirable reasons up to 1603, it frequently behaved as if it were; even now, the "seat" of government, the Houses of Parliament, is still located in London, its capital, often just abbreviated to "Westminster" or "Downing Street." The danger is then one of underestimating and undervaluing the radical differences in history and sensibility of those who feel themselves "governed" with insufficient representation. But this is precisely why the other kingdoms have often wished to separate from England, or at least to have many of their own powers devolved to them—or, as many see it, given back to them—as, in 2014, with the vote for the "independence" of Scotland. Those who signed the 1707 Treaty of Union, for instance, were later derided by the Scottish poet Robert Burns with "We're bought and sold for English gold,/Such a Parcel of Rogues in a Nation" (referring to the bribery of some Scottish politicians)—a feeling still shared by some members of the "Yes camp" in 2014.[41]

Although the contemporary cultural complexes among the different members of this Island Home could perhaps playfully be brought to life through analogies to the dynamics of a dysfunctional family, it is more fruitful here to explore the way the different imaginative kingdoms, which make up the political union of the United Kingdom, or, more loosely, Britain, were *complicit* in the building and maintaining of the "British Empire." Here, it has to be said at the outset, that the smaller island of Ireland was the first victim of English and Scottish colonialism, beginning with the Anglo-Norman invasion in the twelfth century and lasting 800 years, almost as long as the Magna Carta itself, that supposed Great Charter of Liberty.

In 1215, the English barons, threatening war against King John, succeeded in placing the power of the king *below* the law, and this has often been heralded as a foundation in the Western traditions of liberty, democracy, and the rule of law, mainly because of the so-called Golden Clauses 39 and 40:

> No free man is to be arrested or imprisoned or disseized [have their property confiscated], or outlawed or exiled, or in any other way ruined, nor will we go against him, except by the legal judgement of his peers or by the law of the land.
> To no one will we sell, to no one will we deny or delay, right or justice.[42]

But, looking more closely, these freedoms were limited to English male landowners. They were not extended beyond these shores, nor to slaves or serfs within them, and they preempted the influence of women by controlling marriage, particularly of widows, and ensuring women had no legal redress against wrongs done to them, except in the case of the murder of a husband. Nonetheless, in restricting the power of the king, the Magna Carta became a symbol of liberty and was an inspiration to the American Founding Fathers who brought it with them from England as the foundation of their own law (though, true to the original, their definition of a "free man" reflected their own priorities and did not extend to the native inhabitants they found there before them). In a supreme irony, however, the Magna Carta—which was the forerunner of the Bill of Rights—was used by "the colonists" as a historical precedent from which to claim their own rightful liberties against King George III—the first colony to achieve equality from its original colonizers—but only by war.

The Selective Remembering of History

It would seem that, generally, in the preceding centuries, all the separate kingdoms that compose the nation of Britain colluded in denying the moral implications of having an empire. Protests from the imaginative literary culture went unheard. Even now we hear much more about how colonizing began—as an "innocent" exploration of new worlds (like the Portuguese, Spanish, Dutch, and French)—and how it was advanced through trade for "mutual benefit" (the East India Company) than we do about how it was conducted and ended: in conquest, theft, betrayal, and a relentless refusal to leave—even after members of these same colonies had fought and died beside Britons during two world wars. The empire seems to have been largely sustained through a mixture of deception—vague references to sugar plantations, Indian silks, African gold, and so forth, initially including a general ignorance as to what they meant—and an even greater self-deception: Greed and arrogance were sublimated as a mission to "civilize," bringing Christianity (and cricket) to benighted souls and bequeathing the English language and the rule of law to those assumed to have little religion and culture of their own. In many countries—Ireland for one—the native language itself was in addition proscribed or discouraged.[43] How many people asked themselves, how we would feel if a country did that to us, and how, therefore, might we imagine those countries to feel?

Rudyard Kipling, often dismissed as the anomalous "Imperialist Poet," wrote a poem, as late as 1899, called "The White Man's Burden," which (in a telling example of the complex known as *reversal*) placed the "heavy harness" on the colonizers not the colonized—"Go bind your sons to exile, to serve your captives' need"—patronizing and dehumanizing those held "captive": the "fluttered folk and wild—Your new-caught, sullen peoples, Half-devil and half-child."[44] The phrase "white man's burden," feeding, as it did, into the self-deceptions of the Victorian age, took off on its own. (Yet, by contrast, *Kim*, his only full-length novel, which had as its heroes both the Anglo-Indian boy Kim *and* his Indian guru, was lyrically embedded in the India he obviously loved.)[45]

Those who are still proud of "the largest empire the world has ever known," "on which the sun never sets," and those who are horrified at the atrocities committed in its name, find their most common ground in the matter of slavery. Even then, William Wilberforce comes first to mind, the great abolitionist of slavery, whose first act, the Slave Trade Act, was passed in 1807, followed by the more complete Slavery Abolition Act in 1833 (typically reminisced as Britain "leading the way").[46] The fact that, by the 1760s, Britain was the foremost European trader in slaves, who were shipped from Bristol and Liverpool in the thousands to work on the sugar plantations of the Caribbean, is by contrast still less well known. One of the estimates puts the number of slaves at 42,000 a year, all suffering the long journey across the Atlantic, chained and shackled in the dark, sold to the Americas, both North and South. Walter Benjamin, the German critic, illustrating his claim that "There is no document of civilization which is not at the same time a document of barbarism," said he once heard the outstanding historian of slavery Orlando Patterson speak in his home island of Jamaica: "'If you want to see the wealth of Jamaica, go to Britain,' he advised, 'Whenever I go to the Tate Gallery [as in Tate & Lyle sugar] I feel a sense of proprietorship.'"[47] The contemporary *Oxford Dictionary of National Biography*, by contrast, says only "Tate, Sir Henry, first baronet (1819–1899), sugar refiner and benefactor."[48] Yet how many Britons going to art exhibitions at the Tate have any idea what the name means and, more generally, where the wealth of Britain in earlier centuries came from?

But what is empire if not enslavement? The British massacre of the Indian "rebel" siege at Lucknow could have made this clear in 1857, were the government able to see it. "One sees what one sees best oneself," as Jung says.[49] The savagery of that and other retributions suggests that the colonists knew *unconsciously* that their presence was unjust—that they were engaged in a form of piracy—but, refusing to make the guilt conscious and so retreating further into denial, they then projected onto the colonized all the ferocity of which they were the instigators, justifying to themselves a superior ferocity in retaliation. Yet, in one sense, they were but enacting the cultural complex of the entire nation, which, like them, would focus on the wrong done to them—the initial siege in which many soldiers were killed—but not on the wrong done to the Indians in the first place, a wrong that asks, in any way it can, for redress. As Joseph Conrad conveys in his *Heart of Darkness* (1899), all you have to do is "look away."[50]

One of the signs of a complex is that ideas and practices, which should be understood in relation to each other, are kept apart so they do not impinge on each other; if they were put together, it would mean that one or the other would have to be given up. There are what the Armenian Greek teacher G. I. Gurdjieff (c. 1870–1949) calls "Buffers" (as that which prevents carriages of a train from bumping into each other) and what we might call a "holding idea" in the unconscious, whose task is to justify the holding of opposing points of view in spite of the fact that they, as it were, dis-imply each other: such as, for example, that freedom is a good in itself, yet good for some people—Britons—but not good for others—people in other lands, not least those whose lands were invaded.[51] We might infer that the holding idea is disguised racism—that the colonized are inferior—an idea in turn held in place by a combination of arrogance and greed. Consequently, when atrocities took place, they invited a dismissive interpretation of "one bad apple," rather than a recognition that these bad acts enacted the shadow of a shared culture of feeling that implicitly allowed them to happen.

A further complication, one that arguably helped to hold imperialism in place, was an overvaluation of hereditary class, more prevalent in earlier centuries but still present today. The insularity of the island character, leading to self-preoccupation and triviality, may, when unconsciously enacted and overvalued, count as a complex. This may be clearly seen in a preoccupation with the class structure of society, whether inherited or not, inevitably impeding the free flow of the imagination that sees through rigid structures, making possible movement and change. In a recent series on television called *Empire*, Jeremy Paxman made the point that the colonists habitually came from the public schools that were themselves structured on hierarchical principles, and this particular culture was continued in the colonies themselves.

I will give one example from the present (2012–2014), known (with a friendly nod to Watergate) as *Plebgate*. To abbreviate as much as possible, and to parody only slightly: A member of Parliament, who happened to be the chief whip, wanted to cycle down Downing Street past No. 10, which is *not allowed*. But it was quicker. A policeman, doing his duty, stopped him (asking him to exit through the pedestrian gate rather than the main gate). The MP swore at the policeman, and the policeman wouldn't take it and, what's more, told tales. The incredibly ungrown-up debate arising from this encounter was whether the MP had called him a "F . . . ing Pleb" or just sworn at him (as one does) *without* using the "pleb-word." Two years, one resignation, many newspaper articles, TV announcements, examinations of CCTV footage, arrests of police informants, and two court cases later, a huge sum of money was transferred to the policeman who, we hope, lived happily ever after. In this comedy of manners, the moral issue—that a representative of the people was rude and abusive to an officer of the people, whatever word he did or didn't actually say—was hardly addressed. It wouldn't have happened in Downton Abbey!

Another sign of a cultural complex lies in its language. George Orwell's analysis of the debasement of collective discourse, in his *Politics and the English Language*, is relevant here: its reach for abstraction, the staleness of its imagery, its lack of precision, and hackneyed phrases "tacked together like the sections of a prefabricated hen-house." Clichés and "dying metaphors" can even "think your thoughts for you, to a certain extent," corrupting language as language in turn corrupts thought.[52] The "white man's burden" manages to do all these things at once.

Yet the history more commonly commemorated in books about the "slave trade" invariably quotes Lord Mansfield, the Chief Justice of the King's Bench, who, in 1772, found *for* the slave Somerset against Stewart—the man who regarded himself as his "owner"—on the grounds that slavery was not supported by British common law (not, we note, that it was a deprivation of a human right in itself). Either Mansfield or William Davy, Somerset's own counsel, expressed the plea in the sentiment of the time:

> The air of England has long been too pure for a slave, and every man is free who breathes it. Every man who comes into England is entitled to the protection of English Law, whatever oppression he may have suffered before that and whatever may be the colour of his skin. Let the black go free.[53]

Although Lord Mansfield's groundbreaking judgment set a legal precedent within Britain (and paved the way for Wilberforce's Act thirty-five years later), it was not extended to those breathing the less pure air of the British colonies. Yet the unconscious cultural complex hidden in plain sight in the imagery was, at the time, less remarkable because it was so widely shared. English air, it would seem, is purified by English law, a boon not shared by those in the colonies who, nevertheless, also had to live under English law—albeit a colonial variant forced upon them in the name of "empire"—the other meaning of *autonomy* being a law unto oneself. The metaphor of air was unfortunate—the gift of life, the breath of life—may not everyone breathe freely of it? "If you prick us, do we not bleed?" Shylock asks.[54]

The Post-War Narrative—a New Story?

The loss of what has been called a "grand narrative" after the Second World War was common to all nations, but did Britain, having, in earlier centuries, too grand a narrative, have more to lose than others? This is not a matter of possessions—that Britain lost its empire, its ill-gotten gains, and its inflated influence on a world stage—it is about the shedding of illusions, not least about itself. What matters is how Britain and all the kingdoms of Britain see themselves, what story the country as a whole tells itself, which is, in part, founded on how its people remember their common past and, in part, perhaps, on how it relates to their archetypal core. Is it possible to contribute to a new mythic image to unify the islanders by bringing some of the earlier complexes of the culture into consciousness? And if so, how?

As we know from personal histories, individuals cannot reach a new story until they have fully accepted what was wrong about the old—which means confronting the shadow of the past—and this would seem true also of cultures, composed of individuals who, in addition to their own shortcomings, have to consider how far they have contributed to the imbalances of the culture of their time. A cultural complex, like a personal complex, would sidestep contradictions in its history and in its image of itself, preferring to focus on its virtues while ignoring its vices. For example, it would take for granted the advantages of its wealth without asking where that wealth came from; it would celebrate its power without considering how it was achieved or how it was practiced; it would value and defend its own freedom without asking itself how it could have been a colonial power for over 300 years without depriving other races and cultures of their own right to that same freedom. Or, conversely, it would recoil and wallow, as one London taxi driver briskly told me, in "post-colonial guilt," which, he continued, paralyzes energy and initiative, indulges in over-compensation and "political correctness," and does not dare to distinguish the good from the bad in its history (a parallel, perhaps, to positive and negative inflation in the individual). The collective memory would still appear to be split, with the negative aspects of empire for the most part denied and repressed into the unconscious and the few positive aspects—if such there were—correspondingly rootless and inflated.

At the simplest level, how could a culture, any more than a person, hope to grow without first acknowledging and repenting of the moral failures in its own history? And without then bringing them into a relationship with the rest of its values, offering the culture a new, deeper, and more realistic dimension of self-knowledge thereby gained, so it could serve the whole in whatever way was needed? In Jungian terms, this would be to confront the collective shadow and draw it, however reluctantly, into consciousness.

But while it seems indisputable that Britain's imperial past asks to be reevaluated, and atoned for, it has first to be generally recognized. Yet, in a 2014 television program called *The British*, the overriding question on which the series turned was "How could Britain come to terms with not being a superpower?" asked in the admiring tones of a further question: "How could a small island become the greatest superpower on Earth?" The tone was mindlessly to glorify, rather than soberly to morally assess, such an "achievement," let alone to ask if it was an achievement at all. Why was the question not framed in the tone of appalling lessons learned from history, lessons to share with other nations, how to look out for modern forms of imperialism, with the same mindset, disguised as, say, unaccountable global corporations or the ever-increasing human imperialism against the Earth? On the contrary, the language, falling into lines such as the "greatest navy the world had ever known" (having just pointed out that the "Royal Navy" began with Captain Cook stealing South American gold from a Spanish ship), was intoned to rising strains of martial music sounding like PR from Big Brother in Orwell's *Nineteen Eighty-Four*. No moral context was given.[55]

Nonetheless—popular media aside—attitudes toward colonialism and imperialism have changed since 1945, but not yet—I would suggest—in a way that allows the culture to thrive. It is as though the culture is suspended, unable to completely embrace its future because it has not fully acknowledged the evils of its past. However, what is entirely new is the debate—its range and extent and depth. In the light of a new multicultural Britain and the 2014 Scottish referendum on independence, many people in politics, and in articles and letters to the newspapers, asked, "What is it to be British?" and "What are British values?" Many, in addition, demanded that we "set the record straight" on our imperial past. One letter to *The Guardian* newspaper in June 2014 from Linda Bellos, a former politician and founder of *Black History Month*, on the "long-term impact of enslavement," may stand for many similar:

> So little of that past is acknowledged. And when it is, it seems to evoke only guilt. What is needed is surely an acknowledgement of the consequences of the enslavement and transportation of possibly 10 million African men, women and children. Britain played a major role in this trade, even if some people like to dwell only on the abolition of the trade. If reparations cannot be quantified in purely financial terms, then at least let us all set the records straight and begin to repair the long-term consequences for West Africa and the Caribbean. As I often remind my English friends, we did not come to the UK because of the weather.[56]

Another sign and symbol of reparation for British colonial history may be seen in the statue of Mahatma Gandhi, standing in Parliament Square outside the Houses of Parliament, close to one of Churchill, who tragically failed to see the justice of Gandhi's cause and refused him the independence he was owed. It is an image of atonement, one of regret and admiration for a man of peace, with a welcome touch of gentle self-parody in its positioning. Such, however, does not extend to the beheader of a king and scourge of Ireland, Oliver Cromwell, who still sits upon his horse, honored, presumably, by some Britons as a symbol of democratic liberty, but, by the Irish, who may be said to have known him best in the massacre at Drogheda (herding 1000 townsfolk, including children, inside St. Peter's Church, locking the doors, and setting it on fire), he is regarded, as Neil Hegarty records in his *The Story of Ireland*, as a "genocidal maniac."[57]

A New Creation Myth as Symbol

Jonathan Freedland, a journalist writing for *The Spectator* and *The Guardian*, suggests that

> For reasons that are not all bad, we have turned 1939–45 into a kind of creation myth, the noble story of modern Britain's birth. We vote for Churchill as our Greatest Briton and revere the Queen in part because she is a direct

link to that chapter in our history, the moment when we were unambiguously on the side of good.[58]

It was also the time when many members of the colonies or the Commonwealth felt more like an extended family than subjects forced against their will, and many gave their lives, side by side with those from the country that had colonized them, in a cause they experienced as common to them all. Given that Britain had not always historically been on the side of their good, the mutual sharing of the challenges of war may have, in many cases, served as a reconciliation and an atonement. Symbolically, it was also the time when the archetypal energies of an island race might justly be summoned in defense of their home. "Without victory is no survival."[59]

Mythically, again, it could be said that the span of the war fell into two modes—death in 1940 and rebirth in 1944—the dual motifs of the symbol of transformation. Initiation rites typically have a "going down" and a "coming up," as, for instance, in the Eleusinian Mysteries of the *kathodos* and the *anodos*, presaging a new vision.[60]

Remembering history as myth, especially in a time of war, may be dangerous, however. As with the retelling of Shakespeare's John of Gaunt's dying words, there is a precise context that cannot be so easily generalized in times of peace. The myth may have encouraged a "narrative of apartness," the "solitary Tommy," whose "finest hour" is ever to face the challenges of life heroically alone.[61] Even in the

Figure 1.2 Beachy Head from the Sea and Air, East Sussex, England (Author: Ian Stannard, from Southsea, England. License: CC-BY-SA-2.0)

affectionate comedy *Dad's Army*, the mixture of old boys and very young lads on the south coast were in no doubt they could prevent the invasion single-handedly if everything didn't keep going wrong. And when, in 1945, Churchill spoke of a "kind of United States of Europe," he envisioned Britain as a friend to the new Europe, not a participating partner within it.[62]

Yet we cannot argue with a symbol, if symbol it be. If it comes from the *collective unconscious*, the challenge is to relate to it on its own terms and participate with it imaginatively, not literally, not forcing the variety of life into its assumed meaning—a meaning we could not in any case fully understand. But we could invoke what we might call our *cultural psychopathology* to guide us—assessing where our imbalances would tend to lie and how they might express themselves, and for this we would turn to our shadow—the unappeased shadow of our imperial past. Where there is less than a full confession of guilt is there not repressed shame? Yet we do not want to swing unconsciously from autonomy over others to insularity among ourselves, moving from one opposite to the other on the same level, unaware that both may belong to this particular cultural complex that can only be "outgrown" by finding our way to a different level of consciousness beyond each of the extremes.

Might Britain's overreaching conduct in the establishing of an empire now be in danger of being falsely compensated by an "over-withdrawing" from a necessary participation with other countries, other cultures? Could it be that we might unconsciously literalize the symbol into "historical facts" that "prove" it in the outer world—"we're better off alone"—without understanding that, as a symbol, it belongs to the inner world and so "is there" to call us toward a genuine autonomy, not over others but over ourselves—the real meaning of freedom? This allows us to have a fully conscious choice whether to engage—or not—and even, incredibly, to ask, could some good have come out of it all?

Easter and Pesach fell on the same day in 2015. It was early spring. It was a sunny day, and, wondering on this, I was walking through the trees in London's Green Park, along with many hundreds of other people, when I came by chance across the Canada Memorial—a memorial to the one million Canadians who had fought in the two world wars—"most of them as volunteers," the plaque said. It is a beautiful low-sloping sculpture by a Quebec artist, Pierre Granche, composed of two slabs of shining red granite, engraved with green-embossed maple leaves, as though they had been flung across it by the wind and settled at random where they fell. The narrow walkway between the two slabs (representing British and Canadian participation) faces the Canadian port of Halifax in Nova Scotia from where many Canadians set sail for Europe. There are two inscriptions beside it, one in English and one in French—the dual languages reminiscent of the original seven-year war between the English and the French, from 1756 to 1763, for supremacy over land that belonged only to indigenous peoples. At the east end of the walkway, a circular bronze casting reads: "In two world wars one million Canadians came to Britain and joined the fight for freedom. From danger shared, our friendship prospers."

Figure 1.3 Canada Memorial, Green Park, London, by Pierre Granche, 2007 (Photography by Kraig Hayden, Journeys with a Camera, Creative Commons)

One hundred thousand of those Canadians gave their lives. Usually a shimmer of water flows over the incline of the polished granite, as though maple leaves (the national symbol of Canada) are floating down a stream, catching the sun as they tilt and turn. But that day was a holiday and the water had been turned off. Children of many nationalities were sliding down it, laughing and shouting and running back up to slide down again, knowing nothing of the black plaque on the side requesting us to show respect by keeping off the memorial—inviting the thought that this joyful play was itself a form of respect. And it seemed for a moment as though the freedoms fought for had, indeed, been won, not only in the war that had gone but also in the heart of the future to come, and I felt the million Canadians would understand.

Notes

1 C. G. Jung, "The Phenomenology of the Spirit in Fairy Tales" (1945), in *The Collected Works of C. G. Jung*, vol. 9i, eds. Herbert Read, Gerhard Adler, Michael Fordham, William McGuire, trans. R. F. C. Hull (London: Routledge & Kegan Paul, 1968), § 384.
2 C. G. Jung, *Memories, Dreams, Reflections* (London: Flamingo Paperbacks, Random House, 1983), chap. 5, pp. 207–208.
3 C. G. Jung, "The Tavistock Lectures" (1935), in *The Collected Works of C. G. Jung*, vol. 18, eds. Herbert Read, Gerhard Adler, Michael Fordham, William McGuire, trans. R. F. C. Hull (London: Routledge & Kegan Paul, 1976), § 371.

4 Percy Bysshe Shelley, "A Defence of Poetry," in *Poems and Prose* (London: J. M. Dent, 1995), p. 279.

5 Thomas Singer, with Catherine Kaplinsky, "The Cultural Complex," in *Jungian Analysis: Working in the Spirit of C. G. Jung*, ed. Murray Stein (Chicago: Open Court, 2010), pp. 23–37. See also Thomas Singer and Samuel Kimbles, eds., *The Cultural Complex: Contemporary Jungian Perspectives on Psyche and Society* (London and New York: Brunner-Routledge, 2004).

6 Thomas Singer, "A Jungian Approach to Understanding 'Us vs. Them' Dynamics," *Psychoanalysis, Culture & Society* 14 (2009): 32–40.

7 C. G. Jung, *Aion* (1951), in *The Collected Works of C. G. Jung*, vol. 9ii, § 17.

8 Northrop Frye, *The Great Code: The Bible and Literature* (New York and London: Harcourt, Brace, Jovanovich, 1982), p. xvii. See also Jules Cashford, *The Moon: Myth and Image* (London: Cassell Illustrated, 2003), pp. 9–11.

9 W. B. Yeats, *Autobiographies* (London: Macmillan, 1973), p. 194.

10 William Shakespeare, *Richard II*, II.i.46.

11 C. G. Jung, "The Structure of the Psyche" (1927/1931), in *The Collected Works of C. G. Jung*, vol. 8, eds. Herbert Read, Gerhard Adler, Michael Fordham, William McGuire, trans. R. F. C. Hull (London: Routledge & Kegan Paul, 1969), § 325.

12 John Keats, *Poems 1817*, *Project Gutenberg eBook of Poems 1817*. June 1, 2005 [eBook #8209]. Most recently updated January 18, 2014. www.gutenberg.org/cache/epub/8209/pg8209-images.html

13 Shakespeare, *Richard II*, II.i.48.

14 W. C. Sellar and R. J. Yeatman, *1066 and All That* (London: Methuen, 1930).

15 Winston Churchill, Wireless Broadcast, May 17, 1940; Speech to the Houses of Parliament, June 4, 1940.

16 D. H. Lawrence, *The Man Who Loved Islands and Other Stories* (Pickering, UK: Blackthorn Press, Large Print Books, 1987).

17 John Donne, "Meditation XVII," in *Devotions upon Emergent Occasions* (1624), in *Donne's Devotions* (Cambridge: Cambridge University Press, 1923).

18 Jung, *Memories, Dreams, Reflections*, p. 358.

19 Yeats, *Autobiographies*, pp. 194–195.

20 William Smith, *A Dictionary of Greek and Roman Antiquities* (London: John Murray, 1875).

21 Prof. Stefano Carta, online discussion, Feb. 16, 2016, at iaap-politics-conf-2014. Permission to quote given by Prof. Stefano Carta.

22 Donne, "Meditation XVII."

23 Shakespeare, *Richard II*, II.ii.40–50.

24 Ibid., II.ii.51–66.

25 C. G. Jung, "The Theory of Psychoanalysis" (1913), in *The Collected Works of C. G. Jung*, vol. 8, eds. Herbert Read, Gerhard Adler, Michael Fordham, William McGuire, trans. R. F. C. Hull (London: Routledge & Kegan Paul, 1961), § 486; and *The Development of Personality* (1954), vol. 17, §§ 159, 335.

26 Dannie Abse, "A Note to Donald Davie in Tennessee," in *Ask the Moon* (London: Random House, 2014).

27 Tom Singer, "Playing the Race Card: A Cultural Complex in Action," in *Sacral Revolutions: Reflecting on the Work of Andrew Samuels*, ed. G. Heuer (London: Routledge, 2010).

28 C. G. Jung, "The Relations between the Ego and the Unconscious" (1928), in *The Collected Works of C. G. Jung*, vol. 7, § 240: "For the development of personality . . . strict differentiation from the collective psyche is absolutely necessary, since partial or blurred differentiation leads to an immediate melting away of the individual in the collective."

29 "The Ten Oxherding Pictures," in Daisetz Teitaro Suzuki, *Manual of Zen Buddhism* (New York: Grove Press, 1960), chap. IV.

30 C. G. Jung, "Adaptation, Individuation, and Collectivity" (1916), in *The Collected Works of C. G. Jung*, vol. 18, §§ 1094–1095.

31 Wolfram von Eschenbach, *Parzival*, trans. A. T. Hatto (London: Penguin Classics, 1980).

32 See the films of Mark Kidel and James Hillman on *The Architecture of the Imagination*, (1994), *The Heart Has Reasons* (1993) (how the heart is imagined by scientists and poets), and *Kind of Blue: An Essay on Melancholia and Depression* (1994) (in defense of melancholy), Calliope Media website. Accessed June 13, 2015, www.calliopemedia .co.uk/

33 Shakespeare, *Hamlet*, III.ii.21–24.

34 Wolfram von Eschenbach, *Parzival*.

35 C. G. Jung, "Problems of Modern Psychotherapy" (1929), in *The Collected Works of C. G. Jung*, vol. 16, eds. Herbert Read, Gerhard Adler, Michael Fordham, William McGuire, trans. R. F. C. Hull (London: Routledge & Kegan Paul, 1966), § 134.

36 R. S. Thomas, "A Welsh Landscape," in *Collected Poems, 1945–1990* (London: W&N, New Edition, 2000).

37 Robert Burns, "My Heart's in the Highlands," in *The Canongate Burns: The Complete Poems and Songs of Robert Burns*, eds. A. Noble and P. S. Hogg (Edinburgh: Canongate Books, 2003).

38 William Blake, "Jerusalem," in *The Poetry and Prose of William Blake*, ed. Geoffrey Keynes (London: The Nonesuch Library, 1961), pp. 375–376.

39 Rupert Brooke, *1914 & Other Poems* (London: Sidgwick & Jackson, 1915), p. 15.

40 W. B. Yeats, *Collected Poems* (London: Macmillan, 1965), p. 44.

41 Poem written in 1791, in *The Canongate Burns: The Complete Poems and Songs of Robert Burns*.

42 Dan Jones, *Magna Carta: The Making and Legacy of the Great Charter* (London: Head of Zeus, 2014).

43 Neil Hegarty, *The Story of Ireland* (London: BBC Books, 2012), p. 78ff.

44 Rudyard Kipling, *Rudyard Kipling's Verse, Definitive Edition* (London: Hodder & Stoughton, 1941), pp. 371–372. The subtitle of Kipling's poem originally read "Written for the US and the Philippines." It was composed for the Diamond Jubilee of Queen Victoria, whose title was "Empress of India."

45 Rudyard Kipling, *Kim* (1901) (London: Penguin Classics, 2012).

46 See Linda Colley, *Britons: Forging the Nation 1707–1837* (New Haven and London: Yale University Press, 2012), who draws attention to the many petitions against slavery in Britain, from 1783 onward, signed by millions of ordinary people, especially women, pp. 284, 360, and 365–366.

47 Walter Benjamin, "Theses on the Philosophy of History, On the Concept of History," *Gesammelten Schriften* 1:2 (Frankfurt am Main: Suhrkamp Verlag, 1974).

48 *The Oxford Dictionary of National Biography* (Oxford: Oxford University Press, 2004).

49 C. G. Jung, *Psychological Types* (1921), in *The Collected Works of C. G. Jung*, vol. 6, eds. Herbert Read, Gerhard Adler, Michael Fordham, William McGuire, trans. R. F. C. Hull (London: Routledge & Kegan Paul, 1971), § 9.

50 Joseph Conrad, *Heart of Darkness* (London: J. M. Dent, 1899). (This tale refers strictly to the Belgian Congo, which he visited himself and described in his *Last Essays* as "the vilest scramble for loot that ever disfigured the history of human conscience and geographical exploration," but it is obviously valid for aspects of any colonial enterprise.)

51 P. D. Ouspensky, *In Search of the Miraculous* (London: Routledge & Kegan Paul, 1975), pp. 154–156. "'Buffers' help a man not to feel his conscience."

52 George Orwell, *Politics and the English Language* (Peterborough, ON: Broadview Press, 2006).
53 Linda Proud and Valerie Petts, *Consider England* (London: Shepheard-Walwyn, 1994), p. 62. The now questionable phrase "the black" would not have been used dismissively by his friend, the writer Samuel Johnson, an outspoken opponent of slavery, who, after his wife's death, employed a freed Jamaican slave, Francis Barber, as his servant, sent him to study at school, and, on his own death, made him his residual heir with an annuity of £70, which enabled him to open a draper's shop in Staffordshire. Michael Bundock, *The Fortunes of Francis Barber: The True Story of the Jamaican Slave Who Became Samuel Johnson's Heir* (New Haven: Yale University Press, 2015).
54 Shakespeare, *The Merchant of Venice*, III.i.66.
55 *The British*, Sky Atlantic TV, June 9, 2012. A Nutopia Production. Series Producers Sam Starbuck and Michael Waterhouse.
56 Linda Bellos, Letter, *The Guardian*, June 19, 2014.
57 Neil Hegarty, *The Story of Ireland*, pp. 117–149.
58 Jonathan Freedland, "British Stereotypes: Do Mention the War, Please!" *The Guardian*, January 26, 2012.
59 Churchill, Speech to the House of Commons, May 13, 1940.
60 See Anne Baring and Jules Cashford, *The Myth of the Goddess: Evolution of an Image* (London: Penguin Books, 1993), pp. 374–390.
61 Freedland, "British Stereotypes." See also "Enemies Within," *The Spectator*, February 11, 2012.
62 Churchill, Speech to the Academic Youth, Zürich, 1946.

Chapter 2

About Two Cultural Complexes

The German Complex of Superiority and the Russian Complex of Feeling Encircled by Hungry Barbarians

Gert Sauer

The following quote comes from colleagues who have taken up the old thread of complex theory from Jung and made a new differentiation between individual and cultural complexes:

> Cultural Complexes are not the same as cultural identity or what has sometimes been called "national character," although there are times, when cultural complexes, cultural identity and national character can seem impossibly intertwined. For instance, those groups emerging out of long periods of oppression through political and economic struggle must define new identities for themselves, which are often based on long submerged traditions. This struggle for a new group identity can get all mixed up with underlying potent cultural complexes which have accrued historical experience and memory over centuries of trauma and lie slumbering in the cultural unconscious, waiting to be awakened by the trigger of new trauma . . . And for some people, their complexes—cultural and personal—are their identity.[1]

As for my work, I would like to add that the Jungian tradition is part of a broader stream of scientific thought: Historians also speak of a "peoples' memory." In her essay on the understanding of the medieval lives of saints, Irene Berkenbusch, a colleague studying the example of Saint Elizabeth of Thuringia, draws attention to some basic rules of psychohistorical interpretation:

> A single person may not be interpreted as an autonomous or isolated unit. Because the individual is embedded in social habits which are liable to social change, the cultural and social context has to be taken into consideration. This counteracts monocausal explanation of an individual's existence.[2]

A little later in her study, Berkenbusch makes it clear that psychohistory is concerned with the mindset or "mentality" of a society as a whole:

> First of all psycho-history is interested in the analysis of a singular I, the individual and [its] beliefs and behaviour, motivations etc. It is about thought content,

DOI: 10.4324/9781032695143-4

while the history of mentality is concerned with the mind-set not of just one person but of a society as a whole within an era. As for the history of mentality, the collective element comes to the fore. The study of the history of mentality has its roots in French historical research. Its founder is Lucien Febvre.[3]

In writing about cultural complexes within the framework of analytical psychology, we should be aware that we are also discussing *collective mentality*. I postulate that "collective mentality" is roughly equivalent to what analytical psychology calls the *conscious attitude* or *collective consciousness*. Here, we must take into account that collective consciousness is a part of the dynamic system of the psyche that includes thought, emotion, and behavior. An individual who is in a cultural complex, along with others in the same group, takes for granted that their point of view is self-evidently the general point of view. They tend to be unconscious of the fact that their point of view is not self-evident to others. Furthermore, the feeling of "self-evidence" is a power that removes its own self-evident content from objective analysis and observation and thus makes it unconscious. This creates an interesting situation: We have to draw attention to the question of why certain things are self-evident to us in order to have a chance to make them conscious. Here, the paradox arises that collective consciousness is often more unconscious than individual consciousness, even though it is a group consciousness.

In its study of cultural complexes, analytical psychology is different from more conventional historical research in that the study of complexes focuses on their three main elements: energy, emotion, and image content. We call the interaction of these elements *psychodynamics*. Psychodynamic interactions create historical and behavioral reality. This can be observed in the doctrinal dispute within psychoanalysis on a grand scale and within analytical psychology on a smaller scale. Any time a group—political, psychological, or spiritual—claims absolute truth for its brand of knowledge, it may truly be in the grip of a cultural complex. This claim of absolute truth is an indication of a great unconsciousness. It is similar to the view of European historiography, which saw "Europe as the hub of the world" for a long time, clearly revealing that this consciousness was under the influence of a cultural complex. The study of cultural complexes is very important to me clinically in practical work with immigrants, as I constantly need to be able to distinguish individual consciousness from collective consciousness. In order to understand individual consciousness, we need to know about collective consciousness and its values.

Two Cultural Complexes as Examples

I wish to consider the *superiority complex* of many Germans and *the complex of being surrounded by hungry barbarians* that preoccupies many Russians. I address both complexes at the same time because the Germans and the Russians have a common, painful, and, in some ways, parallel history, as each country constituted its first real national identity at the same time. I first spoke about this subject at a three-country conference in 2008. In 2013, at the beginning of the Ukrainian crisis, I was shocked by the politics of the representative of the European Union, which revealed, once again, the power of those repetitive complexes. Unfolding events demonstrated Western blindness to history and its own shadow of believing in its inherent superiority. The West showed no awareness of Russia's deeply rooted complex related to the fear of being surrounded and attacked. These mutually interactive complexes of Western superiority and the Russian fear of being surrounded have come to full flower in the ongoing destruction of human lives in Ukraine. The history of Germany and Russia amply demonstrates that cultural complexes are persistent and relatively constant. It is, of course, my hope that careful consideration of how engrained and potent these complexes are might help a bit in preventing further entanglements and trauma.

As part of my own self-evident view of the world, I have to draw attention to my own pair of glasses: I have a stake in both the German and Russian cultures. I grew up in Germany. My mother was a Russian refugee from the 1918 Russian Revolution. My father was a German Prussian. He died young, and thus my inner culture became Russian. In my own analysis, I had to work out the shadows of both countries, including their imperialistic shadows. At the same time, my dual experience gave me the opportunity to be both subjective and, at times, objective about both cultures, which has allowed for greater clarity on occasions. Before beginning this analysis, I feel it important to mention that cultural complexes are not necessarily shared by all members of a group.

The Complex of German Superiority

The European Football Championship of 2008 was an amusing example of how the ideas of some Germans about the supremacy of their team just bubbled up. It was quite embarrassing to witness the victory celebration in Berlin wherein the German runners-up could not handle their defeat graciously. Instead, the German fans had to denigrate the victorious Spanish team with verbal abuse and crude gestures. Sports are often an excellent barometer of collective mentality and emotion; they also reveal underlying cultural complexes. In his book *Grüezi Gummihälse*, with the beautiful translated subtitle *Why the Germans Sometimes Are a Pain in the Neck*, the Swiss journalist Bruno Ziauddin writes, with a large dose of Swiss self-irony, the following remarkable words about German football:

> Germans are as per self-assessment world export champions, world champions in collecting aluminum . . . and football world champions. . . . Someone so pushy in only taking the absolute, the greatest, the highest and the very best as his guiding principle, deserves to be once again reminded of his own finitude and fallibility.[4]

Later in the same chapter, Ziauddin zeros in on the German feeling of supremacy, which, as I noted previously, is intimately connected to the term *self-evident*:

The feeling of having the monopoly on the truth is very German. Admittedly I also have met with some know-it-alls among the Swiss. Interestingly those were always the ones who were especially well-meaning towards the Germans. Self-irony does not belong to the core competencies of the Germans.[5]

Ziauddin quotes an article from the Austrian weekly magazine *Profil* about the *Marmeladinger* as the Germans are sometimes called in Austria:

Not just a few of the reported statements of Germans had a whiff of unintentional hilarity. In such a way a German professor of Romanic literature at the University of Vienna was filled with indignation because she felt that "objective criticism" and the "drafting of clear objectives" was seen as "the arrogant habit of a German who is above it all." I dare to assume: the unshakable German conviction tends to be that one's own opinion, one's world view, one's own way of doing things and one's behaviour are completely "objective," "factual" and "goal-oriented" and are qualities which will compellingly contribute to the welfare of the community. Challenging such positions must be based on a fallacy or a flaw of character of the challenger. This pitiless self-confidence and sense of mission is much more widespread in Germany than anywhere else.[6]

Ziauddin also gives a typology of "the superior German":

- The dashing-looking Prussian
- The Perwoll German (*Perwoll* being the brand name of a light-duty detergent)
- The conceited German

To me, the last one seems to be the most appropriate for our subject. As Ziauddin notes:

The conceited German. Aggressive variation of the Homo Perwoll. Like him he has completely come to terms with the past. But he makes an aggressive show of his moral superiority. Strong in his opinion. Convinced not to be a know-it-all, but, of course, he does know what is best. He is completely objective. He supports recycling and is against climate change. He does know everything about Switzerland, even before he has ever been there (source: *Der Spiegel*): He sees a Swiss as a hillbilly, bourgeois, financed by the money of despots, in the evening at ten sharp "the pavement is rolled up," only the USA are worse (Bush, warmongering, imperialism, religious fundamentalists, racial hatred).[7]

At this point, Ziauddin makes a psychologically interesting statement: He argues that the complex of superiority is connected to a truth complex. It attaches itself to behaviors always connected with a sense of mission or purpose. Of course, the feeling of superiority can, in some cases, be a defense mechanism stemming from a feeling of inferiority. The defense of superiority is then acted out through the necessity of an important mission.

This feeling of superiority linked to a sense of knowing the truth and being on a mission should be uppermost in our minds when we think of this German cultural complex. While working on this chapter, I was invited one day to a birthday party for a seventy-year-old. Seated at my table was another senior man who soon introduced himself as a veteran of World War II. We started talking. In 1940, when he was twenty-six years old, he went to war and, in the year 1949, he was released from being a prisoner of war. He told me how his military training and the earlier Hitler Youth indoctrination and education had taught him that Russians were subhuman. When, in the war, he saw a group of Russian POWs (prisoners of war) with their shorn heads, they matched those preconceived stereotypes. For him, the Russians were indeed subhuman, as the Nazis had shown in their propaganda. Only when he found pictures of family celebrations and other memorialized events in deserted houses in occupied Russia did doubt arise. If I remember correctly, he came from a home that had been originally oriented toward communism or socialism, but he had been strongly influenced by National Socialist propaganda and was, in this respect, an example of the National Socialists successfully influencing Germans to believe they were superior.

We could err now if we assumed that the superiority complex of the Germans, as much as it was based on National Socialism, has been overcome. Ziauddin and others—including the German press, which reflects collective attitudes—give ample evidence that the German superiority complex is alive and well. Here is how I would frame my hypothesis about this cultural complex:

> The German complex of superiority exists throughout German history. It finds expression in the present as a continuing feature in German speech, writing, thinking, and feeling as well as in the inner and outer dealings with other non-German groups. It had its apex in the ideology of the so-called Third Reich. But it was present long before this and remains operative in the contemporary German psyche. I formulate this notion with an eye to German history because there are many preexisting ideas that separate the racist ideology of the nineteenth century from the roots of the German superiority complex before that time.

Many Germans have always been proud of the parliamentary convention in the Paulskirche (St. Paul's Church) in Frankfurt in 1848. In regard to my subject of the German superiority complex, a speech on Poland at that convention by Carl Friedrich Wilhelm Jordan, the representative of Eastern Prussia, is noteworthy:

> Our right is no other right than the right of the stronger, the right of the conqueror. Yes we did conquer, but these conquests happened in a way that they cannot be given back any more. . . . The superior power of the German tribe as compared to most Slavic tribes, perhaps with the exception of the Russian

one, is a fact which has to impose itself on any unbiased observer, and against such a fact based on natural history. The last act of this conquest, the notorious division of Poland was not, as it was called, a genocide. It was nothing else but the proclamation of a demise that already happened, the funeral of an already decaying corpse, which could no longer be tolerated among the Germans.[8]

Today, such words have the scent of psychosis in our consciousness, but, at that time, those words generated political action and behavior.

A key phrase in the analysis of the German superiority complex is "The German Colonization of the East." This notion was created by German historiography to indicate the imperial expansion of the German Reich and its population into the Slavic East. The term *colonization* originated when the European powers wanted to share the world among themselves and founded colonies wherever they went in the name of spreading civilization. Today, this same impulse sometimes flies under the banners of *human rights* and *democracy* rather than *colonization*.

In the earliest German history, from the time of Emperor Otto the Great, we read the following in August Nitschke's essay on *The Early Christian Empires*:

At the same time Otto's Margrave Gero invited thirty Slavic rulers to a banquet, feasted them regally, lulled them into a sense of security and made them drunk; then he let them all be slaughtered. Another Slavic prince was allowed to flee from captivity, but bribed with money, he let all other princes of his tribe be slaughtered and handed the corpses over to Otto of Brandenburg.[9]

A further personal narrative of this German "colonization of the East" came to me on a lovely evening in Carnavé in Lithuania as I sat with two Lithuanian colleagues, Grazina Gudaite and Goda Ruksaite, at the foot of a hill on which once stood the capital of Lithuania. Grazina told us of how, in the early Middle Ages, the knights of the Teutonic Order, who had conquered Eastern Prussia and had wiped out the Baltic Prussians there, had raided and plundered the town, murdered the people, and then burned the town to the ground. It was not any different then: The imperial subjugation of the territories east of the river Elbe was executed and justified in the name of being a superior civilization.

On another occasion, I stood above the river at Frankfort/Oder with a good friend. Viewing the Polish side of the river, his expression became dreamy, and suddenly he saw the old Neumark and he—an outspoken friend of Poland—said: "This was essentially German." But it was not!

For examples in the press of the German superiority complex, I have chosen to look at the coverage on Russia in the *Badische Zeitung*, the only opinion-forming newspaper in Freiburg. Elke Windisch, staffer at the *Badische Zeitung*, shows in her reports as a correspondent on Russia how the German complex of superiority is alive and well today. I quote from her sardonic report on Russian president Dimitri Medvedev, which appeared under the headline: "A Faithful Servant Switches Over":

> When Medvedev crusaded against legal nihilism during his election campaign in front of track workers at the Siberian town of Krasnojarsk, not a single hand was raised for applause. Not even when he explained what he meant: A disrespect of laws and judicial decisions. . . . When Medvedev tries to connect to the people in the way of western politicians there is little response. "Ivan Average-consumer" does not want a sovereign who can be touched, but one to worship. A czar and a martinet. One like Putin . . . Elderly women are wild about Dima (Medvedev). In the erotic dreams of the younger ones is Vladimir (Putin).[10]

Beneath Windisch's sardonic description of President Putin is the German stereotypical prejudice about the obedience of everyday Russians to authority, and it can be read as a masterpiece of the superior democratic perspective of a typical German correspondent. It seems more and more that they need a sidewinder to replace their own shadow of Ivan the Terrible.

There is another revealing piece from the *Badische Zeitung*, which includes a map by the editorial department in an article by Windisch: The map represents Europe and the Mediterranean.[11] It includes five large, warlike arrows showing how gas and oil are transported from Russia to Europe, highlighting for Western readers Russia's display of power.

This map illustrates a most sensitive issue about Russian's oil economics and its impact on Germany and other European countries. In her article accompanying this map, Windisch asserts that Russia is pursuing a neo-imperial strategy with its oil politics.[12] Her report is flawed and poorly researched in that she does not mention the Bulgarian, Greek, and Italian treaties with Russia, and they are omitted from the map. She also omits the fact that Russia feels continually extorted by Ukraine and Belarus, which have received bargain prices. Russian also feels threatened by Poland, Latvia, and Lithuania, which have the potential to block the transfer of raw materials to and from Russia. She does not report Russian viewpoints about these facts. The warlike arrows of the map suggest the "danger from the East," which echoes the ominous warnings not only of Hitler's Third Reich but also of Wilhelm II who declared: "People of Europe protect your most sacred goods."

From these fears, warnings, and beliefs, we can see that the German complex of superiority has a twofold foundation and justification in respect to its eastern neighbors: first, the Russians are a threat, and, second, the Germans are better than the Russians and need to civilize them.

At this point, I must mention the use in German of the key phrase *Polish economy*. For Germans, the phrase *Polish economy* symbolizes ineffectiveness and chaos. It states the challenge that the Germans faced in bringing order and rule to the Polish people. The phrase and its sinister effect on the course of German–Polish history are well known. In this respect, it followed that, as soon as the Germans occupied Poland in World War II, the Polish elite had to be annihilated. Their existence obviously stood against the German feeling of superiority.

The Germans' cultural complex of superiority over the European East is intertwined with religious as well as geopolitical and economic motives. Earlier in history—at the beginning of the Middle Ages (around 600 CE)—the heathens of the East needed to be led to salvation by the Western German Christians. Later, in 1054, when the Roman and Orthodox Eastern churches split, the Orthodox heretics of the East needed to be corrected by Western European crusaders raiding Eastern Europe. In the name of being more civilized, the Germans could fulfill their expansionist visions for the acquisition of resources and markets. The maps of the Middle Ages in Central and Eastern Europe demonstrate this.

The Germans did a good job of depicting the 1919 Treaty of Versailles after World War I as being inhuman and degrading of German dignity. Just a year earlier, however, in 1918, the Reich forced Russia to accept the far worse Treaty of Brest-Litovsk in which Russia sacrificed Riga, Lithuania, Livonia, Estonia, and some of White Russia and Ukraine to Germany. These lands had great economic importance as they were among the most fertile farming areas in Western Russia and would come to support Germany's military effort in the West. Germany's plans for the colonization of the East under Hitler had already been well formed by the Second German Reich (1871–1918), as demonstrated in an exhibit organized by the German Research Foundation in 2006:

> The national socialist plans for the East followed ideological concepts: Eastern Middle Europe, inhabited by different people, had to be ethnically homogenized— first and foremost to the exclusion of the Jewish population. Connected to this project of forcible "Umvolkung" [i.e., change of population] was the hope of making the East, as settled by Germans, the origin of a renewal of the German people. Such visions had a long history. In the Second Empire and against the background of a vigorous modernization dynamic around 1900, Germany had already opened itself to thinking in ethnic categories. Modernization had changed ways of life, everyday habits, and values with an unprecedented force. It had also awakened fears of a "degeneration of the German substance." "Redemption" from this vexing experience of change seemed to lay in the return to eternal values of a rural folklore.[13]

In the discussions about the goals of war during World War I, those nineteenth-century visions concretized in military action. Statements like those of the liberal historian Friedrich Meinecke—"Could not also Courland . . . be made usable to us as a rural land of colonization, if we deport the Latvians to Russia? In former time this would have been thought of as a mere fantasy, and yet it is not infeasible"—can be viewed as opening the minds of the later National Socialists to a policy of exterminating not only the Jews but also the Balts and Slavs. They show how seriously the German bourgeoisie thought about creating new soil for the German people.[14]

Just how intense those visions were can be proven by the fact that the German Empire financed Lenin and actually even smuggled him into Russia by train through Germany and Sweden, as has been reported in *Der Spiegel*.[15] He was the ultimate secret weapon against Russia. Smuggling Lenin into Russia gave the Germans a way to undermine the Russian Empire. Such facts are often forgotten in Germany. Poorly differentiating consciousness is always a clue to the effectiveness of a complex.

Beginning with the so-called Northern Crusades to the East in the Middle Ages, the German Livonian and Teutonic military orders joined forces with the Christian kings of Denmark and Sweden against the pagan peoples living around the southern and eastern shores of the Baltic Sea. Likewise, in the Middle Ages, the Catholic Premonstratensians set out from Magdeburg to spread Western Christianity as a religion of higher value. These medieval groups lend evidence to the centuries-old, powerful idea of German superiority that justified expansion into Eastern Europe. Even the Reformation makes no exception to this idea of German superiority; the cultural complex emerges in the work of Martin Luther. Luther based his antisemitism on this notion of German superiority and the inspiration of his faith, which appears in his treatise *On the Jews and Their Lies*. Luther offered his "superior" German insights:

> [the Jews are a] base, whoring people, that is, no people of God, and their boast of lineage, circumcision, and law must be accounted as filth. They are full of the devil's feces . . . which they wallow in like swine.[16]

These self-righteous ideas coupled with expansionist dreams are a prominent part of the German cultural complex of superiority, which is reflected in the notion that Germans are specially blessed by God himself. For instance, the second verse of the hymn "Wake up, wake up you German land" reads:

> God honored you, Germany, highly with his word of blessing,
> bestowed you with a great light and let you be invited to his realm,
> which is eternal, there have you been invited to, he wants to heal your harm.[17]

Of course, many other nations have claimed such special status in God's creation, although the current edition of the German hymnal reflects the good sense of having deleted this verse.

But it certainly brings to mind the Ziauddin quote: "The feeling of having a monopoly on the truth certainly is something very German."[18] Examples of this attitude are abundant in the operas of Richard Wagner, such as *Lohengrin*. Consider also these two quotes from C. G. Jung, both taken from letters written in 1944. On January 12, 1944, Jung wrote to Arnold Künzli: "You have got the spirit . . . then the spirit appears in the shape of the devil, as the horrible fate of Germany demonstrates."[19] And, on January 15, 1944, he wrote to Emma Pelet and included himself in his analysis: "We all have the fiery devil inside of us, who broke through and gained power in Germany, thanks to the limitless unconsciousness and arrogance of the individual."[20]

Since the Middle Ages and the Reformation, the German complex of superiority has been connected to a deep longing for a monopoly on the truth and to the desire for geographic, economic, and spiritual expansion into other lands to fulfill the mission of bringing the higher German civilization to other people. In the German psyche, truth became an absolutist concept that did not allow for a true dialogue. Wilhelm Grönbech, a Danish research scientist of Germanic culture and mythology, offers the following understanding of the collective German psyche and behavior: "It is all about being in the entourage of the right prince."[21] The content and the princes are changing; the behavior stays the same.

The Russian Complex of Feeling Encircled by Hungry Barbarians

This age-old cultural complex of feeling encircled by angry barbarians became manifest again with the outbreak of the Russo-Georgian war in the last days of August 2008 and is now exploding like a volcano in the crisis in Ukraine. I am deeply afraid of Western politicians who are uninformed about the Russian fear of encirclement and invasion. The Russian cultural complex is reflected in a newspaper map from *Argumenti i Fakti*, a widely published Russian newspaper that strives to give objective coverage. The headline is a perfect statement of the Russian cultural complex: "The War Is at an End. They Encircle Russia."[22]

The map, which shows the region around the Caspian Sea, is totally opposite to Elke Windisch's map in the previous section. Here, Russia is encircled by Western military expansion—Georgia, Ukraine, the Baltic states, middle Asia, and so on. The map also pictures NATO and American weapons pointing from Afghanistan to Iraq and to Turkey and from Georgia toward Russia. The writer of the article cannot understand why no one in the West can appreciate why Russia had to intervene against the aggression of Saakashvili, the so-called pro-Western, pro-NATO president of Georgia from 2004 to 2013.

About 200 years ago, Alexander Pushkin wrote the famous and immortal fairy tale of the Golden Cockerel. The rooster is the protector of the land of Czar Dadon who is killed by an anima/queen named Schamachan. A wise old man, an astrologer, had given Dadon the golden rooster. It was placed on the rooftop of the palace and always called in the direction from which the enemy would be arriving.[23] The rooster can be seen as a medieval radar system, symbolizing the historical need of Russia to protect herself from every direction.

In this context, it is easy to understand how the American plan to install a radar system in the Czech Republic and Poland in the name of fighting the war on terror triggered the age-old cultural complex of Russia feeling surrounded by enemies. Sergej Wladimirowitsch Bodrow, a well-known Russian film director, said in an interview with the newspaper *Argumenti i Fakti* how negative he deems this complex to be, even though he only ascribes it to the previous Soviet era:

> We should at long last overcome the deeply rooted Soviet complex, that in the West no one is loving us, that they would like by any means to defraud us and to insult and humiliate us. We should stop to think that we are always surrounded by enemies.[24]

Der Spiegel conducted an interview with Aleksandr Isayevich Solzhenitsyn. In response to a question about the cooling down of Western and Russian relations, he answered as follows:

> In Russia, just as in the West, the cherished hopes are not in accord with reality. When I came back to Russia in 1994, I experienced an idolisation of the western world and of the constitutional order of very different countries . . . This mood changed after the brutal NATO-bombing of Serbia. A thick black line was drawn which will never be possible to erase again, and I believe, that it is drawn through all the social classes of the Russian society. Added to this were the attempts of NATO to draw parts of the disintegrating Soviet Union into its sphere, especially and most painfully—the Ukraine, a closely related country, with which we are connected by millions of family ties. . . . Until then the West had been seen as a knight fighting for democracy. Now we had to realise disappointedly that western politics are mainly guided by pragmatism, a rather often selfish and cynical pragmatism at that. The West . . . quickly got used to the thought that Russia had almost become a country of the Third World and would stay like this forever. When Russia regained strength the West panicked.[25]

Solzhenitsyn represents a conservative part of Russian society, strongly oriented to history and tradition, whereas Bodrow represents the more liberal, intellectual, internationalistic-oriented group. As one can see from their respective quotes, however, both are talking about the same phenomenon.

German correspondents and experts took up the subject in Peter Scholl-Latour's 2007 book, *Russia Surrounded: The Empire of Putin between NATO, China and Islam*, which was published as a best-selling title on the *Spiegel* list.[26] Even those who do not share Scholl-Latour's conclusions became aware that he formulates the problem as it unfolded historically. The essence of his thesis is that Russia is historically conditioned to fear enemies from all sides. Gabriele Krone-Schmalz has been the ARD correspondent (the foremost German television station) in Russia for a long time. In her book *What Happens in Russia*, she analyzes with a keen eye the blind spots of Western politicians and media. She also accurately perceives the deceit of the pragmatic and selfish West by quoting the then American Secretary of State Condoleezza Rice who said in 2007: "It is ridiculous that ten antiballistic missiles and some radar systems in Eastern Europe will threaten the Soviet strategic system of deterrence and everybody knows this."[27]

Krone-Schmalz and her colleague Philipp Zelikow wrote a book in 1997, in which they commented on the conditions of German reunification. She reported that the American Secretary of State at the time, James Baker, had said the following:

> Baker promised Scevardnadze and Gorbachev "ironclad guarantees, that neither the jurisdiction nor any troops of NATO would be moved to the East" if Moscow would agree with the membership of unified Germany in NATO. This

phrasing is, according to Condoleezza Rice, also to be found in letters of the government of G. W. Bush senior to Gorbachev.[28]

Gabriele Krone-Schmalz wrote furthermore:

What appalled me at the time, was the fact that German politicians of the first rank called the projected expansion of NATO to the East in confidential conversations one of the biggest mistakes of foreign policy in postwar history while in official statements they claimed the opposite. If you look at it from a political point of view, not an economical one, and if it had been the goal to take the farewell to the confrontation of East versus West seriously, then, in this situation, there would have been just one possibility: It would have been the task of all the concerned parties to come up with new security-structures for our world.[29]

And Gabriele Krone-Schmalz has reiterated these arguments with great sadness in her new book entitled *To Understand Russia: The War on the Ukraine and the Arrogance of the West*.[30] Such a new security structure would have made a conscious effort to avoid rekindling the old Russian cultural complex.

Let us take a closer look at Russian history in order to better understand the origins of the cultural complex of feeling encircled by hungry barbarians. In maps of the Kievan realm of old Russia in the twelfth and following centuries, you can easily see why Russia developed this cultural complex. When the Mongols came, and Russia was defeated from the east, Lithuanian, Polish, German, and Swedish crusaders were simultaneously coming from the west to take their part of the loot. This pattern has continued throughout Russian history.

N. M. Karamzin, the most important Russian historian of his time, lived from 1766 to 1826. His twelve-volume *History of the Russian State* is part of the backbone of common knowledge familiar to every Russian and was republished in 2007. The underlining theme of his work is simple and clear: When Russia is strong and united, it can withstand the threats from all sides. This is based on the recurrent Russian experience that, when it is defending itself against an enemy coming from one direction, enemies from the other side of the realm would attack from behind. A classic example of this experience was that of Alexander Newskij who fought off the Swedes as well as the Livonian Teutonic Order of the Sword from the west between 1240 and 1242. The German Teutonic Order first sought to extinguish the old Baltic Prussians and then expand into the Baltic lands and, from there, into Russia, always in the name of the True Faith, as directed by Rome. Both groups— the German Teutonic Order and the Livonian Teutonic Order—had tried to conquer parts of Russia at the very time when a vast region of Russia had been subjected to the Mongolians attacking from the east. In the course of these struggles, Alexander Newskij became a national saint and the savior of the fatherland. He achieved this by making an arrangement with the Mongolians that kept his back free. The famous film *Alexander Newskij* by Sergej Eisenstein depicts the Teutonic Knight as a Western barbarian who, possessed by his conviction of having righteous Roman values, recklessly commits atrocities in the Russian town of Pskow. Like all of Eisenstein's other films, this one belongs to the treasures of Russian culture and communicates deep collective memories and emotions.

In his chapter on Russia from the eleventh to the thirteenth century, Karamzin writes about the time the Polowzer from the southeast were defeated. The besetment by this steppe people is known to every Russian because of the famous opera *Prince Igor* by Alexander Borodin. Karamzin describes how, all at the same time, the attacks of the Polish were fended off, the Galician nobles repelled the attacking Hungarians, the Kama Bolgars lost interest in further fights in the east, and the Teutonic Order could not advance further into the east.[31]

As mentioned earlier, Alexander Newskij had to play the Asian card and bear the Mongolian Tartaric yoke so his forces would be available to defend against the Swedes. At the same time, Lithuania and then the Polish-Lithuanian Commonwealth took possession of, and subjected, territories of Western Russia.

With the gradual strengthening of Moscow and the final shaking off of the Mongolian Tartaric sway by the Muscovite grand dukes in the fifteenth and sixteenth centuries, a time of Russian consolidation began. Karamzin lists the various foreign powers that, since the reign of Grand Duke Ivan III (Ivan the Great, 1462–1505), could no longer threaten Russia: Lithuania, Sweden, the Empire of the Khans, and the Ottoman Empire.[32]

However, with the end of the Rurikids dynasty, which lasted from 852 to 1598, Russia became engulfed in turmoil and was occupied by Poland in the time of the so-called *smuta* ("Time of Troubles"). On November 4, 2005, Russia inaugurated a new national holiday, Unity Day, to commemorate the popular uprising led by Kuzma Minin and Dimitry Pozharsky that led in 1612 to the expulsion of the Polish occupiers from Moscow. This also marked the end of the Time of Troubles and foreign intervention in Russia. At this time, the Romanovs became the czars, and their reign began a restrengthening of Russia. This era had been preceded by a time during the Rurikids' rule when every prince wanted to be his own master, about which Karamazin wrote: "Is it, under such circumstances, really surprising, that the barbarians conquered our fatherland?"[33]

Karamazin observed that, after the Napoleonic Wars, only a strong Russian government could protect Russia from the threats of the surrounding barbarians. Western historiography usually forgets that Western Europeans are seen as the barbarians by the Russians, even though Russians are appreciative of high Western culture. And German society as a whole has never fully acknowledged the psychic and physical destruction that Hitler's Germany brought to Russia. These attacks contributed greatly to the historic feeling of the Russian people that they are encircled by dangerous enemies, a potent cultural complex that can erupt in the Russian psyche at any time and cause a virulent and politically unstable situation within Russia and in the international community. Contemporary commentator Georges Sokoloff writes about how this ancient fear of encirclement affects the current Russian psyche in his *Métamorphose de la Russie, 1984–2004*:

Vladimir Putin and the group of people who polished his outer image, knew how to take advantage of the added national mortifications of Russia in the second half of the year 1999. They converted them into a program of national reawakening. The mortifications arose out of the extortion by the terrorists in connection to the confrontation with the Chechens. They also arose out of the severe accusations of the Western press because of international financial scandals. And finally out of the disdain of the great ones of the world for the former great power of the East.[34]

Another contemporary Franco-Russian observer, Hélène Carrère d'Encausse, describes in her book the necessity of modern Russia to become aware of its Eurasian will to survive. She bases her argument on another famous Russian historian— Wassilij Kliutschevskij—and quotes him as follows:

In his course on Russian history the great historian Kliutschevskij summarized the development of the Russian (state). In doing this he quoted the permanent necessity of this state to defend itself against the outer World. In other words the compulsion of conforming to its own national interests. He added: "Russia was formed in the 14th century under the pressure of a foreign yoke; it consolidated and expanded in the 15th and 16th century while fighting for its survival in the West, the South and the South-West. Wassilij III was one of the great architects of the unification of the Russian territories and of the formation of the Russian state. The fight for survival in the 16th century was especially the work of Ivan IV, who was called 'The Terrible.' He defeated the heirs of the Golden Horde, but also fought with western states, who dominated the access to the Baltic Sea: Livonia, Lithuania and Poland, and he fought in the East, where he conquered Siberia."[35]

The Russian complex of feeling surrounded by hungry barbarians is deeply rooted in Russian history and in the Russian psyche. It is connected with the repetitive experience of national suffering and profound disappointments at the hands of so-called friends and enemies who, in the name of idealistic goals, sought their own gain at Russia's expense. The incidents in South Ossetia, Georgia, and Ukraine demonstrate that specific events can activate the cultural complex at any time.

Conclusion

Both the German cultural complex of superiority and the Russian cultural complex of fear of being encircled by hungry barbarians are more or less anchored in collective consciousness. But they are both linked to deeper, unconscious emotions, images, and historical memories that can have destructive sociopolitical consequences. The knowledge of cultural complexes seems to be not only vital for psychoanalysts who are working with individuals but also essential to a more thorough awareness of politicians, diplomats, businesspeople, journalists, and everyday citizens. Only the open exchange of collective memories in open discussions can create awareness and consciousness of different views and meanings. Here, I will give two hopeful examples:

- There was a German–Polish exchange of books describing their mutual history as well as an attempt to change purely nationalistic and arrogant agendas in a committee that had to revise schoolbooks on history during the 1990s.
- In what seems like a long time ago, in 2000, my dear friends of the Polish Association and my dear friend Jörg Rasche from Germany created a weekend with our English colleagues to engage in conversation about personal and cultural history. It was an excellent exercise in listening, even when it was not pleasurable. We told our familiar histories, embedded in the histories of our culture.

Notes

1 Thomas Singer and Samuel L. Kimbles, eds., *The Cultural Complex: Contemporary Jungian Perspectives on Psyche and Society* (London: Routledge, 2004), p. 5.
2 Irene Berkenbusch, "Vita of Saints in the Middle Ages under the Point of View of Psychohistory," in *Meetings with Literatures. Festschrift for Carola L. Gottzmann on her 65th Birthday*, eds. Petra Hörner and Roswitha Wisniewski (Berlin: Weidler, 2008), p. 158.
3 Berkenbusch, p. 158.
4 Bruno Ziauddin, *Grüezi Gummihälse, warum uns die Deutschen manchmal auf die Nerven gehen* (Reinbeck bei Hamburg: Rowohlt Taschenbuch, 2008), p. 142.
5 Ziauddin, p. 116.
6 Ziauddin, p. 101.
7 Ziauddin, p. 25.
8 "Drang nach Osten," Wikipedia. Accessed April 23, 2014, at http://en.wikipedia.org/wiki/Drang_nach_Osten
9 August Nitschke, "Frühe christliche Reiche," in *Propyläen der Weltgeschichte, vol. 5, Golo Mann und August Nitschke*, eds. Golo Mann and August Nitschke (Berlin, Frankfurt am Main: Propyläen, 1986), p. 337.
10 Elke Windisch, "A Faithful Servant Switches Over," *Badische Zeitung*, May 3, 2008, p. 3.
11 The map from *Badische Zeitung* represents the transfer of gas from Russia to Western Europe. It also shows warlike arrows directed against Europe. See www.badische-zeitung.de/der-muehsame-weg-zu-mehr-unabhaengigkeit
12 Elke Windisch, "Pact against the West," *Badische Zeitung*, May 3, 2008.
13 Paraphrased by author from Isabel Heinemann, Exhibition Supplement, "Wissenschaft, Planung, Vertreibung, Der Generalplan Ost der Nationalsozialisten" (Science, Planning, Expulsion: The General Plan for the East of the Nazis), in *Ausstellung der Deutsche Forschungs-gemeinschaft* (Exhibition of the German Research Foundation), 2006, p. 7.
14 Exhibition Supplement.
15 "Revolutionär seiner Majestät," *Der Spiegel 50*, March 12, 2007.
16 Martin Luther, *On the Jews and Their Lies*, 54, 67, 29; cited in Robert Michael, *Holy Hatred: Christianity, Antisemitism, and the Holocaust* (New York: Palgrave Macmillan, 2006), p. 111.

17 "Wake Up, Wake Up You German Land," *EKG*, hymnbook of the Protestant Church of Germany.
18 Ziauddin, *Grüezi Gummihälse*, p. 116.
19 C. G. Jung to Arnold Künzli, January 12, 1944. From *C. G. Jung, Letters*, vol. I (Olten, Freiburg: Walter, 1981), p. 422.
20 C. G. Jung to Emma von Pelet, January 15, 1944, p. 423.
21 Wilhelm Grönbech, *Kultur und Religion der Germanen* (Darmstadt: Wissenschaftlichen Buchgesellschaft, 1980).
22 "The War Is at an End. They Encircle Russia," *Argumenti I Fakti* (Arguments and Facts), no. 24, 2008.
23 Alexander Pushkin, *The Fairy Tale of the Golden Rooster*, illustrated by Iwan Bilibin (Frankfurt am Main: Insel Bilderbuch, 1976), p 3.
24 Sergej Wladimirowitsch Bodrow, Interview in *Argumenti I Fakti*, no. 27, July 2008, p. 10. Original in Russian, translation by Gert Sauer.
25 Aleksandr Isayevich Solschenizyn, "Spiegel Gespräch: 'Mit Blut geschrieben,'" *Der Spiegel 30*, July 23, 2007, p. 101.
26 Peter Scholl-Latour, *Russia Surrounded* (Berlin: Ullstein Taschenbuch, 2007).
27 Gabriele Krone Schmalz, *Was geschieht in Russland* (Munich: F. A. Herbig, 2007), p. 175.
28 Schmalz, p. 175.
29 Schmalz, p. 182.
30 Gabriele Krone Schmalz, *Russland verstehen der Kampf um die Ukraine und die Arroganz des Westens* (Munich: C. H. Beck, 2015).
31 N. M. Karamsin, *Istoria Gossudarstwa russkowo* (History of the Russian State) (Moscow: Äksto, 2007), p. 240.
32 Karamsin, p. 833
33 Karamsin, p. 992. Original in Russian, translation by Gert Sauer.
34 Georges Sokoloff, *Métamorphose de la Russie 1984–2004* (Paris: Librerie Arthème Fayard, 2003), p. 573. Original in French, translation by Gert Sauer.
35 Hélène Carrère d' Encausse, *L'Empire d'Eurasie* (Paris: Fayard, 2005), p. 29. See also the interview in *Rossijskaja Gaseta*, August 8, 2008, no. 168. Translation by Gert Sauer.

Chapter 3

Russia, a "Therapy" for the West?

Luigi Zoja

Translated from the Italian by John Irving

Remorse and Nostalgia

Octavio Paz, poet and essayist, referred to anthropology as "the remorse of the West."[1] By adopting this point of view, a whole current of studies takes on a significance that extends well beyond its specialistic importance. Anthropology is not only the study of a few surviving premodern peoples; it is also the blob of melancholy that secretly torments the Euro-American West—now a universal model as a result of globalization—for its elimination of human qualities that are not geared to efficiency.

I am using this example to suggest that Russia arguably recurs in Western discourse not only because it presents itself today as a rival, but also because it represents much of what our modernity has lost—and for which it is thus nostalgic.

The West's Relations with Russia

Why do we speak about Russia so often? In postmodernity, talk is mostly of economics. As an economic antagonist of the West, the Russian Federation is little more than a gnat: Its GDP (gross domestic product) is 20 percent lower than Italy's,[2] even though it has more than double the population and a territory so vast it contains virtually infinite natural resources. It has been dubbed a filling station with nuclear weapons, and its missiles are a reason for fear. A nuclear war is only being avoided because of what we assume to be implicit, a "balance of terror" like the one that prevented armed conflict between the West and the Soviet Union during the Cold War (in those days known as MAD—mutually assured destruction).[3]

Moreover, Russia is sometimes referred to in fairly benevolent terms, especially in Italy. Why this should be is another question we have to ask ourselves. In the present international situation, establishing who the aggressor is in the conflict between Russia and Ukraine is arguably easier than it has ever been since Hitler's day. Relative benevolence may thus be not so much a current phenomenon as a historical residue of the "Italian exception" that persisted throughout the Cold War. Italy, in fact, was the only country in the West in which the opposition was

DOI: 10.4324/9781032695143-5

dominated by a Communist Party, a fact that made its international position between the United States and the Soviet Union ambiguous and hampered any real possibility of government alternation.

Today, however, not only in the Italian narrative but also in the German one, it is often possible to detect an attitude of extreme caution, verging on indulgence, toward the positions assumed by Russia, attacks on neighboring countries included. German television news—the quality reporting of the Second Channel, ZDF, in particular—tends to attribute this to a form of "German sentimentalism" that impedes any overly hostile attitudes toward Russia. We must acknowledge, therefore, how three generations on, a problem of collective psychology—a semiconscious "debt" or a sense of guilt for their attack on the Soviet Union, a key event in World War II—still lingers in these two former Nazi–Fascist Axis allies. Insofar as it recalls two already familiar facts, this comes as only a relative surprise for psychoanalysts.

First, studies of collective traumas and their long-term persistence have evolved. Today, we know a great deal about their consequences in the third generation of Shoah survivors. Moving on to the United States and the problems of the African American population, they are still affected by and analyzing the scars of slavery more than a century and a half after its abolition.[4] Research is based not only on individual psychiatry but also on a broader vision that embraces anthropology, sociology, and the Jungian concept of the collective unconscious.

Second, identifying the *long-term* consequences of the Nazi–Fascist Axis's attack on the Soviet Union demands both a historical-political approach and a psychological one, which the layperson may struggle to share. In a state of catastrophe such as war, common trauma leaves wounds not only among the attacked, *but also among the attackers*, as we can tell today from the albeit-limited number of studies that are coming out of the Ukraine–Russia conflict.

The Words of Svetlana Alexievich

The questions I am asking sum up a central point in Svetlana Alexievich's Nobel Prize acceptance speech. The Soviet Union disappeared virtually in a moment, but that did not mean there were suddenly no "reds" left in the world, especially among the elderly. No matter how large it is, a state can disappear more or less rapidly. But this in no way corresponds to the disappearance of the need for a utopia, which, in the Soviet case, had controlled the birth of the state itself.[5]

In turn, the cultural space on which the experiment was built conjures up something far greater and more complex than the mere nostalgia of those who felt themselves to be Marxists.[6] It is a temporal, spatial, psychological, primary dimension for human beings, but it is being increasingly repressed, erased, and underestimated in the daily life of the West.

Returning to Svetlana Alexievich, in her speech she said, "We live faster than ever before."[7] It thus becomes clear that what this Belarusian writer is telling us does not concern the citizens of the former Soviet Union alone. Worn out by consumerism and ephemerality, even cultivated Westerners may believe they are feeling "nostalgia for Russia" when they think back with regret to the days of committed intellectuals who always viewed the country with curiosity, often with indulgence or sympathy. The new twenty-first-century populist, on the other hand, expects to rediscover the appeal of indisputable authorities such as the czar, Stalin, or Putin there. Certain strong attractions—which we are unable to define but whose influence we perceive—have more complicated and older roots than the lacerating twentieth century that preceded us.

Premodernity and Lack of Boundaries

The melancholy and dismay at the immensity typical of people fascinated by Russia today also existed in the Middle Ages, the seventeenth century, and the nineteenth century, the century of Romanticism. They existed centuries before Marx. Over the last few generations, they have been removed from the lived experience of Europeans on account of the hurry for and expectation of concrete results that are inevitable consequences of globalization and the Americanization that entails. But it is precisely a "slow pace" and an unconcern for acceleration that have differentiated traditional Russian culture from the West and that continue to do so today.

It is significant that this should also apply to the art we regard as being the most quintessentially modern, namely cinema. Explaining how he came to make *Ivan's Childhood* (1962), his smash-hit debut film, Andrei Tarkovsky speaks of his rapport with the short story on which it was based, *Ivan*, by Vladimir Bogomolov. He was seeking not merely to reproduce the plot, but to capture the *rhythm* of the story. The title character is a boy shattered by the war, yet his character and feelings are described, not by the action thereof, but by its opposite, namely the *pauses between actions*.[8]

It is possible to view this difference between cultures from a general perspective. The West's passage to modernity has highlighted a spatial-temporal divergence from Russia in the principal creative activities: cinema, theatre, and the figurative arts.

Let us set the Russian soul beside the more specifically European world, using the concept with which Max Weber distinguished the traditional mind from the modern. The latter entails *Entzauberung der Welt*: the disenchantment or dismay of the world, which is reduced to a container in which agents are clear, identifiable, and lay—almost scientific, even when looking at moral qualities.[9]

This modern logic is lacking in the works of Dostoyevsky, one of the figures most associated with the "Russian genius." Evil is ever present but cannot be identified using the clear-cut categories of the Ten Commandments. Evil is a human potential that preexists norms, and Dostoyevsky is psychology before psychoanalysis. For the characters of Raskolnikov and Stavrogin, in Dostoyevsky's novel *The Possessed*, their moral uncontrollability is in more than one respect related to the lack of boundaries of the steppe and the never wholly complete Russian capacity to transform a millenary past into a present with coherent modern structures.

We Westerners must be careful not to use reductive post-Weberian criteria, a mistake we make in even the most banal, commonplace occurrences. It makes no sense to say that "Russians are melancholy, so they drink too much vodka" and, circularly, "Russians drink too much vodka, so they become melancholy." Many Italians also drink too much: Sometimes they grow sad; sometimes they grow exuberant. Alcohol determines a change in emotions, not in their content. It is never extraneous to the subject's lived experiences and cultural conditioning.

It is natural for us in the West to read Dostoyevsky because he is an extraordinary narrator. But, half-consciously, we also read him because the evil that runs through his work *did not experience the Enlightenment,* even though cultivated Russians, who often spoke French fluently, were familiar enough with Enlightenment philosophy. This evil is thus external to us Westerners: It has something of Weber's magic about it, of which we are all deprived, and it distresses us and fascinates us at one and the same time.[10]

If forming into definable units is extraneous to the Russian soul, it is not because it is incapable of combining with Western philosophy and science: On the contrary, the greatest experiment of transformation into an equal and "modern" society in the history not only of Russia but also of humanity was precisely the application of the theories of a German Jew, Karl Marx. But much older and more decisive than that of the Bolshevik, indeed the czarist, state are the lived experiences that in fiction, and even earlier in oral culture, merge the unlimited dilation of time with the lack of boundaries of space that is perceptible in geography: "The land of Russia was soil before it was a nation."[11]

Even non-specialists are familiar with one of the most concrete differences between Nazi *lagers* and Stalinist gulags: The latter, which were situated at immense distances from Europe and the sea—save for those in the frozen Arctic—had barely any need for fences. Unlike a barrier, the infinity of space cannot be cleared by resorting to expedients.

The Infinite Unity of Space and Time

The Westerner is short-winded and suffocates inside the boundaries of place and time, which are intertwined. The European bourgeois who sees Chekov's *The Cherry Orchard* for the hundredth time does so not *despite* knowing perfectly well that nothing at all is going to happen in the play, but *precisely because*—half-consciously—they need to take part in a time flow in which nothing happens: that is, something that has been an original, ordinary, physiological condition for the normal, or at least the natural, human being for millennia. But human beings who live in the present, be they Russian or Western, have seen industrialization and modernization seize this reassuring container from their grasp almost before their eyes, without them even noticing.

The Russian classics do not speak of immensity alone: Endeavoring to contain it, they overflow with pages. We are unlikely to say: "During the holidays I'm going to read *War and Peace* or *The Brothers Karamazov*." "This year . . ." or "Over the next few years . . ." is more likely.

When we Westerners decide to watch a film by Tarkovsky or Sokurov, we are fully aware that we will not find an infinitesimal fraction of the dynamism and action—not to mention the killings—of a Hollywood movie. Maybe we have heard praise for the two directors and sense that their creations are driven by non-commercial criteria. What we don't know is that we are making this choice partly because, irrespective of our culture and conscious convictions, intoxicated by the "productivity compulsion," our nature and our unconscious are seeking a modicum of peace and quiet in an anti-hysteric, antimanic space.

As I have suggested from the start, not only the individual but also all Western culture (and, today, certainly the most modernized strata of Russian society) is pursuing a way of correcting the one-sidedness of this anxiety.

In the twin immensity of space and time, the real Russia naturally has boundaries. Yet, more than in other places in the world, in Russia the narrative blurs and dissolves its real borders, chipping away at them, making them hard to define. Traditional tales and songs have always teemed with characters seeking to withdraw from the immensity of space, but after a lifetime of roaming they still find themselves in Russia.[12]

So what about time? Under the czar and the Soviet regime, citizens were not allowed to have real opinions about the future, which belonged to the halls of power. Despite that, it may have been unforeseen for the state itself.

The Unforeseen

Vasily Grossman's description is hard to beat:

> And then, all of a sudden, on 5 March 1953, Stalin died. This death was like an invasion: it was a sudden irruption into this grand system of mechanised enthusiasm, of carefully planned popular wrath, of popular love organised ahead of time by district Party committees.
>
> Stalin's death was not part of any plan; he died without receiving personal instructions from Comrade Stalin himself. In the freedom and capriciousness of death there was something explosive, something hostile to the innermost essence of the Soviet State. Confusion sieved minds and hearts.[13]

If the future cannot be foreseen, the past existed and ought not to be alterable. But the Russian specialist Stephen Kotkin harbors doubts on this point.[14] Under the various regimes in Russia, it has always been conventional to present the future as radiant. It is the past that has always been unforeseeable.

Infinity and Reality

After these remarks on what extends beyond borders, now let us look at a centuries-old dynamic—hence, at a process that, in theory, can be defined historically. Let us observe, that is, the most important stages in the long process of union and opposition between Russia and Ukraine with the present-day facts.

In 1868, a czarist decree established an interesting case of preventive legislation by declaring that the Ukrainian language had never existed and never would.[15] In the course of history since then, extreme-right national regimes have forged mythical bonds with the past to justify their present aggressiveness. Returning to the example of the Axis powers, fascism invented a would-be continuation from the Roman Empire, whereas Nazism did the same with the Germanic tribes of Arminius who brought the Empire down. These apparently psychological operations did not save the two regimes from disrepute and ultimate downfall.

In 1931–1932, Stalin had weakened Ukraine with mass crop requisition, causing the *Holodomor*, which Ukrainians and others today regard as intentional genocide by famine.

Nikita Khrushchev subsequently spread the myth that Ukraine had decided to merge with Russia in the past. To celebrate the myth's 300th anniversary, the then leader of the Soviet Union transferred the sovereignty of the Crimea from Russia to Ukraine, which is its territorial and, hence, economic continuation. Its demographic continuation was already assured by the fact that, after World War II, the Tartars, a people who had inhabited the Crimea for centuries, had been accused of siding with the Germans and deported to Siberia.

Males and Females Today

Speaking of historical processes that can also be measured in numbers, in nonimaginary Russia the "production of new life," which the citizens of nations perform naturally by giving birth to children, has reached an all-time low: Not only do the former Soviet states (and ethnic groups) view each with suspicion, the gap between men and women is also one of the widest in the world.[16] At a rate of four women murdered for every 100,000, the number of femicides is infinitely higher than in Western Europe. In Latin countries, traditionally male chauvinist, the rate is higher only in Latin American countries such as Colombia (4.2 per 100,000) and Brazil (4.3), where crime is often out of control. In Italy, the rate is 0.4, in Spain 0.5.[17]

Russian divorce and abortion rates are among the highest in the world. Given the relatively risky lives of males, what with their high consumption of alcohol and other substances, in the twenty-first century Russia has recorded one of the widest gaps between male and female life expectancy: from twelve to fourteen years.[18]

The result of all this is a very high percentage of fatherless children who grow up with their mother and often, given the physical and age proximity between the generations, with their grandmother: the proverbial *babushka*, the anti-Hollywoodian antihero of *Alexandra*, one of Sokurov's film masterpieces. As in Tarkovsky's *Ivan*, here there is no shooting, no bloodshed: Everything boils down to the waiting. If we describe it as a *Russian war film*, the accent should fall on *Russian*, not on *war film*, as we might expect in Europe or America.

The important studies that have accompanied the development of American society over the centuries (suffice it to recall those of Margaret Mead and Daniel
Patrick Moynihan) tell us that, in different societies (or the ethnic groups that make
up a macro-society such as America), the cultural and economic development of
the various groups is directly proportional to the presence of fathers. At the top of
the US ladder are Asians and Jews, where the father is rarely lacking. On the bottom rung are African Americans, where the figure has been absent since the time of
slavery and continues to be so with the mass incarceration of Black males. Using
this very well-known analogy,[19] one would not be too mistaken if one summed up
Russia's failure to modernize by saying that the country is inhabited by the African
Americans of Europe.

The Unconscious Needs of Culture and
Western Nostalgias

Ultimately, the complex charm that whatever we perceive as Russian exercises on
us cannot be put down to objective and aesthetic elements alone. Dostoyevsky and
Tolstoy are, of course, pinnacles of literature, as are Tarkovsky and Sokurov of
cinema, but the veneration we heap on them also says a lot about the psychological
imbalance of the West. What is activated in our unconscious when we view Russia,
as is inevitable, from a distance?

According to Jung:

> The more one-sided the conscious attitude, the more antagonistic are the con-
> tents arising from the unconscious, so that we may speak of a real opposition
> between the two. In this case the compensation appears in the form of a counter-
> function, but this case is extreme.[20]

As a consequence:

> The unconscious compensation of a neurotic conscious attitude contains all the
> elements that could effectively and healthily correct the *one-sidedness of the
> conscious mind* if these elements were made conscious.[21]

Psychoanalysis came into being at the turn of the twentieth century when Freud
noted that the excessive repression of sexuality in "well-bred" women led them to
the neurosis—more specifically, hysteria—with which their psychophysical whole
rebelled precisely against that *one-sidedness*. In this medical and Freudian concep-
tion, the problem may boil down to a sum of individual cases. But what interests
me today is to stress, like Jung, how *the one-sidedness of all our Western culture*
may force it into preferences that risk writing off the charm of anti-Western or anti-
American cultures as "only" aesthetic, literary, or sentimental. This yearning for
Russian immensity also tells us how immense our shortcomings are.

In fact,

> The collective unconscious, being the repository of man's experience and at the same time the prior condition of this, is an image of the world which has taken aeons to form. In this image certain features, the archetypes or dominants, have crystallized out in the course of time.[22]

At this point, the question is: Are space and time that spread toward infinity specific archetypes (or dominants) of the Russian soul, or do they belong to the human soul in general?

On the one hand, we sense the infinite exerting attraction and, at once, terror on all human beings. Precisely to dominate the absolute unknown, sooner or later every culture imagines an omnipotent God and heroes of infinite strength. Does this mean that the God and the heroes were already there, that they are a universal archetype?

On the other hand, the magic of the infinite, for which we postmodern Westerners have felt acute regret as long as we have lived in a world in which everything is measurable, materializable, and finite, appears to manifest itself above all in the Russian landscape, in the irreversible sadness that every Russian epiphany leaves in our ears and in our eyes.

This magic sounds barely credible if it is expressed in the language of the West: We "the disenchanted" may be the first not to believe in it.

But, if sorrow comes from the mysterious otherness that lives on beyond the steppe, it moves us and convinces us, like a dream, like everything that is relatively indefinable because it comes more from the unconscious than from objective and rational information.

Svetlana Alexievich sums up the mystery with poetical-political but bitter words: "Suffering is our capital, our natural resource. Not oil or gas—but suffering. It is the only thing we are able to produce consistently."[23]

This meta-tragic and meta-Christian capacity fills us with ecstasy, perhaps even admiration, irrespective of any sentiment of sharing or repulsion that may inspire the system in which it has manifested itself down the ages.

Notes

1 Octavio Paz, *Tiempo nublado* (Barcelona: Seix Barral, 1986), I, p. 1.
2 GDP, World Bank, https://data.worldbank.org/indicator/NY.GDP.MKTP.CD
3 I have called the new situation MAD 2. See Luigi Zoja, *Paranoia. La follia che fa la storia*, 2nd. ed. (Turin: Bollati Boringhieri, 2023), Preface.
4 See, for example, Èlodie Grossi, "New Avenues in Epigenetic Research about Race: Online Activism around Reparations for Slavery in the United States," *Social Science Information* 59, no. 1: 93–116. https://journals.sagepub.com/doi/full/10.1177/0539018419899336; Rachel Yehuda and Amy Lehrner, "Intergenerational Transmission of Trauma Effects: Putative Role of Epigenetic Mechanisms," *World Psychiatry* 17, no. 3: 243–257. www.ncbi.nlm.nih.gov/pmc/articles/PMC6127768/

5 See the introduction to my *Utopie minimaliste*, 2nd ed. (Milan: Chiarelettere, 2021).
6 I believe it is correct to use this term and not *communist*. Using the two as equivalents is a Eurocentric and modern-centric deformation. The societies proposed by Plato, many pre-Columbian American societies, and other non-European cultures were also based on common property.
7 Svetlana Alexievich, "On the Battle Lost," Nobel Lecture, given in Stockholm, Sweden, December 15, 2015, www.nobelprize.org/prizes/literature/2015/alexievich/lecture/
8 Andrei Tarkovsky, *Sculpting in Time* (Austin: University of Texas Press, 1986).
9 Max Weber, *Politik als Beruf—Wissenschaft als Beruf* (1919). Published in English as "The Politician's Work" in *Charisma and Disenchantment*, eds. Paul Reitter and Chad Wellmon (New York: New York Review Books, 2020).
10 It is significant that my Italian copy of *The Devils* (Fyodor Dostoyevsky, *I demoni* [Turin: Einaudi, 1993]) includes *Il male in Dostoevkij* (Evil in Dostoyevsky), a long essay by the leading Italian philosopher Luigi Pareyson.
11 See Marco Belpoliti, "Putin e l'animo russo. Intervista con Gian Piero Piretto" [Putin and the Russian Spirit: An Interview with Gian Piero Piretto], *Doppiozero*, October 13, 2014, www.doppiozero.com/putin-e-lanimo-russo-intervista-con-gian-piero-piretto. Piretto is a historian, one of Italy's major Russian experts.
12 Ibid., pp. 19–21.
13 Vasily Grossman, *Everything Flows* (1970) (London: Vintage Books, 2011), p. 26.
14 "A Historian of the Future: Five More Questions for Stephen Kotkin," *Uncommon Knowledge*, YouTube, February 10, 2023, www.youtube.com/watch?v=3ww4ofe0v70; "Five More Questions for Stephen Kotkin: Prigozhin Mutiny Edition," *Uncommon Knowledge*, YouTube, July 11, 2023, www.youtube.com/watch?v=M5z5HUS4tmM
15 Timothy Snyder, "The Making of Modern Ukraine," Fall 2022, https://online.yale.edu/courses/making-modern-ukraine, Lecture 22.
16 Alexander Etkind, *Russia against Modernity* (Cambridge, UK: Polity Press, 2023). Chapter 6 examines these data, which come from a number of international sources.
17 World Population Review, https://worldpopulationreview.com/country-rankings/femicide-rates-by-country
18 Etkind, *Russia against Modernity*.
19 See also my *The Father: Historical, Psychological and Cultural Perspectives* (2000) (New York: Routledge, 2018), Chapter 4.
20 C. G. Jung, *Psychological Types, The Collected Works of C. G. Jung*, vol. 6, eds. Herbert Read, Gerhard Adler, Michael Fordham, and William McGuire, trans. R. F. C. Hull (London: Routledge & Kegan Paul, 1971), § 694.
21 C. G. Jung, "On the Psychology of the Unconscious," in *The Collected Works of C. G. Jung*, vol. 7, eds. Herbert Read, Gerhard Adler, Michael Fordham, and William McGuire, trans. R. F. C. Hull (Princeton: Princeton University Press, 1969), § 151. Italics added.
22 C. G. Jung, "Archetypes of the Collective Unconscious," in *The Collected Works of C. G. Jung*, vol. 9i, eds. Herbert Read, Gerhard Adler, Michael Fordham, and William McGuire, trans. R. F. C. Hull (Princeton: Princeton University Press, 1969), § 187.
23 Alexievich, "On the Battle Lost."

Chapter 4

The Mysterious Russian Soul

Elena Volodina

> You cannot grasp Russia with your mind.
> —Fyodor Tyutchev, *Stikhotvoreniya* [Poems] (December 10, 1866)

Russia is a vast country—more like a whole continent, not just a country. Its expanse is thrilling. Russian culture has imbibed the influence of the West and the East, including Byzantium, Christianity, and Slavic pagan creeds. This culture reflects the geographic and climatic variety of the vast lands of Eurasia. "Russia's hugeness is its metaphysical quality, not just a parameter of its empirical history. Russia's horizontality and the immeasurability of its lands is the internal dimension of the soul of the Russian nation."[1]

The Russian soul is often depicted as mysterious, containing a deep secret. Poet and essayist Joseph Brodsky speaks of "ambivalence" being "the chief characteristic of my country."[2] The mystery is rooted in a distant past in which the Russian nation formed as a spiritual entity. Back then, people felt part of nature, and nature was part of them. Ancient Slavic nations were in a state of spiritual connection to the world, a state that Jung called "participation mystique."[3] These nations' profound and resilient spirit, capable of a metaphysical perception of nature, was enriched by a harmonious interaction with it. Nature was relished for its beautiful soul; the entire Russian culture is permeated by poetic perceptions of the land and the natural environment.

In the tenth century CE, authorities began to impose the Christian faith on the Russians. The Christian myth flowed powerfully into public perceptions, pushing the ancient Slavic worldview into the background. However, the great forests preserved, in their depth, the connection between humans and nature. Ancient rites survived, as did folktales and ballads, herbal ornaments on fabrics, and animal designs on ovens and wooden huts.

Because Slavic mythology never fully developed and has remained in an embryonic state, it was not fully assimilated by the Christian myth and has reached us in the form of folktales and beliefs. This is what the mystery of the Russian soul amounts to: the simultaneous coexistence of two worldviews. One is the dominant, consciously perceived Christian worldview, and the other is unconscious of its own

DOI: 10.4324/9781032695143-6

existence—the ancient Slavic worldview, which, given its unconscious character, is capable of powerfully possessing the collective soul of the Russian nation.

Whether collective or individual, in the Russian soul, there is always an expectation of the miraculous. In just a bit, a miracle will happen, and our lives will change radically: We shall become healthy and rich, and we won't need to do anything for it. Ancient Russian ballads, *bylini*, and Russian folktales also nurture this hope. The most celebrated and powerful of the *bogatyrs* (epic heroes) is Ilya Muromets, who spent his first thirty-three years lying on a stove unable to walk, after which he miraculously got to his feet and was given superhuman strength.

The protagonist of *By Will of the Pike*, a popular folktale, is a poor fool named Yemelya, who goes to fetch some water from a hole in the ice and catches a pike with his bare hands.[4] In exchange for her freedom, the pike gives him the supernatural ability to grant all his wishes. From that point on, Yemelya does what he pleases. Eventually, he marries a princess and becomes rich and influential. The Russian poet Alexander Pushkin used the same motif in *The Tale of the Fisherman and the Fish*: An old man catches a goldfish in the sea and then sets it free.[5] In return, the goldfish grants the fisherman his wishes. A Russian saying goes "Fools are lucky." These fools—the protagonists of folktales—are simple-minded people who commit absurd actions contrary to common sense. A folktale fool can catch a fish and then release it although his family back home is starving. The fool lives in close connection with the unconscious and understands life intuitively. As a result, he interacts with the world efficiently, making the world come to his aid to grant all his wishes.

In these folktales, we can see that an encounter with the miraculous requires touching water and getting acquainted with the creatures that live in it. The protagonists of *By Will of the Pike* and *The Tale of the Fisherman and the Fish* are in a state of mystic participation in nature. Just as pagans keenly perceived the miracle of nature—the miracle of water, the miracle of wind, rain, and sun—so is the Russian soul permanently fine-tuned to the miraculous and always prepared for an encounter with the numinous.

The only female deity in the Russian pantheon, Mokosh, is also associated with water and moisture. Slavic nations worshipped the fertilizing, healing, purifying, and oracular powers of water; they had special rites to worship water.[6] Folktales make frequent mention of *dead* and *living water* used to treat the sick and even resurrect the dead. To this day, pagan rituals are carried out on the eve of the Feast of St. John the Baptist, called *Kupala* [bathing] *Night* in Russia. The rituals involve dancing and collective bathing in rivers and lakes. Water is a universal symbol of the unconscious. Deep in the collective unconscious of the nation lives a creative principle that makes miracles happen. The collective anima animates the nation, endowing it with the ability to feel keenly and anticipate the future.

Inside the Russian soul is a deep urge to encounter the numinous. It's like being possessed by a cosmic spirit. Not long ago, a fragment of the sash of the Holy Virgin was brought to Moscow from a monastery on Mount Athos in northern Greece; it was widely advertised as an opportunity to heal one's body and obtain one's wishes. Thousands of people lined up for eighteen to twenty hours in the freezing cold to get a chance to touch the relic. This longing reflected a purely pagan desire for a miracle and had little to do with Orthodox Christianity, if only because another fragment of the very same sash is on permanent display in a nearby church in Moscow, and very few people pay attention to it.

In a positive sense, the desire for a miracle enables considerable spiritual accomplishment, of which history knows many examples, such as the holy old men who were held in great esteem in medieval Russia. Moreover, we find many mentions of the passions and excesses of the Russian character, the desire to tease fate and stretch one's luck. One dangerous game that plays at the brink of life and death is called *Russian roulette*. There is a Russian expression that translates as "faith in Russian serendipity"—another way of wishing for a miracle. The negative aspect of this characteristic is that people are passive and do not want to work every day in order to achieve what they desire. They want to get it all at once "by will of the pike"; this explains the popularity of financial schemes that promise to make one rich overnight. When the miracle fails to happen, some people fall into black despair and sometimes even take their own life. Others slide into a state of apathy, which goes hand in hand with the famous Russian sloth.

In the realm of Russian culture, there is a phenomenon known as the *Great Russian Literature*—a literature that formed over just one century, the nineteenth, but managed to attain the height of a universal phenomenon. Great Russian Literature emerged as a replacement for a realm, by then almost forgotten, populated by superior and inferior pagan deities and for the poetic world of Russian nature. The forgotten ancient Slavic soul was reborn as the literary soul. As Russian philosopher Ivan Ilyin puts it, "Russian poetry is the all-national voice of the Russian soul. In the poetry, the soul has perceived its historical mission, its achievements and failures, its virtues and sins."[7]

Russian literature opened up new dimensions of the human soul. The Russian fate assigned a spiritual mission to Russian fiction: In Russia, the creative quest was best manifest in the form of fiction, which became a gauge of the achievements and failures of Russian spirituality. Russian classical literature was a spiritual ministration: This was how Russia saw itself and how it was perceived by society. Its subject matter was not just art or culture, but the tragedy of human existence in Russia. "Just like Russian culture on the whole, Russian Literature corresponded to the vastness of Russia itself: it could only come to be in a huge country with limitless horizons."[8]

Russian literature was the most profound and brightest reflection of the Russian soul. It did not portray real-life historical conflicts or characters, but rather the existential conflicts of its time. Its characters were not social types but personifications of ideas present in the drama of the Russian psyche. The world of Russian classical fiction is an objective truth and value, a living, moving organism. After the 1917 revolution, Russian literature could no longer develop freely: It was, in a way, mothballed, becoming a huge cluster of stored energy. In the twentieth century, we lived behind an iron curtain, and Russian literature was our connection to the Russia of yore, to our roots. The Great Russian Literature became a myth in itself, with a strong energy of its own.

Russian classical literature is the spiritual heritage belonging to the entire nation. All Russians, whether they like it or not, live in this realm and are thereby tied together into some kind of entity. The realities of the world out there become cultural realities, which exist inside the psyche. All the characters of the great Russian novels, with their quests, toils, and joys, live within the collective national unconscious and represent collective aspects of autonomous, emotionally charged complexes, which can, under the right circumstances, constellate and take a person over completely. By becoming conscious of these complexes, the national character becomes conscious of itself. "Russian poetry has contained the most profound ideas of Russian religious thinking and Russian philosophy, and has itself become an organ of national identity."[9]

Widely known cultural complexes include those of Raskolnikov, Anna Karenina, and Oblomov. Who are these fictional characters who have given their names to these complexes? Rodion Raskolnikov, from Fyodor Dostoyevsky's *Crime and Punishment*, is a complicated and ambiguous personality: at once both a cruel murderer cold-bloodedly testing the theory of the Superman and a heartbroken penitent whose heart is brimming with love.[10] The very name, *Raskolnikov*, is symbolic, because the word *raskol* means "split" in Russian. There are several types of splits in his personality: murder versus love of one's neighbor, theory versus life, crime versus pangs of conscience. The Raskolnikov complex is also characterized by a division between the immediate experience and self-observation or reflection. Rebellion against the world order and against God coexists with a quest for religious faith, eventually leading Raskolnikov to humility. He breaks the moral law and falls because he has moral standards and a conscience.

The Anna Karenina complex, named after the protagonist of Leo Tolstoy's *Anna Karenina*, is mentioned when someone is unable to control his or her passions and commits suicide.[11] The problem is that people suffering from this complex fail to manage their lives, not just their passions. Anna was unable to live with her husband comfortably and stably; this relationship made her feel abused and oppressed. She was an openhearted person who felt others keenly and empathized with them. She suffered from loneliness in her family and hoped that love would fill her world; instead, love made her lose the world and herself as a result. The story of love turned out to be a story of death. Anna's tragedy is that she could not suffer the duality of her love for her son and her love for a man. She felt guilty, and this tremendous guilt crushed her. This story is also about freedom and responsibility for oneself and one's family.

The complex named after Oblomov, the protagonist of Ivan Goncharov's *Oblomov*, is that of a talented man who is afraid to live his life.[12] Oblomov literally does not get out of bed for the first fifty pages of the novel. Oblomov's case can be interpreted as that of a nonviable psyche with an unresolved maternal complex, or as a paralysis of individual will. It can also be understood as a keen perception of the unconscious, in which case the passiveness and contemplation represent supreme wisdom and a drive toward the transcendental.[13]

There are a multitude of other cultural complexes—even the complex of the Great Russian Literature itself. Many young girls in love feel influenced by Tatiana Larina, the female character of Alexander Pushkin's *Eugene Onegin*, expressed as a powerful urge to write a letter to the object of one's desire.[14] This connection makes a girl's feelings more elevated and meaningful. Her love becomes poetic, filled with the energy of nature and of previous generations.

A whole range of female characters are called *Turgenev's girls*, after the author Ivan Turgenev who created them. The most powerful image in this group is that of Liza Kalitina in *Home of the Gentry*.[15] Liza is an exemplary constant lover; for her, love is just as sacred as her principles about good and truth. When, as a result of her personal drama, she learns that she cannot be united with the man she loves (his wife turns out to be alive and returns to Russia), she finds only one road for herself in the world: to become a nun and purify her soul. Nowadays, when a woman is called "a Turgenev's girl," the connotation is usually a negative one, that of pride and arrogance. In reality, however, Turgenev created holistic characters, marked by dignity and high moral standards; he showed the beautiful soul of a Russian woman.

The anguish of losing meaning in midlife is called an *Uncle Vanya complex* after the protagonist of the play of the same name by Anton Chekhov.[16] A woman's suffering the lack of meaning in life can be seen in *The Three Sisters* by the same playwright.[17] Whereas Uncle Vanya entertains no hopes for change or renewal and blames himself, his mother, and the idleness of his youth for his wasted life, the three sisters expect their lives to change dramatically, once and for all, provided they move to Moscow. They believe in a sacred place—called Moscow—where they can be happy. The tragedy is that they are well aware they will never return to Moscow. Doomed to live in an unjust world and keep up appearances, they prefer pain to being insincere to themselves, preserving the love of life in the absence of love around them.

The opposite may also be true—namely, that the great Russian authors did not create or discover these complexes but only described and named the complexes that already existed among the Russians. Indeed, one can hardly assume Russians only became apathetic after reading *Oblomov*. They were already in the grasp of this complex: They had no idea how to adapt to the world, how to apply their talents and their "crystal-clear soul."

We may still be living in a literary realm. Everything the authorities and the bureaucrats are now doing, the entire machinery of corruption and despotism, has been depicted in the nineteenth-century writings of Mikhail Saltykov-Shchedrin and Nikolai Gogol in such exact detail that it is as if they were describing our present-day lives. The powers-that-be as well as ordinary people feel this fact keenly and painfully. For example, a Moscow newspaper decided to decorate the city with quotations from the Russian classics, including Saltykov-Shchedrin and Tyutchev. The banners were removed on the orders of the Moscow government after less than a day. No explanations were given; probably, the authorities felt exposed and feared being found out, just as the mayor did in *The Government Inspector* by Gogol.[18]

There is a reason why Joseph Stalin called fiction writers "engineers of the human souls" and why he tried to structure the souls by establishing himself as a god. Soviet literature imposed an ideological goal upon people and preached that attaining that goal was the duty of every person. The propelling power of the imposed sense of duty brought about a silent inner rebellion, expressed in the form of profound indifference and obedience to fate. The national soul is still unable to deal with the collective trauma that it experienced in the twentieth century. For seventy years, the Russian nation lived without a moral standard, in a country where all human values were trampled on and one's life was constantly under threat. The crimes of the regime had tragic consequences for the society as a whole and each individual in particular. Any person living in contemporary Russia suffers from the aftermath of Stalin's regime.

One of the functions of culture is to deal with trauma. Getting in touch with the energy of pre-communist Russia before it was raped by the Bolsheviks would be beneficial. Connecting to one's ancestors and getting their help would be good. Russian literature could greatly assist with this, if it were not for unexpected barriers. A matter now being discussed in Russia at the very highest level of government is reducing literature classes in secondary schools. Apparently, literature is one of the authorities' main concerns: They want to limit the next generation's access to the realm of classical Russian literature, thereby preventing it from becoming aware of the role and the mission of the person, the nation, and the state.

In the theater, the prevailing fashion is to refurbish classical plays by ruining and distorting the author's message and failing to bring it home. The viewer is thus isolated from the source and prevented from becoming aware of and experiencing his or her complexes. The crippled, traumatized play, with its meaning gone, falls apart like a derailed train.

Meanwhile, we all recognize quotations when we hear them. Russians firmly believe that foreigners have only a superficial understanding of Russian literature and, therefore, take a relaxed view of their interpretations. Foreign directors generally believe the three sisters are too passive. What could be easier than buying a ticket to Moscow? And yet, one cannot get away from oneself, and the provincial city simply cannot do without the three sisters. Likewise, one can get out of Russia, but one cannot get away from it. Those who have left suffer from nostalgia; those who have stayed say every day, "Enough—time to leave this place," but they know they never will. One has to sustain the constant tension between the urge to flee the country and the impossibility of leaving it behind.

Life in Russia is still hard and joyless in the material sense. The corruption and cynicism of contemporary authorities leave the new generation without moral guidance. Russians are said to have severe, unsmiling faces. Indeed, every family has accumulated endless pain and humiliation in its history; survival in the dangerous darkness of real life requires such qualities as cruelty and ruthlessness.

Apparently, in Russia, the Shadow has engulfed the bright side of life: love, kindness, honor, beauty, and joy.

This explains why present-day Raskolnikovs plan murder and robbery with calculation and cynicism but are then unexpectedly overwhelmed by guilt and compassion. The contemporary Anna Karenina consciously marries a rich, successful man; possessing every comfort of life, she fails to realize she needs love as well as money and social standing. People are tormented by guilt without realizing they have only wronged themselves and now feel guilty for a wasted, loveless life in which money, possessions, and social success were substituted for love. Modern young people read few classics, but this does not protect them from actualization of the complexes that are rooted in the nation's collective unconscious.

In the darkness of Russian life, amid filth, violence, poverty, and injustice, there is a growing painful, distressing awareness of the world's imperfection. This is why Russian characters have this longing for wholeness, a thirst for light, and an inability to express love. Russia's vast, unlimited expanse is reflected in Russian characters. Their souls are filled with love that finds no outlet. They are tormented with guilt for what they did and didn't do. They are unable to withstand the pressure of the world; openhearted and honest, they seek love and freedom. Their souls are anguished and restless. Sustaining this kind of stress is hard, and the soul cries for help. Some find salvation in drink, which lets one forget it all for a while but kills more people every day. Some keep hoping for a miracle but expect it to come from without, like Assol, the protagonist of Alexandr Grin's *Scarlet Sails*, who sits on the seashore for years, gazing into the sea and waiting for a miracle ship with scarlet sails. Perhaps it is time to become aware of oneself and start making one's own miracles? As Alexandr Grin put it:

> I have understood one simple truth. It consists in making one's miracles with one's own hands. When what a person fathoms most is a five-kopeck coin, it's easy to give it to him. But when the soul contains the seed of a fiery plant— a miracle—make it happen if you can. The person will have a new soul, and so will you.[19]

Against the background of increasingly pragmatic lifestyles, dominated by brain power and material success, longing for truth becomes more acute every day. Emotions suddenly break free in a truly pagan rebellion against externally imposed rules. One's soul rushes to the vast plains, the forests, and the rivers, where the pike splashes its tail, where love lives and miracles happen.

Notes

1 Nikolai Berdyaev, *Sudba Rossii* [The fate of Russia] (Moscow: Sovetskiy pisatel, 1990), p. 60.
2 Joseph Brodsky, *Less than One: Selected Essays* (New York: Farrar, Straus & Giroux, 1986), p. 10.

3 C. G. Jung, "General Aspects of Dream Psychology" (1916/1948), in *The Collected Works of C. G. Jung*, vol. 8, ed. and trans. Gerhard Adler and R. F. C. Hull (Princeton: Princeton University Press, 1975), § 507.

4 "Po schuchjemu veleniju" [By the will of the pike], in *Russkie narodnie skazki* [(Russian Folk Tales]) (Moscow: Detgiz, 1981), pp. 36–48.

5 Alexander Pushkin, "Skazka o rybake i rybke" [The tale of the fisherman and the fish], in *Collected Works*, vol. 3 (Moscow: Pravda, 1981), pp. 320–325.

6 Alexander Afanasyev, *Poeticheskie vozzreniya slavyan na prirodu* [The poetic outlook on nature by the Slavs], vol. 1 (Moscow: Soldatenkov, 1868), pp. 170–206.

7 Ivan Ilyin, "Rossiya v russkoj poesii" [Russia in Russian poetry], in *Collected Works*, vol. 6 (Moscow: Russkaya kniga, 1997), p. 352.

8 Berdyaev, *Sudba Rossi*, p. 18.

9 Ilyin, "Rossiya v russkoj poesii," p. 353.

10 Fyodor Dostoyevsky, *Prestuplenie i nakazanie* [Crime and punishment], in *Collected Works*, vol. 2 (Moscow: Lexica, 1996).

11 Leo Tolstoy, *Anna Karenina*, in *Collected Works*, vol. 8–9 (Moscow: Khudozhestvenaya literatura, 1982).

12 Ivan Goncharov, *Oblomov*, in *Collected Works*, vol. 3 (Moscow: Lexica, 1996).

13 Natalia Baratoff, *Oblomov: A Jungian Approach. A Literary Image of the Mother Complex* (Bern: Peter Lang, 1990).

14 Alexander Pushkin, *Evgenij Onegin* [Eugene Onegin], in *Collected Works*, vol. 4 (Moscow: Pravda, 1981), pp. 6–155.

15 Ivan Turgenev, *Dvoryanskoe gnezdo* [Home of the gentry], in *Collected Works* (Moscow: Sovetskiy pisatel, 1986).

16 Anton Chekhov, *Dyadya Vanya* [Uncle Vanya], in *Collected Works*, vol. 13 (Moscow: Nauka, 1988), pp. 61–116.

17 Anton Chekhov, *Tri sestry* [Three sisters], in *Collected Works*, vol. 13 (Moscow: Nauka, 1988), pp. 117–188.

18 Nikolai Gogol, *Revizor* [The government inspector], in *Collected Works*, vol. 4 (Moscow: Akademiya nauk, 1940).

19 Alexandr Grin, *Allye parusa* [Scarlet sails] (Moscow: L.D. Frenkel, 1923), p. 132.

Part 2

Cultural Complexes Emerging in the Context of Europe Divided and at War

Chapter 5

A Tale of Two Referenda

Convulsions in the Post-Brexit United Kingdom and in Ukraine

Ann Kutek

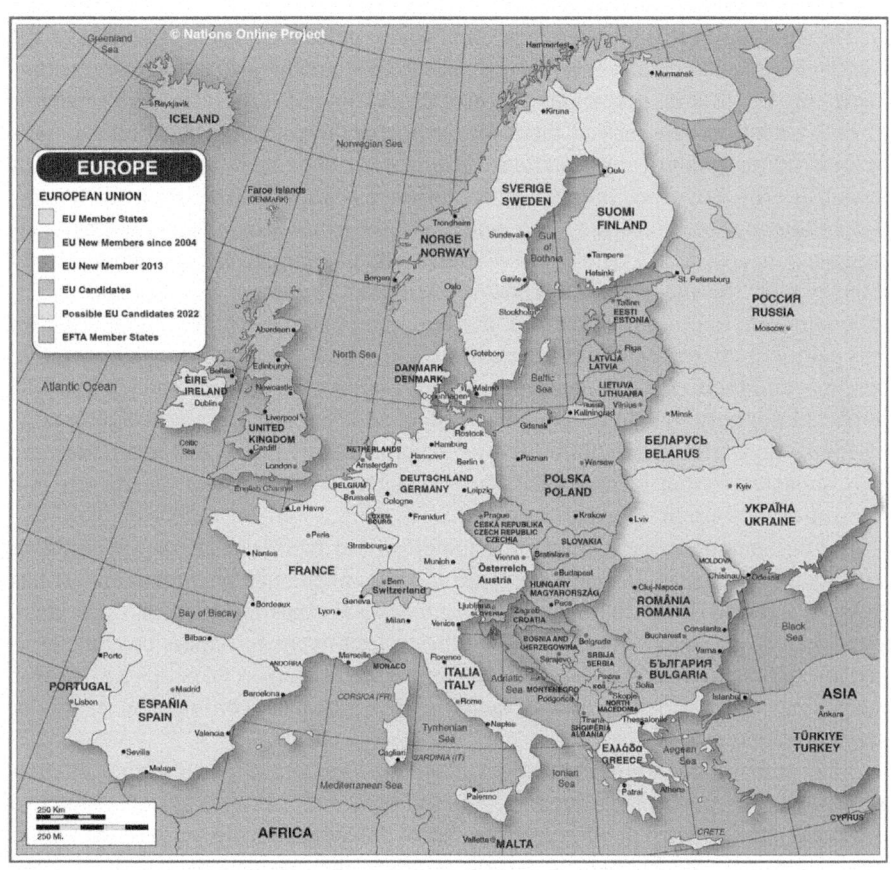

Figure 5.1 Contemporary Europe in 2022 (Source: Nations Online Project 2022, www.nationsonline.org/oneworld/europe_maphtm)

DOI: 10.4324/9781032695143-8

Coming upon the first edition of this volume, the reader can only be enriched by the erudition of the authors and editors and the depth of their analysis of the myriad tribes that have peopled the peninsula of Europe, from archaic times to the present. Yet, next to these lasting achievements, blood-soaked conflicts, the rewriting of narratives, and the multiplicity of truths that gave rise to them, these times are redolent of warring siblings and the absence of a real or imagined parent to calm emotions and restore equanimity. This updated contribution is focused on current tumultuous events at two extremities of Europe, the borderlands that are the United Kingdom to the west and Ukraine in the east. It is necessarily subject to limitations of scope, as already defined, notably by Jules Cashford and Gert Sauer. Moreover, it emanates from a psyche formed in Great Britain with a hinterland in Central and Eastern Europe, with French acculturation,[1] and informed by current complexes erupting on Europe's edges.[2]

The purpose of this chapter is to eschew any personal analysis of some of the leading figures in the current turmoil, an absurd and unethical urge, however tempting it may be. It is instead an attempt to extract some of the psychosocial features of each situation and subject them to a reflection inspired by the thinking tools of an evolving analytical psychology, in a manner accessible to the nonspecialist reader. It will, however, involve a little effort to confront ideas such as the *collective unconscious, complex, individuation*, and *symbol*, complemented by post-Jungian concepts such as the *political psyche* and *gender psychology* and how they interact with the theory of the *cultural complex*.[3] Equipped with a cursory historic perspective on both situations, the hypothesis is that striking commonalities and parallel patterns can be discerned in each, which have made their respective conflicts and their consequences almost predictable.[4] In addition, each scenario is impacted not only by geography, the weather, and "accidents," but also, crucially, by the ill-understood and ill-constrained capabilities of the digital age.[5] They are also impacted by the little-studied booty of culture—the looting of artifacts and imposition of foreign heraldry.[6]

Having emerged from the seismic tumult of the twentieth century, *Europe*, at seventy years old, is a recent political and organizational phenomenon.[7] It has enjoyed a period of relative stability, *pace* the bloody balkanization of Yugoslavia. Then, barely into a new timeframe, at either extremity, historic passions have broken through again to see a renewed cycle of harm inflicted on its peoples as well as the planet's environment, led, once again, as in most earlier conflicts, by swarming males.[8] Why is this?

The nature of the harm at one end, for Ukraine, is essentially existential, whereas at the other, for the United Kingdom, it is on the face of it about a spiral related to a profound narcissistic wound, related to loss of power and significance in the world. From both, one dominating motivation emerges: the preservation of sovereignty, or of the self, as Jung has it.[9] So apparently similar impulses have propagated effects that curtail, devastate, or reverberate in ordinary people's lives throughout the continent and well beyond it in this globalized world. Such events invite urgent interrogation into human ethology, gender, and enactment, including into the fourth estate with its outright misinformation and risky parodies, while policymakers and strategists could be well employed reviewing patent omissions in understanding and in forward planning.[10]

Individuation—Selfhood—Sovereignty

If one were to pick one thing among his lifelong studies and interests that mattered above all others to Jung, then surely it has to be *individuation*. Louis Zinkin, analytical psychologist and student of group processes, asserts, "For Jung it was undoubtedly the greatest human endeavour."[11] We need not be detained here by the many definitions and paradoxes attached to the idea in its clinical or theoretical contexts. Suffice to say, it means becoming who one truly is or was meant to be; alternatively, it stands for self-actualization.

The question then arises, what is understood by a "self" or even a "group of selves"? I am with Zinkin in his search for clarity and coherence:

> The self comes into existence only through the interaction with others and the form it takes, the sense the individual has of being or having a self, will depend greatly on the culture in which he or she has been brought up. It is created, made and formed not by any single act but by a continuing interaction with others. This does not imply it is fragile. In certain cultures it may be very strong, in others weak and uncertain.[12]

He arrives at this view not having sought a static proof borrowed from metaphysics; rather, he treats it as an experimental assumption based on observation not of one individual who claims to know she or he has a self, but of "groups of people [. . .] and, how it comes about that they seem to talk to each other without too much difficulty as if they know what they mean by the self."[13] Whereas Zinkin views becoming "real through recognition by other people," Jung's panoply of explanations for the social conventions of his time, he argues, are the likely result of the relational deprivation of his own early life, especially his disappointment with his father in the context of a sleepy part of Switzerland. He was a solitary child and adolescent.[14] Added to this, notes Zinkin, was the philosophical background of Jung's classical education, the need for God images, which "led him to trivialise the social dimension."[15] Zinkin's constructivist position amounts to straying from Jung's system of polarities between the collective and the personal, and from his emphasis on the "age-old timeless, placeless and thus context-free nature of the deepest levels of the unconscious."[16]

Along with some of Jung's followers—among them, Henderson, with his cultural unconscious, Hobson, with his view of dialogue, Redfearn, with his many selves, or Samuels, with his pluralism—Zinkin compensates for Jung's intellectual deficiencies in respect to the collective unconscious by moving closer to Erving Goffman's social psychology. As the present volume attests, a further development of a constructivist approach has been achieved with the idea of the cultural complex.[17] Zinkin does not, however, entirely abandon Jung's hypotheses about the unconscious and the self. Instead, he conjugates the emergence of any one self, as of all the other selves, from the existence of language, and language is not possible without a culture, and culture is always shared. To have a self and to have a chance to individuate with it, he believes, means making a claim, but

> it is a claim which can readily be validated by others within the same society and what is claimed, that is, what a person means by having a self will depend on the notion of the self shared by his or her particular society.[18]

It is, therefore, predicated on a cultural consensus.

Another of Jung's foundational concepts was that of the *complex*. It is highly pertinent to individuation and to the present discussion. It was the result of his try-ing to make sense of observations during his renowned word association tests in the early 1900s, when patients displayed emotional disturbance over certain words. He named this a *complex indicator* as a potential sign of an unconscious psychological conflict.[19] The idea has since passed into common currency and is now much used in trauma work with patients. What Jung discovered and managed to describe was the *feeling tone* and seeming *autonomy* of complexes. He commented wryly that not only do people have complexes, but "complexes have [them]." He explains:

> Every constellation of a complex postulates a disturbed state of conscious-ness . . .The complex must therefore be a psychic factor which in terms of energy, possesses a value that sometimes exceeds that of our conscious inten-tions . . . And in fact, an active complex puts us momentarily under a state of duress, of compulsive thinking and acting, for which under certain circum-stances the only appropriate term would be the judicial concept of diminished responsibility.[20]

In short, complexes arise at varying degrees of heightened moments of emotional arousal throughout life. They need not be wholly negative, and their original occurrence is not necessarily remembered. Although sometimes damaging or obstructive, they are inevitable in the development of the self, in childrearing, and in education. We can regard them as largely unconscious internal "traffic lights." In social contexts, they can become shared complexes or responses, which can often evolve into shared beliefs, opinions, ideologies, phobias, and practices. We are, after all, creatures of habit, including those whose role is to be stubbornly contrarian.

When I move my interrogation from the particular of selfhood to the general phenomenon of the group, the level of complexity grows exponentially. Self-hood, in the case of the evolved communities we call nations, can make a claim to statehood. The point about statehood, in modern terms, is it can make a further claim to sovereignty, which is a sign that its people consider themselves to have an "individuated identity" (see the upcoming discussion of F. H. Hinsley), tested by the effectiveness of its ability to preserve the self-determination of its constituent people and the exercise of political power among other states. As history shows, the evolving differentiation between those two words—*nation* and *state*—is that nations arise from a deeply shared identity and language, grown organically over centuries—and, indeed, with distinct cultural complexes—without necessarily becoming states. Such would be the case of the nomadic Roma, Ashkenazi Jews, the Sámi people of Scandinavia, or the Boykos, Hutsul, and Lemkos peoples of the Carpathian Mountains.

A state, on the other hand, is a construct not necessarily coterminous with a nation and can be made up of several nations or states that have been either subjugated by another state or entered into a more or less voluntary pact to work together for continued survival. It is a sort of marriage. Switzerland is one European example of such a long-standing arrangement, as is the United Kingdom or the historical Republic of Two Nations. The latter was a 400-year-old collaboration between the huge Grand Duchy of Lithuania and the Kingdom of Poland that ended late in the eighteenth century and contained the territory we know now as "Western Ukraine."[21] More recent examples would be Germany, Italy, the former Yugoslavia, and the Russian Federation.

We arrive at the common and central bone of contention in this tale of two entities: It is the perception of sovereignty and the exercise of sovereign power.[22] It is an elusive concept, and, although it is not usually the concern of analytical psychologists or psychoanalysts in their theoretical discourse, their primary clinical preoccupation is precisely with each patient's achievement—at a micro level—of symbolic sovereignty in the self. At the macro level, F. H. Hinsley, cryptanalyst and late Cambridge professor of history of international relations, in a striking parallel wrote in 1966:

> The concept of sovereignty will not be found in societies in which there is no state. Far from arising at once with the emergence in a community of the forms of the state the concept will not have appeared until a subsequent process of integration or reconciliation has taken place between a state and its community. It will infallibly have struggled to the surface, on the other hand, whenever and wherever that process has advanced to a certain point. And then, once the concept has emerged in any society, its further development will have been ultimately linked with further changes in the relations between the society and its government.[23]

The language resonates with Jungian notions of the relations between the ego and the self and, hence, with the idea of individuation.[24] Wilfred Bion, the psychoanalyst and pioneer of group observation, has condensed the hypothetical nature of all these relations. He came up with a snippet of theory formulated to help him, and us, represent communication in the area of "containers" and what might be "contained." He states: "Communication is about a relationship between meaning and its expression, between emotion and its expression,"[25] where meaning or emotion is contained by the mode of expression, the "container." Furthermore, he suggests there could be three ways whereby this communication may occur. He calls these distinct patterns of relating either *commensal*,[26] symbiotic, or parasitic and defines them as follows:

> By "commensal" I mean a relationship in which two objects share a third to the advantage of all three. By "symbiotic" I understand a relationship in which one depends on another to mutual advantage. By "parasitic" I mean to present a relationship in which one depends on another to produce a third, which is destructive of all three.[27]

These very brief and schematic characterizations can apply as much to relations between aspects of the self, to those between individuals and groups, as to relations between political entities such as states, something I shall endeavor to demonstrate in what follows.

Britannia

In what follows I return to two signal definitions from Bion:

1. True thought requires neither formulation nor thinker.
2. The lie is a thought to which a formulation and a thinker are essential.[28]

As a sovereign state, the United Kingdom has arguably individuated and has grown accustomed to punch above its weight since the loss of empire. But, on several parameters, the United Kingdom is definitely in steep decline. At the time of writing, on January 31, 2023, three years after the United Kingdom left the European Union (EU), the International Monetary Fund said the UK economy would shrink by 0.6 percent and perform worse than other advanced economies, including Russia, as the cost of living continued to hit households. It did not mention Brexit in its report as a factor for the United Kingdom not performing as well as comparable states.[29] In 2020, with the onset of the COVID-19 pandemic, Britain already lost 10 percent of GDP.[30] A further decline has occurred in environmental and food standards as they diverge from the EU. The hurriedly, and possibly illegally, assembled Northern Ireland Protocol, which wedges the province in the Single Market with a border between two parts of the United Kingdom, produces endless anomalies such as titanium oxide, a food additive banned by the EU but allowed in Great Britain. As a result, Northern Ireland will not accept imports of foodstuffs containing it across the Irish Sea.[31] In the aftermath of the protocol, negotiations over Britain's post-Brexit participation in the EU Horizon research program have all but collapsed, grants to top universities have ceased, and many researchers have left the country.[32] Politically, the referendum result has added fuel to the objectives of the ruling Scottish National Party (SNP), making the breakup of the United Kingdom no longer just a pipe dream.

The result of the advisory referendum on Great Britain's and Gibraltar's continued membership in the EU dawned on the nation early on June 24, 2016. It was a close-run thing, to most people's surprise, by a simple majority. The winners were the "Leavers," a loose coalition of those holding anti-EU sentiment from across several political parties. The nations of Scotland and Northern Ireland voted to remain, but the English vote carried the day. The prime minister, David Cameron, kept his promise to resign should his Remain in the EU proposal lose. He was gone later that day, and a transition period of four years began in order to allow for forty years of institutional accretions to be dismantled and new "global" relations set up. As it turns out, there was no plan what to do in the event the Leave campaign won, since the prime minister had banned the Civil Service from planning for a failure in his policy. He assumed reason would triumph, and the disgruntled Leave campaign would lose.[33] Likewise, the Brexit campaigners within and without the Conservative Party were not expecting to win and were mulling the idea of a second referendum to come. The formal exit took place on January 31, 2020.

The debate about the United Kingdom's membership of the European Economic Community (EEC) had continued unabated at least from the time of joining in 1973. Membership was confirmed by referendum in 1975. Despite Britain's enormous political and trade advantages[34] and her contribution to the project through her institution-building capacities and support for a rules-based world order, there has been a vociferous Eurosceptic tendency, such as the Bruges Group, which, although working mainly with Conservative politicians, has attracted some Labour politicians to its fold, and of late the European Research Group (ERG), centered on the right wing of the Conservative Party. In addition, elements who had left the party coalesced around a series of other political groupings, notably the UK Independence Party, whose main aim was for the United Kingdom to leave the EU. The principal arguments deployed against Europe can be reduced to three:

- Uncontrolled immigration
- The cost of membership
- The loss of sovereignty

After the extension of EU membership to former Warsaw Pact states in Central and Eastern Europe in 2004, the Blair government, unlike other member states, chose to accord immediate freedom of movement into the United Kingdom to citizens of new member states. As a result, more than a million, mostly young, Central Europeans took up the offer in short order and immigrated to fill the shortfall in employment in a range of sectors, including agriculture, construction, hospitality and social care, and the digital and finance industries. They joined the already settled European communities of Italians and especially the French: In 2012, London was said to be the sixth largest "French city."[35]

The "new" Europeans settled where work was to be had according to or below their actual skills, in the farthest reaches of Scotland, the cabbage fields of Lincolnshire, and urban areas bristling with startups. A majority were engaged in manual labor and went to some places where foreigners had not disturbed the peace of rural communities since the last Viking invasion in 1066. Many brought their young families, set up their own grocery shops, and swelled Roman Catholic Church membership to unprecedented levels.[36] Since Brexit, large numbers have returned to their native lands in the EU, citing falling living standards, insecurity, and xenophobia among reasons for leaving. However, net immigration into the United Kingdom has grown, only now from non-EU states.

Peter Ricketts, a seasoned diplomat with access to the inner workings of government in Britain for almost half a century, has laid out a credible account of the confluence of ideology, the myth of empire—we might say cultural complex—and the lack of a written constitution with the changing character of the British governing elite. He surmises that

> the lack of effective checks and balances on a prime minister, coupled with a preference for conviction politics over strategic thinking led [him] to make the fundamental error, for which [he] will always be remembered. . . . Cameron cannot have been fully aware of the depth of anger and alienation bubbling in the country . . . or that the referendum would ignite this explosive mixture of grievances.[37]

Cameron overlooked, as had centrist politicians elsewhere in Europe and in the United States, that populist grievances get allied to identity politics, threats to

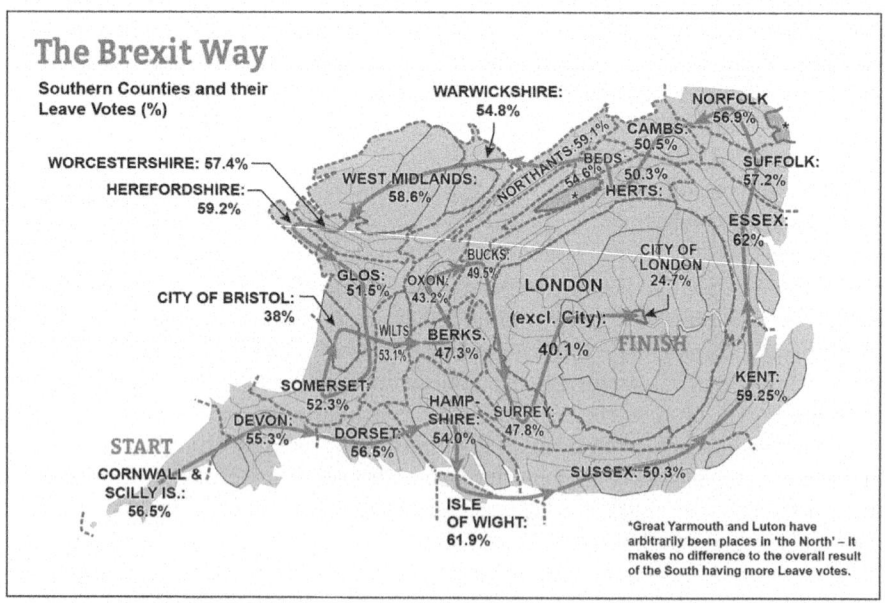

The Brexit Way

Southern Counties and their Leave Votes (%)

WARWICKSHIRE: 54.8%

NORFOLK 56.9%

CAMBS: 50.5%

WORCESTERSHIRE: 57.4%

HEREFORDSHIRE: 59.2%

WEST MIDLANDS: 58.6%

NORTHANTS 59.1%

BEDS: 54.6%

SUFFOLK: 57.2%

BEDS: 50.3%

HERTS:

ESSEX: 62%

BUCKS: 49.5%

CITY OF LONDON 24.7%

GLOS: 51.5%

OXON: 43.2%

LONDON

CITY OF BRISTOL: 38%

WILTS 53.1%

BERKS. 47.3%

(excl. City): 40.1%

FINISH

KENT: 59.25%

SOMERSET: 52.3%

HAMP-SHIRE:

SURREY: 47.8%

DEVON: 55.3%

DORSET: 56.5%

54.0%

START

CORNWALL & SCILLY IS.: 56.5%

ISLE OF WIGHT: 61.9%

SUSSEX: 50.3%

*Great Yarmouth and Luton have arbitrarily been places in 'the North' – It makes no difference to the overall result of the South having more Leave votes.

Figure 5.2 The Brexit Way: A walking route through the areas of the United Kingdom that supplied the majority of Leave votes despite having a minority of voters

sovereignty, and so on, and are more easily exploited by tub-thumpers such as Nigel Farage in the United Kingdom, Viktor Orbán in Hungary, and Donald Trump in the United States. Apparently, a commensal relationship was falsely presented as parasitical, in Bion's terms (see Bion's two ideas noted at the beginning of this section).

An association formed in my mind with a memory of an office party where a woman senior manager arrived with a cake she had baked. It was a tall, round, many-layered confection, and expertly finished. The gathered throng fell into a hush as a junior manager, doubtless compulsively helpful, approached it with a long kitchen knife and was about to plunge it into the center, when its chef skillfully wrenched the knife away and proceeded to cut her pièce de résistance into parallel strips. "That way," she added gruffly to the hapless junior and all present, "it will go much further and the slices are less likely to collapse." This reproof laid bare an unexpected lesson in alleged cake physics and, especially, protocol, of which more later.

Allied to this, Danny Dorling, professor of geography at Oxford University, studied the breakdown of Brexit voting patterns and revealed that most Leave voters were middle class, over fifty years old, overweight or obese, and lived in the south of the country, usually in the shires.[38] They also swayed the vote in Wales because they had retired there and had bothered to vote (unlike many less privileged natives who had benefited from EU aid programs, such as rural bus services, but did not vote). In other words, they comprehensively trounced the numbers of all other Leave voters in the country.[39] Dorling has moreover put forward the striking hypothesis that the self-belief of the British ruling class is partly fostered by the (misleading) prewar history textbooks still used in public schools, themselves an embodiment of the mainly English cultural complex, designed to mold future leaders and administrators of the former British Empire.[40] These textbooks paint a glowing picture of Britannia's role in the world and largely omit the grand-scale exploitation of subject peoples (see Chapter 1 from Jules Cashford). This goes some way to explain the fantastical grandiloquence about global Britain proclaimed on Leave campaign buses and repeated by leaders of the three consecutive Conservative post-Brexit governments as it visibly sinks beneath the waves.[41] In the words of the Thomas Arne anthem, "Britons never will be slaves,"[42] except politically to the United States and economically possibly to China, in compensation for the Boxer Rebellion.

Ukraine

Boris Johnson's demonstrable personal connection with Volodymyr Zelensky and the people of Ukraine did not inspire this chapter, except in the way that two people may meet on the escalators, one traveling up, the other down. It was rather the common complex to plow on regardless, to tolerate overweening entitlement in sections of their elites, closing an eye to corrupt practices, plus the immense failure to check on reality and to plan accordingly. Edward Lucas,[43] a British observer of

Central and Eastern Europe, itemized remarkably, at the start of the Ukrainian invasion, the warning signs leading to the conflict and how Western Europe left itself
and its neighbors avoidably exposed.[44] What may have brought the United Kingdom and Ukraine latterly together was also a certain sense of kinship, structurally,
on account of neighboring "leviathans."[45]

In the 1570s, Kostiantyn Ivanovych Ostrozky, who ruled the land of Galicia–
Volhynia—which already had a long history, albeit under the hegemony of the
Grand Duchy of Lithuania sealed by the 1569 Treaty of Lublin—planned a mo-
mentous cultural project: to publish the Bible in Church Slavonic. The Ostroh Bible
came out in 1581 before such a text appeared either in Constantinople or Moscow
and indicated the prominence of Ukraine in the Orthodox world.[46] It appeared half-
way between Tyndale's first English translation of the Bible, published in Antwerp,
and the Authorized King James Version in 1611. In 2019, the Orthodox Church of
Ukraine—one of several Orthodox churches in Ukraine—declared its autocephaly[47]
from the Moscow Orthodox patriarchate to the wrath of its patriarch Kirill, a strong
supporter and influencer of Vladimir Putin and his Ukrainian project.[48] Could this
have been a contributory casus belli?

Oleksandr Cherednychenko, writing in 2009, asserted that today's Ukraine
shares with practically all post-colonial nations the challenge of establishing a
national identity. Moreover, ethnic Ukrainians number 75 percent of the country's
population, in line with the indices of most unitary states.[49] Its tradition of statehood dates back to the ninth century, marked by the foundation of Kyivan Rus.
Somewhat aided and abetted by visiting Vikings, in the following 200 years it
expanded to empire status, stretching from the Baltic in the north to the Black Sea
in the south, from the Volga basin in the east to the Carpathian Mountains in the
west. In 1147, the Kyivan prince Yuri Dolgorukiy established a colonial settlement, which he named *Moscow* after the local river. Kyivan Rus, as a state, was
recognized internationally among peers such as Byzantium and the kingdoms of
France, Hungary, and Norway, not least owing to royal marriages, notably of Anne
of Kyiv who married Henri I of France. The Tartar invasion of 1237–1241 caused
the fall of Kyiv and shifted the state to its western province of Galicia–Volhynia,
where, under a religious pact with Rome, Dmytro Romanovytch was crowned king
of Galicia by the Pope in 1253.[50]

In respect of the common aberration of using *Rus* and *Russia* as equivalent
terms, and thereby adducing the emergence of Russia to the birth of Kyivan Rus,
the French historian of Ukraine, Daniel Beauvois, asserts that the only state per-
taining to Eastern Slavs in the ninth century was Kyivan Rus, whereas what was
to become Russia was known at its inception as *Muscovy* and was, for over 200
years, a vassal of the Golden Horde. It does not emerge as independent and a separate branch of Eastern Slavs until the course of the fifteenth and sixteenth centuries, freed of the Mongol invaders and having learned well from their marauding
ways. It is only around 1475 that there is documentary reference to *Russian* lands,
and it is when Moscow is recognized as having hegemony among Eastern Slavs
(identified by their adoption of Orthodox religion) and after subduing neighboring

Figure 5.3 Principalities of the later Kyivan Rus, after the death of Prince Yaroslav I c. 1056, superimposed on a map of modern Europe (Attribution to SeikoEn CC BY-SA 3.0 Wikipedia)

principalities. They are distinct from other Orthodox Slavs, or Ruthenians, sometimes known as "Red Ruthenians," who group around the neighboring states made up of Balts and Western Catholic or minority Protestant Slavs. The term *Ukraine*

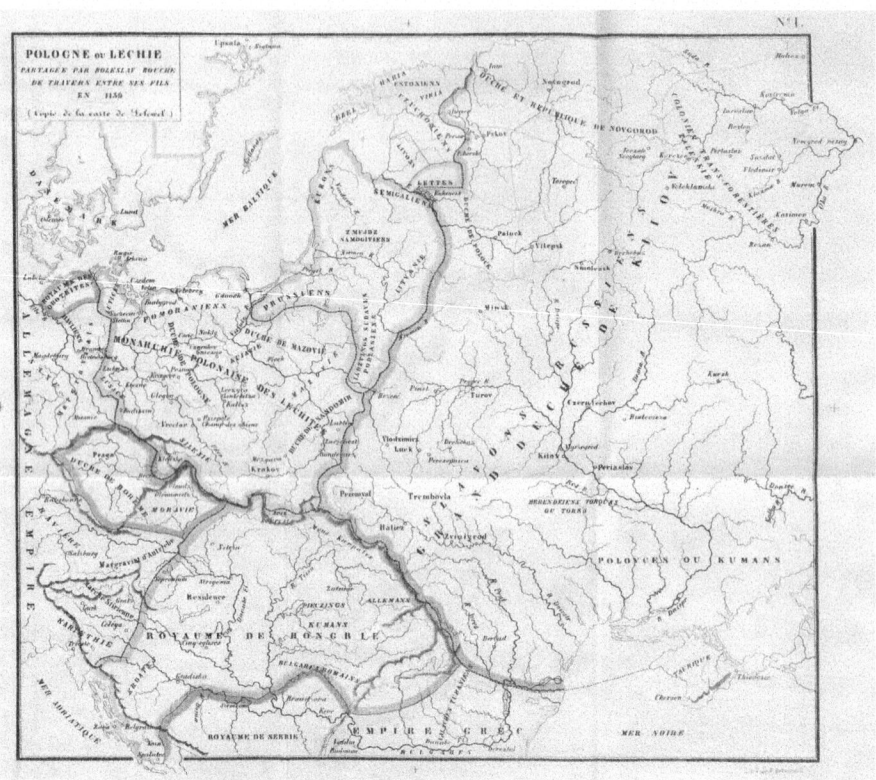

Figure 5.4 Kyivan Rus in 1139 from an 1860 map by cartographer Joachim Lelewel
(Public domain)

appears as a synonym of *Rus* in the twelfth century, specifically in a geographical context, to denote the confines of territories governed by Kyiv. Beauvois contends that a false equivalence is practiced in Russian historiography to make Russia's statehood appear older than it is and amounts to pirating a neighboring heritage.[51]

Nevertheless, the attacks by the Golden Horde from the east put paid to the statehood of Kyivan Rus. In exchange for security and survival, it sought refuge with, and became a "tenant" of, the neighboring, expanding state in the west, namely the Grand Duchy of Lithuania and the Kingdom of Poland, which were in ever-closer political union from the fourteenth century onward owing to their common interest in preserving their northern and eastern frontiers against Teutonic, Muscovy, Ottoman, Tartar, and eventually Swedish invasions. That union was signed in Lublin and was consulted as a model by Elizabeth I of England who was contemplating her own realm's union with the Kingdom of Scotland.

Kyivan Rus elites meanwhile, as is the wont of oligarchs today, soon gravitated to the center of political power and became absorbed among Lithuanian and

Polish magnates, some adopting the then trendy Calvinism, most though adopted Catholicism and the language and sartorial fashion at court. Kyivan Rus (Ukrainian) identity and the soul of the nation were consigned to the ways and collective memory of the common people and did not reassert itself until the seventeenth century with the foundation of the *Hetmanate*, otherwise known as the Cossack state, in 1645, led by Bohdan Khmelnytsky, which sowed the seeds of democracy and abolished serfdom. Khmelnytsky took on the Turks and the Poles; however, the ill-starred rapprochement with Moscow and the Treaty of Pereyaslav in 1654 deprived it of independence and autonomy and turned a portion of Ukraine into a Russian protectorate. Renewed attempts to free itself under Hetman Mazeppa, by forming an alliance with Charles XII of Sweden in 1709, were met by tough reprisals from Peter the Great. Despite producing a wishful constitution in 1710, under Hetman Orlyk, never implemented, the Hetmanate was liquidated by the recently enthroned Prussian Catherine in 1764, and serfdom was reintroduced.[52] The rest of Ukraine remained in the Commonwealth of Two Nations until its own imminent partitioning.

The Lithuanian–Polish political union[53] survived until 1795 when a sufficient number of its very own restive magnates committed high treason by upending their state as they sought preferment from their eastern neighbor, the irresistibly seductive and expectant powerful Empress Catherine and her agile lieutenants. She was ready and waiting to cut up the cake over three phases, beginning in 1772, according to her precise whim, and shared it with two of her neighbors.[54] Indeed, she married off Potemkin's beloved niece,[55] Alexandra Engelhardt, to the Polish magnate Hetman Francis Branicki and as a dowry gave them the newly acquired Ruthenian/Ukrainian city of Bila Tserkva.[56] It was always going to be a family affair. In 1791, the city was placed in the Pale of Settlement, which encompassed parts of seven contemporary nations, including large swaths of Ukraine but excluding Greater Russia. It became a buffer territory, where Jews and other conquered peoples were permitted to scratch a living oppressed by high taxation and beset by starvation.[57]

A second attempt at a restoration of a modern Ukrainian state took advantage of the ferment of World War I and the Russian Revolution. A revived Hetmanate under Skoropadsky took form between 1917 and 1920, but it was subdued by Bolshevik forces seeking to preserve the territory of the former Russian Empire. It also had to contend with the renascent claims to statehood from neighboring Poland in 1918—hence the Polish–Ukrainian War, which asserted Polish hegemony over Western Ukrainian territory and a brief measure of cultural relaxation. Ukrainian claims to statehood were in practice delayed for another seventy years. Worse was still to come on the Soviet side of the border with the genocidal famine of 1932–1933 and attacks on Ukrainian culture and identity carried out systematically.[58]

In Galicia meanwhile, on the Polish side, the Ukrainian majority saw the continuation of the National Democratic Alliance with its Austrian roots. In 1929, this all changed with the emergence of the Ukrainian Military Organization, a clandestine network led by Colonel Konovalets, active in the 1918–1919 war for independence in Eastern Ukraine. It turned into a political party called the Organization of

Ukrainian Nationalists (OUN); its ideology was radical nationalism. The ideology of creating a "new man" was the brainchild of a former Eastern Ukrainian social democrat, Dmytro Dontsov, who never joined the OUN but shaped a new generation of activists. Historian Serhii Plokhy observes: "The OUN, at best a marginal force on the Ukrainian political scene, proved the ability to influence that scene far beyond its actual political weight."[59] Its terrorist tactics broke through in 1933, with the assassination of a Soviet diplomat in Lviv as a reprisal for the famine in Soviet Ukraine, and in 1934, with the assassination of the Polish interior minister, Bronisław Pieracki, in reprisal for Poland's pacification policy toward militant Ukrainians.[60] The organizer of the killings was a twenty-five-year-old Lviv Polytechnic graduate, Stepan Bandera, who headed the OUN in Galicia. Bandera was tried in Warsaw and sentenced to death, but this was commuted to seven life sentences in 1936. With the simultaneous invasion of Poland by Nazi Germany and Soviet Russia in September 1939, the chaos in Polish prisons allowed Bandera to go free. Bandera collaborated with the Nazis but was also imprisoned by them for proclaiming an independent Ukraine in 1941.[61] In 1943, under Nazi occupation, the OUN instigated the "Volhynia Massacres," which spread to Galicia and the Lublin area, when some 133,000 unarmed Poles and other minorities, including Jews[62] and especially women and children, were butchered by the Ukrainian Insurgent Army (UPA). In their terms, this was ethnic cleansing in preparation for a future homogeneous Ukrainian state.[63] Ukrainian nationalist terrorism and killings continued sporadically until 1947, then under the Soviet regime. Subsequently, the undoubted fascist Bandera, confounded with nationalism, became the touch paper for nationalist sympathies, which were used as a pretext by Russia to intervene in Ukraine from 2014 onward.[64]

Paradoxically, the carve-up of Europe occasioned by the Treaty of Yalta (1945) after World War II, hosted and led by Stalin, with Roosevelt and Churchill in attendance, brought about the territorial aggrandizement of Ukraine to a status it had not had since the fourteenth century, on condition that it stayed firmly in Stalin's back pocket. Its vast fertile lands became the "breadbasket" of Europe, and its eastern mineral resources contributed to the Soviet industrial infrastructure. Added to this was unrivaled access to the Black Sea and its connection to the Mediterranean and beyond. In 1954, Nikita Khrushchev, the Soviet leader, himself of Ukrainian heritage, "donated" the Crimean peninsula to be administered as a part of Ukraine in a symbolic gesture. It made no palpable difference to existing power structures because Ukraine was treated as an integral state/province of the USSR and, incidentally, shared in its inherited grandiose heraldic tradition and distinctions.[65] It was a recipe for a continuing symbiotic relationship, as Bion describes it.[66]

Barely thirty years later, after the fall of the Berlin Wall and *perestroika* and *glasnost* in Moscow, the stage was set for the collapse of the Soviet system of government. The détente under President Yeltsin made it possible for Ukraine to seize another opportunity to achieve its national aspiration for statehood. On December 1, 1991, 90 percent of Ukrainians voted for national independence and sovereignty in a referendum.[67] In 1994, Ukraine took the decision to denuclearize its arsenal, and this was ratified by the Budapest Memorandum, with security guarantees from the United States, the United Kingdom, and Russia. A democratic constitution was promulgated in 1996. In practice, however, self-government for Ukrainians, with an immature civil society in a globalized world, was an immense challenge, and the default position became political and economic power brokering among the ruling elite, some of whom had retained connections with Russia, while others sought fresh economic opportunities in the West. None of this was part of a government plan, and corrupt deals became the order of the day as foreign influences came into play from the North and the West. The Orange Revolution of 2004 asserted a democratic manifesto for Ukraine.

In 2013, under the fourth elected Ukrainian president, Victor Yanukovitch, a popular revolt against the covert practices of the ruling class took to the Maidan, the main square in Kyiv. It overturned the idea of a passive people content to be Western stooges or to accept the concocted nineteenth-century myth that the Russian Empire had been made up of "Great Russia and Little Russia," united by a shared history and language. Even a cursory survey of the Russian and Ukrainian languages demonstrates that Russian speakers cannot understand written Ukrainian for the reason that the Ukrainian language is much closer to Polish and Belorussian than it is to Russian.[68] It explains continued Russian attempts throughout history to abolish Ukrainian as a tongue and to break up its communities by systematic population shifts of Russians into Ukraine's geographical perimeters and native Ukrainian deportations into Russia, reminiscent of archaic animal herding on the steppes of Eurasia. The Maidan Revolution expressed young Ukraine's desire to rejoin the European family of sovereign states rather than flip back into being a Russian fiefdom.

In 2014, following the ousting of Yanukovitch, Russia invaded the Crimean peninsula and annexed it. In the Donbas region, an armed conflict of attrition was started by Russian-speaking Ukrainian citizens, supported by forces from Russia opposed to the Ukrainian state, with the claim that their freedoms were being suppressed by Nazi-sympathizing elements in government and they therefore needed protection. The Minsk Agreements were drawn up late in 2014 to stop the fighting, but in vain. A further agreement was drawn up in Minsk in 2015, mediated by Angela Merkel of Germany and François Hollande of France, under the aegis of the Organization for Security and Co-operation in Europe (OSCE), but that too failed. In May 2019, Volodymyr Zelensky was elected sixth president of Ukraine. Meanwhile, it is seeking candidate status to join the EU. It is also considering applying for NATO membership. Until the invasion of Ukraine in February 2022, it has been one of the top producers and exporters of cereals and vegetable oil, especially to developing countries, some on the verge of starvation as climate change takes its toll.[69]

On February 24, 2022, forces of the Russian Federation invaded the territory of sovereign Ukraine as part of a "special military operation," having massed on Ukraine's borders for some months. The world and most Ukrainians were taken by surprise. The anticipated short blitzkrieg did not materialize, and the invading columns got mired in the mud. A full-scale war developed, and millions of Ukrainians were displaced as their homes were toppled, families were split across borders, and many civilians died. The military losses on both sides have been considerable. Two years on, Zelensky continues in office, and the NATO alliance has just about held in its torpor and is supplying material to Ukraine with some delay, if not reluctance. Fuel prices have rocketed in Europe; the Russian economy is being sanctioned, as are leading individuals. There is no sign of peace negotiations. The invaders loot Ukrainian cultural heritage under cover of fire. Masculine might demands its rights as women are ritually raped, and children, adults, animals, and the planet bleed.

At the time of writing this piece, I was waiting at a bus stop one wet evening in a deserted London street when I noticed the other person waiting was a small woman, heavily laden with bags and struggling to open a bottle of juice. A conversation developed where she told me in halting words she had been working late, as a nanny. Her accent suggested an Eastern European provenance. Ukrainian, I ventured. "Russian and Bulgarian" came the swift retort, not impressed with my error, "that Zelensky making all the trouble," she added for emphasis. To pacify my quizzical look, "but," she added, "the people I work for are half Ukrainian and half Russian" and, getting into her stride, "the wife went to Cambridge," she offered as the bus rounded the corner and we boarded. The conversation reached its natural end.

Interrogation

Among the things to emerge from the foregoing is the common element of surprise: the so-close result of the Brexit referendum and the West's ability to be so comprehensively deceived by the personal resolve (complexes) of Vladimir Putin and his circle. There was no anticipation or preparation for either. It was assumed that the Russian leader was "someone you could do business with," since his decades-long exposure on the international stage suggested he was familiar, that Western leaders had the measure of him, and therefore he was almost a "friend." I would venture that this and the aforementioned torpor in the United Kingdom and its neighbors are attributable, in Jungian terms, to an *abaissement du niveau mental* in the collective Western political psyche. It is a lowering in the tone of consciousness, a diminution of will, a kind of loss of soul.[70]

The loss of soul could, in part, be attributable to the interface between humans and machine. It may be reaching saturation for human attention and our usual functioning as biological creatures. The digital revolution has brought apparent convenience and speed of communication but with a background of ubiquity and coercion. The coercive aspect is exploited by commercial and political marketing and by organized crime. It may be that people are simultaneously addicted to, and besieged by, the technology around them. This is manifestly interfering with the natural ability to feel, reflect, and relate to the outside world.

What this means in practice is richly illustrated by Peter Ricketts as he recalls Harold Macmillan's statecraft or the art of creating power. In contrast to the current crop of Conservative leaders, as he took on the premiership following the Suez debacle in 1956, he commissioned an eminent panel chaired by the cabinet secretary to "try to forecast what state the world would be in 1970 and what role the United Kingdom would be able to play in it," with particular reference to its relationship to Europe and the United States. The report pulled no punches about the threat posed by the EEC (without the United Kingdom in it) as a growing power bloc. Given the United States' historic predilection for a united Europe, Ricketts wrote in 2022,

> In a message that still has salience today [the panel] warned that "Anglo-American partnership is not a law of nature" and Britain would need to show that it was capable of giving second place to its own interests in order to show that it was contributing to wider US objectives.

And, quoting from the report,

> One basic rule of British policy is clear. We must not find ourselves in a position of having to make a final choice between the United States and Europe. It would not be compatible with our vital interests to reject either the one or the other, and the very fact that the choice was needed would mean the destruction of the Atlantic Alliance.[71]

Macmillan responded with a memorandum of his own in 1960, making a sustained intellectual effort to turn grand strategy into operational policy. This I would class as a call to a "commensal" relationship where two objects share a third to the advantage of all three.[72]

Today's Conservative leaders shun continuity and pick their advisers often from journalism or political friendship circles. They rely on machine-driven "war gaming," operated usually by young technicians to spew algorithms for action, all bereft of feeling and informed intuition. Eminent experience is dissipated as soundbites on the ocean of the media. Is it a wonder we are where we are?

Finally, the evidence before us suggests overwhelmingly the gendered nature of politics, power rivalries, the acquiescence to war and its conduct; it also reflects humanity's attitude to the exploitation of the planet and its biodiversity. It is also about who controls the (public) narrative.[73] As on the comedy circuit, the default comedian is a man; at most, women are props. If women are by default treated as fruits of the earth or practically as objects whose freedom is curtailed, again by default, then it is by the male of the species. This is neither nurturing nor friendly; it is endlessly coercive, parasitical, and, as Bion states, ultimately destructive to all involved. So in Ukraine, invaders resort to the ritual of rape of women and the deportation of some two million people, of whom about three hundred thousand are children wrenched from their families, for reeducation and erasure of their identity within the Russian Federation.[74] Of course, men on the path to individuation are revolted by these occurrences, just as there are women who cannot help but to resort to violence and oppression. The term *default* indicates it is largely unconscious and so common as to be banal, and to that extent it may be classed as a variant of the cultural complex.

There are clues to be found about the impulse to gendered dominance and violence toward the other in the social and psychological literature. For one, as psychologists Carol Gilligan and Naomi Snider have put it, the influence of patriarchal systems has been to convey to a large proportion of men that they are the only ones with a self and, to most women, the belief that their lot is to be selfless.[75] Sociology professor Mino Vianello judges, in addition, there has been a progressive erosion of empathy in certain male individuals:

> We are forced to agree that females and males have helped each other to survive over the millennia regardless of the gender distinction and despite the prohibitive conditions caused by epidemics and famines after the last glaciation . . .
>
> We need therefore to ask ourselves why and how with the relatively recent advent of homo sapiens-sapiens, that is with the affirmation of reflexive thought favored by a relatively secure sedentary context, this empathic charge suddenly short-circuited, and why the male has since that point been the absolute manager of power in public life with all the destructive consequences that characterize history (what Marx called "prehistory": a condition that denies the individual the possibility to bring under his control the free development and realization of his personality).[76]

For another, Shakespeare's insights, just like hypotheses formed from the findings of work in the clinical consulting room, highlight repeated patterns of relating that can be traced to developmental processes which seem to dam the possibility of developing a genuine self capable of individuation. If it is the case that many parents have been conditioned to relate in specifically unhelpful ways toward their babies, especially male ones, then there could be a problem of epidemic proportions. It is not about blaming women again. It is about the trans-generational transmission of faulty attitudes, just as faulty genes occur from time to time.

In his day, Jung found a striking illustration of this problem in a speech by Cassius in Shakespeare's *Julius Caesar*:

> Come, Antony, and young Octavius, come!
> Revenge yourselves alone on Cassius,
> For Cassius is aweary of the world—
> Hated by one he loves, braved by his brother,
> Checked like a bondman, all his faults observed,
> Set in a notebook, learned and conned by rote
> To cast into my teeth. O, I could weep
> My spirit from mine eyes! There is my dagger,
> [*offering his dagger to Brutus.*]
> And here my naked breast; within, a heart
> Dearer than Pluto's mine, richer than gold.

If that thou be'st a Roman, take it forth.
I that denied thee gold will give my heart.
Strike as thou didst at Caesar, for I know
When thou didst hate him worst, thou lovedst him better
Than ever thou lovedst Cassius.[77]

The theatrical and hysterical outburst, for our purposes, serves as a symbol of sacrificing kinship with an allegedly beloved kin nation and yielding to an aggressive compulsion. Jung comments:

Cassius is infantile because he has freed himself insufficiently, or not at all, from his childish environment and his adaptation to his parents, with the result that he has a false reaction to the world. . . . He is so identified through his close ties with them that he behaves like his father or mother. He is incapable of living his own life and finding the character that belongs to him. . . . The psychologically valuable fact to be elicited here is that Cassius is infantile and identified with his mother [e.g. Russia]. . . . So far as his emotional life is concerned, he has not yet caught up with himself [that is, separated and individuated] as is often the case with people who are apparently so masterful towards life and their fellows [e.g. neighboring sovereign nations], but who have remained infantile in regard to the demands of feeling.[78]

On the same theme, Jean Knox, clinician and analytic researcher, has described what happens when the development of a fully mature and reflective sense of self-agency is inhibited in a person, and how this can lead to a distortion where there is a fear of love and relationship. She believes these problems arise when parents are fearful of their infant's separation-individuation process, and they use the child to remain as a constant psychic mirror for themselves. As the children grow, they fear not only all subsequent relationships as threats to their own subjectivity, but also that, if they individuate, it will cause the destruction of their objects and they will be stranded on their own. This kind of rearing pattern accounts for a range of attachment problems, such as addiction, avoidance, ambivalence, and disorganization, with the possibility of aggression and worse.[79]

This is typically rooted in the person's experience, as Knox observes, that a relationship is always coercive, that one person is directly controlling and dominating another. In turn, she associates the maintenance of this expectation with a particular form of communication between caregiver and child (it could be a father figure) where there is a predominance of indexical communication, in which words are controlling actions and are not truly symbolic communications. A patient afflicted in this way can be released by experiencing alternative modes of symbolic communication in a favorable analytic setting.[80]

In sum, the burden of this chapter has been to show how the complexity behind two intractable contemporary situations is ultimately and comprehensively rooted in communications and the complexes that keep them in their grip, personal or cultural. Whether we deal in truths, distortions, or outright lies delivered coercively, the manner in which we communicate with babies and among ourselves impacts the development of individuals, groups, and nations whose aspiration is surely to maintain identity and culture and to steward the biosphere and hand them on securely to future generations. In practice, a combination of willful ignorance, poor parenting, lack of compassion or empathy, plus the many and varied accidents, such as natural disasters,[81] bring about injustice and collapse the social order. A fear-driven destructive libido—often anxious about abandonment or its corollary, insignificance to the point of disappearance—gives way to mayhem and violence.[82] All of it is down to the nature of communication. There exists mediation, a bridge, sometimes in the form of a silent embrace in the stillness, which could be a route to transformation and rebirth. For that to happen, we need to reflect and, as the poet wrote while World War II raged, not cease from our exploration (of symbols),[83] for which there are no shortcuts,

> This is the use of memory:
> For liberation—not less of love but expanding
> Of love beyond desire, and so liberation
> From the future as well as the past. Thus, love of a country
> Begins as an attachment to our own field of action
> And comes to find that action of little importance
> Though never indifferent. History may be servitude,
> History may be freedom. See, now they vanish,
> The faces and places, with the self which, as it could, loved them,
> To become renewed, transfigured, in another pattern.[84]
>
> T. S. Eliot
> "Little Gidding," *The Four Quartets*

Notes

1 Theodore de Korwin Szymanowski, *L'avenir économique, social et politique en Europe*, ed. H. Maro (Paris 1885/8). Reissued as Teodor Korwin-Szymanowski, *Przyszłość Europy w zakresie gospodarczym, społecznym i politycznym. L'avenir économique, social et politique en Europe* in French–Polish Parallel Text, edited with notes and postface by Radosław Żurawski vel Grajewski, Ministry of Foreign Affairs (Warsaw: The Library of European Unity, 2015); Joseph Redfearn, *My Self, My Many Selves* (London: Academic Press, 1985).

2 Joseph Redfearn, *The Exploding Self—The Creative and Destructive Nucleus of the Personality* (Wilmette, IL: Chiron, 1992).

3 Thomas Singer and Samuel L. Kimbles, *The Cultural Complex: Contemporary Jungian Perspectives on Psyche and Society* (Hove & New York: Routledge, 2004).

4 Anthony Stevens, *The Roots of War: A Jungian Perspective* (St. Paul, MI: Paragon, 1989).

5 Robert Fox, "Ukraine Knows Winning the Information War Gives It the Edge on the Frontline," *Evening Standard*, November 23, 2022, www.standard.co.uk/comment/ukr aine-russia-war-information-vladimir-putin-twitter-elon-musk-volodymyr-zelensky-b1041997.html; Max Hänska-Ahy and Stefan Bauchowitz, "Tweeting for Brexit: How

Social Media Influenced the Referendum," in *Brexit, Trump and the Media*, eds. John Mair, Tor Clark, Neil Fowler, Raymond Snoddy, and Richard Tait (Bury St. Edmunds, UK: Abramis Academic, 2017), pp. 31–35.

6 Heraldry and the awarding of gongs can be the misuse of symbolism as a diversionary tactic.

7 Martin Westlake, "Europe's Dystopian Futures: Perspectives on Emerging European Dystopian Visions and Their Implications," *Review of European Studies* 12, no. 4 (2020). This is an excellent, if selective, survey of mainly English-language literature from the post- 1945 period.

8 Ann Kutek, "Warring Opposites," in *Jungian Thought in the Modern World*, eds. Elphis Christopher and Hester McFarland Solomon (London: Free Association Books, 2000).

9 C. G. Jung, "After the Catastrophe" (1945), in *The Collected Works of C. G. Jung*, vol. 10, eds. Herbert Read, Gerhard Adler, Michael Fordham, and William McGuire, trans. R. F. C. Hull (London: Routledge & Kegan Paul, 1968), § 413.

10 Peter Ricketts, *Hard Choices: The Making and Unmaking of Global Britain* (London: Atlantic Books, 2021).

11 Louis Zinkin, "Your Self: Did You Find It or Did You Make It?" *Journal of Analytical Psychology* 53, no. 3 (2008): 389–404.

12 Zinkin, p. 394.

13 Zinkin, p. 395.

14 Ann Kutek, "Jung and His Family—A Contemporary Paradigm," in *Jungian Thought in the Modern World*.

15 Zinkin, p. 396.

16 Zinkin, p. 404.

17 See Singer and Kimbles, *The Cultural Complex.*

18 Zinkin, "Your Self," p. 404.

19 Marcus West, "Complexes and Jungian Archetypes" *London Spring*, August 12, 2015, www.londonspring.org/what-is-a-complex-in-jungian-psychology/

20 C. G. Jung, "A Review of the Complex Theory" (1934), in *The Collected Works of C. G. Jung*, vol. 8, eds. Herbert Read, Gerhard Adler, Michael Fordham, and William McGuire, trans. R. F. C. Hull (London: Routledge & Kegan Paul, 1969), § 200.

21 Robert Frost, *The Oxford History of Poland–Lithuania, vol. I, The Making of the Polish–Lithuanian Union, 1385–1569* (Oxford: Oxford University Press, 2015).

22 Ann Kutek, "On Sovereignty" (Unpublished manuscript, University of Oxford, 1969).

23 F. H. Hinsley, *Sovereignty* (London: C. A. Watts, 1966), p. 22.

24 C. G. Jung, "The Transcendent Function" ([1916]/1957), in *The Collected Works of C. G. Jung*, vol. 8.

25 W. R. Bion, *Attention and Interpretation* (London: Karnac, 1988), p. 95.

26 *Commensal* is from the Latin root, *mensa*, table, meaning sharing a table.

27 Bion, *Attention and Interpretation*, p. 95.

28 Bion, p. 104.

29 "UK Expected to Be Only Major Economy to Shrink in 2023—IMF," *BBC News*, January 31, 2023, www.bbc.co.uk/news/business-64452995 31.01.2023

30 Ricketts, *Hard Choices*, p. 184.

31 "Brexit and Food. How Is It Working Out?" *The Food Programme*, BBC Radio 4, January 29, 2023.

32 Anna Fazackerley, "Brexit Causes Collapse in European Research Funding for Oxbridge," *The Observer*, February 4, 2023, www.theguardian.com/education/2023/feb/04/brexit-causes-collapse-in-european-research-funding-for-oxbridge-universities

33 Ricketts, *Hard Choices*, p. 134

34 Ricketts reports that studies of trade flows repeatedly show that trade roughly halves as the distance between countries doubles. Ricketts, *Hard Choices*, note p. 252.

35 Lucy Ash, "London Sixth Largest French City," *BBC News*, May 30, 2012, www.bbc.co.uk/news/magazine-18234930

36 Many of the EU arrivals were Lithuanians and Poles, traditional adherents of the Catholic church. At the peak before Brexit, there were over one hundred Polish parishes across Britain. According to the Polish Catholic Mission in England and Wales, after Brexit, there are seventy parishes covering two hundred towns. The Catholic Church, Bishops' Conference of England and Wales, www.cbcew.org.uk/home/the-bishops/polish-catholic-mission-in-england-and-wales/

37 Ricketts, *Hard Choices*, pp. 134–135.

38 Danny Dorling and Sally Tomlinson, *Rule Britannia: Brexit and the End of Empire* (Hull, UK: Biteback, 2020).

39 Danny Dorling, "Brexit and the End of the British Empire," Atlantic Fellows for Social and Economic Equity programme and the International Inequalities Institute at London School of Economics, YouTube video, March 29, 2019, www.youtube.com/watch?v=AM5-Ihrztc4

40 Dorling, "Brexit and the End of the British Empire."

41 Ricketts, *Hard Choices*, pp. 206–207, referencing Boris Johnson's speech on February 3, 2020, at Greenwich.

42 *Britannia Rules the Waves* composed in 1745 to words by Thompson.

43 Lucas is the past Moscow bureau chief of *The Economist*.

44 Edward Lucas, "Russia InFocus with Edward Lucas," *New Debate*, YouTube video, April 8, 2022, www.youtube.com/watch?v=VyTfH_lD3tI

45 There is, however, a theory, that, if the United Kingdom had not left the EU, a full-scale invasion of Ukraine may not have taken place.

46 Serhii Plokhy, *The Gates of Europe: A History of Ukraine* (London: Penguin Books, 2016), p. 70.

47 Referring primarily to Eastern national churches, *autocephaly* is independence from patriarchal authority.

48 "Orthodox Brothers on Collision Course," *Orthodox Times*, January 10, 2023, https://orthodoxtimes.com/orthodox-brothers-on-a-collision-course/

49 Oleksandr Cherednychenko, "Identité linguistique et identité nationale sous la mondialisation: le cas d'Ukraine" in *Sprachliche Individuation in mehrsprachigen Regionen Osteuropas*, ed. Klaus Bochman (Leipzig: Leipziger Universitatsverlag, 2009).

50 Oleksandr Cherednychenko, "L'Ukraine après le Maïdan: une nouvelle identité," *Cahiers Sens Public* no. 17–18 (2014): 75–84.

51 Daniel Beauvois, "Les Russes ont capte l'héritage de l'Ukraine a leur profit," *Libération*, December 11, 2004.

52 Cherednychenko, "L'Ukraine après le Maïdan: une nouvelle identité," p. 78.

53 Lithuanian–Polish political union was arguably a historical blueprint for the EU. See Kutek, "On Sovereignty."

54 Poland, Lithuania—the main protagonists—and their tenants—Latvia, Estonia, Belarus, Moldova, and Ukraine—and their Jewish lodgers, among other minorities, disappeared from the map of Europe as nations until the conclusion of World War I and were shared between Russia, the Habsburg Empire, and Prussia, where Catherine originated. The erstwhile landlords and their tenants did not emerge in possession of their individual statehoods until after the fall of the Berlin Wall, at least two centuries later.

55 Potemkin is said to have been Catherine's secret "consort."

56 Bila Tserkva is the largest city in Kyiv Oblast.

57 Korwin Szymanowski, *L'avenir économique*; Wikipedia, s.v. "BilaTserkva," last modified September 22, 2023, 19:57 UTC, https://en.wikipedia.org/wiki/Bila_Tserkva

58 Plokhy, *The Gates of Europe*.

59 Plokhy, *The Gates of Europe*, p. 239.

60 Poland's pacification policy was a series of measures taken against Ukrainian militant activists in 1930.

61 Bandera was assassinated by KGB agents in Munich in 1959 while living in West Germany.

62 They included Jews, Russians, Czechs, Georgians, and those Ukrainians who hid potential victims of the terror.

63 Timothy Snyder, "The Causes of Ukrainian–Polish Ethnic Cleansing 1943," *Past & Present* no. 179 (2003): 197–234.

64 Viktor Yushchenko, third president of Ukraine, awarded Bandera the status of "Hero of Ukraine" in 2010. This was later rescinded by the Ukrainian parliament.

65 Scottish nationalists could argue that this is exactly analogous to how England has dealt with Scottish demands to return to their former statehood before they pooled (or pawned) their sovereignty in 1707.

66 Bion, *Attention and Interpretation.*

67 The Crimean vote for Ukrainian independence was 54 percent.

68 Michel Malherbe, *Les Langues de L'Humanité. Encyclopédie* (Paris: Bouquins, 1998), p. 1620.

69 "Ukraine Agriculture Production and Trade," US Department of Agriculture, April 2022, www.fas.usda.gov/sites/default/files/2022-04/Ukraine-Factsheet-April2022.pdf

70 For definitions, see ARAS, s.v. "abaissement du niveau mental" https://aras.org/concordance/content/abaissement-du-niveau-mental

71 Rickett, *Hard Choices*, pp. 120–121.

72 Bion, *Attention and Interpretation.*

73 Mino Vianello, "The Origin of War," Private communication, 2022.

74 Doug Klein, "Victory Over Russia Is the Only Way to Rescue the Kidnapped Ukrainians," *The New Republic*, December 7, 2022. The theft of children and the monstrous attack on their sense of self were practiced by the Nazi regime in WWII and more recently by the Videla regime during the "Dirty War" in Argentina. *The Mothers of the Disappeared* is the most famous ongoing protest against this practice.

75 Carol Gilligan and Naomi Snider, *Why Does Patriarchy Persist?* (Cambridge, UK: Polity Press, 2018). Quoted in Angela Saini, *The Patriarchs: How Men Came to Rule* (London: 4th Estate, 2023).

76 Vianello, "The Origin of War."

77 Shakespeare, *Julius Caesar*, Act IV, scene III.

78 C. G. Jung, "The Battle for Deliverance from the Mother" (1956), in *The Collected Works of C. G. Jung*, vol. 5, eds. Herbert Read, Gerhard Adler, Michael Fordham, and William McGuire, trans. R. F. C. Hull (London: Routledge & Kegan Paul, 1968); *The Collected Works of C. G. Jung*, vol. 10, eds. Herbert Read, Gerhard Adler, Michael Fordham, and William McGuire, trans. R. F. C. Hull (London: Routledge & Kegan Paul, 1967), §§ 429–431. Apparently feeling insufficiently sovereign, we could surmise.

79 Jean Knox, "The Fear of Love: The Denial of Self in Relationship," *The Journal of Analytical Psychology* 52, no. 5 (2007): 559–560.

80 Knox.

81 On February 6, 2023, an earthquake struck Turkey and Syria causing destruction across a huge swath of land and thousands of deaths across frontiers and boundaries, while, in juxtaposition, Russia plans its next military offensive on Ukraine and more death and destruction.

82 Jung, "The Battle for Deliverance from the Mother."

83 C. G. Jung, "Symbols of the Mother and of Rebirth," in *The Collected Works of C. G. Jung*, vol. 5.

84 Jung.

Chapter 6

The War of Symbols

Dmytro Zaleskyi

Introduction—War and Trauma

Let us start with February 24, 2022, although we all know that the war really began much earlier. We have been in this state for eight years now.

On the one hand, it seems that February 24 happened only yesterday. Yet, while experiencing the first minutes of the war, there is, right next to those feelings, the completely opposite perception that a huge amount of time has passed and that we, and the entire country, are now totally changed. In this state, the idea of the past and the future disappears; there is an obsessive fixation on the present and a feeling that one lacks coherence of thought, making it very difficult to focus attention on completed narratives. It is very difficult to reflect "here and now." It is even more difficult to accurately reproduce memories. This lack of focus even expresses itself in small things; for example, it is impossible to watch an entire movie, or finish a book; even listening to all the verses of a song is impossible, and it is definitely hard to finish writing presentations!

There are the mood swings often described for traumatic states—for instance, rapid changes in mood from manic activity to hypersomnia. Another manifestation is obsessive browsing through the news on phones, sometimes continuously. This further aggravates the time split. Information is "swallowed in lumps," without narrative linking and therefore losing the sequence of time.

I have also observed a polarization of attachments. There can be a feeling of becoming closer, to the point of fusion, to loved ones and strangers who have shared in this difficult situation. On the other hand, there can be a distancing of oneself from others, sometimes even very close friends. These attachment dynamics can transform one's analytical position, even to the point of losing it altogether. Indeed, mutual regression of the analyst and patient and the total inappropriateness of interpretations work in the metaphor of "both being in the same lifeboat," and threats to immediate survival, everyday life, and the social fabric create a situation where the very possibility of maintaining therapy becomes the content of the therapy. It can be a way of going through the trauma together and returning to the analytic relationship at a deeper level, or it can be the end of the therapeutic relationship.

DOI: 10.4324/9781032695143-9

All these aspects add up to the experience of a borderline gray zone. Such liminal space causes deep terror and, at the same time, it can inspire a passion based on the justice of the struggle. After about three or four weeks, it seemed that I, and most people around me, were gradually coming out of this "traumatic state of consciousness." It is true that some people may remain in this traumatic state much longer, so that it slowly acquires the signs of post-traumatic stress disorder (PTSD). I would like to understand more about this critical point, this bifurcation where some people return to active existence and the sense of life, whereas some remain, in fact, in a traumatic state. This in-between state. As Shakespeare's Hamlet said:

The time is out of joint—O cursèd spite,
That ever I was born to set it right![1]

History and Genocide

Turning now to the historical context of the war, the Russian Federation (RF) and Ukraine are linked by a long historical period of being one state, first as the Russian Empire and then the USSR, which also very quickly turned into an empire. Despite many important differences, the common Soviet experience unites us. In the last thirty years, however, our paths have diverged, as most Ukrainians hoped, forever.

On the one hand, it was during the imperial period that Ukraine, like many countries that stepped out from empires, established itself with its modern borders. On the other hand, in the period from 1914 until 1945, it is estimated that every second man and every fourth woman died a violent death in Ukraine. According to other, more conservative estimates, demographic losses in Ukrainian lands in the years 1914–1945 amounted to about 15 million people.[2] Comparison of life expectancy in Ukraine and in the "old Europe" shows that residents of Ukraine lived an average of six to twelve years less. However, in 1932–1933 and 1942–1943, this difference reached the catastrophic gap of thirty to forty years. The war years of 1942–1943 are not surprising. Although 1932–1933 were peaceful years, they were the years of the *Holodomor* (the Great Famine). In a relatively short period of time (1932–1947), several genocides took place on Ukrainian lands. (*Genocide*, according to the definition by the author of the term, Rafal Lemkin, consists of acts of mass violence that threaten the existence of entire groups, either through physical destruction or by creating conditions under which they could not reproduce as a group with its own culture and identity.[3]) Such genocidal acts included the following:

1. Liquidation of the "Kurkuls" (well-off peasants) as a class in 1930–1931 (through collectivization)
2. The Holodomor of 1932–1933
3. The so-called Polish and Greek operations of the NKVD (Soviet Security Services)
4. The Holocaust of the Jews

5. Liquidation of the Roma
6. Mass exterminations of Soviet prisoners of war by the Nazis in 1941–1944
7. Destruction of the Polish population by Ukrainian partisans (Volyn massacres) as well as extermination of Ukrainians by the Polish underground
8. Three mass deportations of (1) Crimean Tatars, (2) Poles from the territory of Ukraine, and (3) Ukrainians from the territory of Poland. The list of mass violence is complemented by Stalin's terror of 1937–1938 and Soviet deportations from Western Ukraine in 1939–1941.
9. The terror of the Soviet government against the anti-communist underground in the western part of the country in 1944–1950

Timothy Snyder refers to the territory between Berlin and Moscow as the "Bloodlands," and Ukraine is in the very center of them.[4] It is true that people from these lands have their own long lists of mass victims, although we still believe that Ukraine's case is unique. And there is also the Chernobyl disaster and the ongoing war to be added to the previous list.

Although Ukrainians actively contributed to the development of the Russian Empire, in view of the cost in human lives, the vast majority of Ukrainians do not wish for an imperial future. Over the past thirty years, Ukrainian society has gained the experience of free elections, democracy, and basic freedoms, which has led to a radical shift in the field of ethics. An open society has made it possible for Ukrainians to see themselves and their history as they are perceived by the world, especially by their closest neighbors in the West. This has been vividly manifested in relation to Poland where mutual blame for past conflicts has given way to reconciliation though mutual acceptance of responsibility and forgiveness. We can see the outcome of this process when Poland, without any hesitation, has supported Ukraine in its distress. We are also sincerely grateful to all the countries of Europe and the world that have united to support us. Without this support, Ukraine as an independent nation would have been doomed.

The collapse of the USSR made it possible to face the terrible reality of the past. Whereas, in Ukraine, this process has continued, in Russia we observe the reverse process, a "mass amnesia," of which a recent manifestation is the ban in 2022 of the society Memorial, which advocated the need for repentance for historical crimes.

Ideology, Ethics, and Symbol Formation

In 2008, the Russian government made a radical turn in its policy, but systemic militarization of the society and the economy had taken place much earlier. The Russian Empire and then the Soviet one have always been deeply ideological states. Traditionally, the key ideological *braces* were developed by a narrow group of people. After the collapse of the USSR, a pragmatic approach prevailed in Russia for a while, but not for long, as old habits die hard. True, the new ideological models were much more modest, such as the conspiracy model developed by A. Aleksandr Dugin (a far-right Russian political philosopher), with its poetic description of the eternal confrontation between the donkey-headed desert god Set (the Atlantic Anglo-Saxon West) and the newborn god Osiris (the Eurasian East).[5] This is a very popular ideological model among some in Putin's entourage and for Putin himself.

But there are other, more serious players among Putin's top brass. We can see Timofei Sergeitsev as one of the significant nonpublic figures. It was his article, published on the eve of the invasion of Ukraine, that called for the total denazification of Ukraine, punishment of dissent, and the collapse of Ukraine as a separate country.[6]

Sergeitsev was an immediate student of Georgy Shchedrovytskyi, who built a certain theory, technique, and movement in the 1960s named methodology. With their seminars and "big games" during perestroika, methodologists worked true miracles, awakening people in large Soviet enterprises from hibernation and making them search for meanings. Everything looked very efficient. They developed a psychotechnique consisting of a set of certain consistent psychological steps, with complete disregard for ethics. It was a truly virtuoso trick whereby meanings were completely isolated from ethics. I understand why. Soviet ethics as such did not exist. Ethics were replaced with a morality based solely on the Persona archetype and an obsession with the Hero archetype, without any chance of integration of this complex. The Hero archetype is the ego without limits, leading only to inflation and the Priapus complex.[7] And now, it is Sergey Kiriyenko, Shchedrovytskyi's student, who manages the territories of Ukraine currently occupied by Russia.

In addition to Shchedrovytskyi, methodology had another father, the mathematician and psychologist Volodymyr Lefebvre, who insisted on the importance of ethics and reflective subjectivity, resulting in a deep conflict between the founding fathers. Lefebvre later developed a binary model of ethical systems.[8]

Ethical System 1 (mature democracies) adheres to the principle that "a compromise between good and evil is evil" (that is, a good result does not justify bad means to achieve it).[9] However—and here lies the paradox—in this system, the "good" individual above all seeks for a compromise with another individual. (One needs to convince the other not to act.)

Ethical System 2 (the USSR and the modern Russian Federation) is based on the principle that "a compromise between good and evil is good" (that is, a good result justifies bad means to achieve it).[10] However, there is another paradox—in this system, the "good" individual above all seeks confrontation with another individual. (One doesn't need to convince; one needs to act.)

In Ethical System 1,

• A bad means should *not* be used to achieve a good end.

In Ethical System 2,

• A bad means *can* be used to achieve a good end.

One can find out which ethical system dominates in a country based on a very simple sign: If moral education is based on prohibition of bad things (don't kill, don't lie), the country belongs to the first system, whereas, if the basis is declaration of the good (be honest, be brave), we are dealing with the second one.

In Lefebvre's binary model, the evil that realizes it is evil becomes the good. Within this ethical system, the Pope apologizes to all those historically offended by Catholicism; his good ratings increase. But the USSR and RF could not afford to apologize for their own "Soviet and Empire" evil, pay compensation to the victims, or talk about their historical guilt. For the second ethical system, this is suicidal! It was sufficient to cautiously admit the fallacy of some of Stalin's actions. And even there, many considered that a disaster. Be that as it may, it turned out that the evil committed by communists was not evil (and Stalin's evil was that he acted against the communists).

The authoritarian regime, having huge media opportunities, takes advantage of the fact that information flows in a coordinated manner from a single center. The budget of the Russian Federation's state-owned media officially equaled EUR 1.3 billion in 2020. For comparison, that would be EUR 24.5 million in Ukraine. The uniqueness of the current situation is that authorities in the RF have completely lost the balancing mechanisms that existed even in the USSR, when the party's power was balanced by the KGB and the army. Currently, the ideology of the RF has only one origin—the FSB (Federal Security Service). Its method of self-realization is very reminiscent of the structure of medieval orders, which also determines the choice of Ethical System 2, according to Lefebvre.

After Ukraine gained independence, I believe, the two ethical systems coexisted in parallel. The Soviet elite were disguised as the new oligarchic authority without any deep internal transformation. According to the principle "Loot defeats the Evil," Ethical System 2 took on one of its most abominable forms, *oligarchic capitalism*, where there was no need even to pretend to strive for the good. Corruption became the key regulatory mechanism of society. My nephew from the Donbas used to say: "Even though with stolen money, what a stadium he has built!"

Civil society in Ukraine developed along a different path. During the past thirty years, we have experienced at least four large-scale public protests that resulted in a victory and a change in power. The latest one was the Maidan Revolution, the Revolution of Dignity of 2013–2014, which finally affirmed the new anticorruption ethic, that prosperity cannot be achieved with unworthy methods.

Lefebvre claims there is a deep gap in understanding between people representing the different ethical systems. In the language of psychoanalysis, this can be described as perverse, inverted ethics. Given that psychoanalysis prevails primarily in democratic countries, the logic of the second ethical system seems perverse to us. I think that the process of symbol formation under Ethical System 2 is also simplified and literalized. A narrow group of elites has a monopoly on formation of collective symbols through psychotechnique projects.

Here's one example: In a village liberated from Russian occupation in the Kharkiv region, our fighters, the Ukrainian Armed Forces (UAF), distributed food. An old lady came out to them with a red flag. The point is that she got it wrong. She mistook our fighters for Russians and approached them with a red flag (see Figure 6.1).

Figure 6.1 Babushka Anya, mistakenly greeting Ukrainian soldiers with a Soviet banner

Our guys were a bit sarcastic, but quite understanding; however, the woman rejected the food products out of annoyance. The video in the Ukrainian media appeared somewhat humorous. The Russian propaganda machine reacted very quickly. This old lady with a flag filled the entire Russian space. You can watch it online. She is sculpted, carved from wood, cast in metal (see Figure 6.2). Somewhere, there is already a monument with the No. 1 Guard, in the classic Soviet style.

Budgets have been disbursed in almost all regions of Russia to promote the new symbol of the "babushka with the flag." But she survived, and there were several interviews with the actual woman and her husband. It turns out that she is not that pro-Russian. She ended up in a hospital in Kharkiv because her house was destroyed by Russian artillery shelling. She strongly resents the Russians, although she is nostalgic for the USSR. You can be sure that these interviews are not popularized in Russia. All in all, one of the interpretations of this image might be "the old empire in its last rush of dying."

Figure 6.3 is another image I'd like to show you. Unlike the Russians, no one artificially promoted this image. The photo spontaneously spread in social media. This is the so-called Borodyanka locker, which became a symbol of the Ukrainian resistance.

Figure 6.2 Babushka with a Flag

Figure 6.3 Kitchen cabinet with a ceramic cock in Borodyanka settlement (Kyiv Oblast of Ukraine), which became a meme and a symbol of persistence against Russian invasion. On April 14, 2022, this cabinet was transferred to Museum of the Revolution of Dignity (maidenmuseum.org)

When Ukrainians look at it, they see a sensible owner who nailed this locker so securely to the wall that it didn't fall off even when a missile hit it. And you can see that even the ceramic figurine of a rooster stayed in place. The rooster is very specific, locally produced. By the way, you can see such a rooster in President Zelensky's office during his interviews.

This image has a certain native authenticity that cannot be devalued. It is not phallic; on the contrary, it generates sympathy, sadness, and nostalgia.

One of the historical legacies of Ukrainians is their consistent inability to exist within the vertical hierarchy of power. The Self-based drive for psychic survival in the Soviet empire forced Ukrainians to concentrate on real relationships in the horizontal plane. It was from the Cossack state that the concept of Ukraine as a separate political community stemmed, dominated by a simplified but extremely democratic tradition. For example, a modern Ukrainian military unit functions to a large extent horizontally. When I served in the Armed Forces in 2015, the guests who came to our battalion said that we had an atmosphere like a volunteer battalion. We took that as the best possible compliment. It meant that you had value, not because you had a title or connections, but owing only to your activity, your courage, your combat qualities that can only be truly appreciated by your comrades.

The Russian army is organized in a completely different way. By the way, the Bucha tragedy—the devastation of the city and its inhabitants and the massacre of Ukrainian civilians and prisoners of war in March 2022—possibly took on such gigantic proportions, among other things, because Ukrainian snipers had killed a large number of Russian officers. Without officers, the Russian army generally turns into a crowd of murderers, rapists, and looters. Moreover, the level of violence was set by FSB officers, who very quickly started "working" with the locals. The Russian structure is absolutely vertical; everything depends on the chief officer—payments, assessment, execution of orders. And the chief officer is under the close control of the FSB.

Symbols and National Identity

A symbol is a living formation that combines the individual and the collective and resonates deeply in the soul. It is impossible to create this via the psychotechnique; the result would be a *simulacrum*, as Jean Baudrillard called it—something that pretends to be a symbol but never becomes one. Mass media usually swallow it, but it is unlikely that this product can ever be a basis for identity.

Simulative symbolic formations can neither provide support for those experiencing a collective trauma nor protect the future generation from psychological traumatization by traumatized adults. An abused younger generation may become the next "client" of authoritarian regimes. The unprocessed trauma of a generation can become the impetus for collective basic assumption groups, as described by Bion: dependence, the search for a messianic leader, and the fight or flight need for an enemy, all of which form an ideal breeding ground for authoritarian regimes. These, in turn, continue the tradition of simulating the symbolic process. A vicious circle!

For Ukraine, I hope, the revolutions of modern times were successful attempts to break out of this cursed circle: first, the student Maidan; then, the "Ukraine against Kuchma" protests; the Orange Maidan in 2004; and, finally, the Revolution of Dignity in 2014. Owing to the link between the sparse dissident generation—those few people who managed to survive the traumatic experience owing to painful self-awareness—and the young post-Soviet generation, which was already less traumatized, they were a success. In this way, a new Ukrainian identity has been forged.

With the work of Thomas Singer, Jörg Rasche, and other Jungian colleagues, the cultural complex has become a widely used concept. For me, now, while I'm observing the stupendous processes that are happening to Ukraine, the question arises: What exactly creates the core of a nation—the cultural complex or the national identity? And how is national identity, manifested through deep national symbols, primarily in artistic form, related to cultural complexes that manifest themselves mostly through unconscious behavioral patterns?

Perhaps, in nations with a more or less good balance of national identity, attention to and awareness of cultural complexes begin to dominate. But, for nations in the process of affirming their identity, the shadow manifestations of cultural complexes are not so energetically intensive. Nations are a rather imaginary entity compared with cultural complexes that manifest themselves mostly through specific unconscious behavioral patterns. National identity touches the very core of the nation, and, in the process of self-awareness, a powerful centripetal force is created. Let's try to think of this process in Michael Fordham's terms. At the peak of self-awareness, the process of reintegration takes place, which is focused on the center, on the conscious idea and unconscious experience of belonging to the nation. During this period of experiencing the development of national identity, marginal, unconscious processes associated with cultural complexes temporarily recede. According to Fordham, over time, we should expect a shift in the opposite direction, toward deintegration. I hope that this will happen after our victory in Ukraine, and we will be able to deal with it.

I suggest that national identity develops primarily by overcoming and integrating collective traumatic experience. Energy is concentrated on the nuclear issues of the nation's survival, which, at the level of the individual psyche, corresponds to the most primary aspect of the Self, the survival Self. Sometimes, it is through the collective experience of war that personal and collective trauma become integrated with each other through the creation of symbols. Mass individual traumatic experiences are sanctified by becoming infused with the collective trauma of generations.

Nations are created through shared identification with symbolic images, the characteristic nature, language, national arts, songs, festivities, and the pantheon of national heroes. Ukraine, in postmodern times, is going through the stage that most European countries went through in modern times. On the one hand, we can rely on the previous experience of the "happy nations"; on the other, modernity and our own history bring completely new challenges. One way or another, a true explosion of creative activities and the art of national self-awareness is taking place in Ukraine. The stories of our individual identity become the current history of Ukraine. Regardless of these processes taking place outside, we need to build on our Ukrainian project—"To Be at Home Inside and in the World"—that was the title of our tenth conference of the Ukrainian IAAP Developing Group (DG) in 2022.

Symbolic creation can generate a renewed state of self-awareness and creative realization. Ukraine, unfortunately, also had the opposite experience—for example, the Holodomor of 1932–1933. One of the gravest crimes in the history of humanity got buried in the collective unconscious, remaining almost unprocessed at the symbolic level. It was strictly forbidden to write or speak publicly about this in the USSR, and so there are very few films, works of literature, or paintings about it. Only after the Orange Revolution in 2004 did this process shift.

National identity, in my opinion, is one of the manifestations of the reflection of the individual Self in the collective unconscious. It is becoming clear to me that a mature national identity is necessary for a democracy to function successfully. But this cannot be created artificially. It must emerge spontaneously from the collective unconscious of the nation by inspiring a growing number of "non-indifferent" citizens to undertake responsibility for the future of their own country.

Notes

1 Shakespeare, *Hamlet*, Act I, Scene 5, ll. 189–190.
2 Yaroslav Hrytsak, *Overcoming the Past: A Global History of Ukraine* (Портал, 2022).
3 Raphael Lemkin, *Axis Rule in Occupied Europe: Laws of Occupation, Analysis of Government, Proposals for Redress*, 2nd ed. (Clark, NJ: Lawbook Exchange, 2008), 79.
4 Timothy D. Snyder, *Bloodlands* (New York: Basic Books, 2010).
5 Jane Burbank, "The Grand Theory Driving Putin to War," *The New York Times*, March 22, 2022, www.nytimes.com/2022/03/22/opinion/russia-ukraine-putin-eurasianism.html
6 Timofei Sergeitsev, "Что Россия должна сделать с Украиной" [What Russia Needs to Do with Ukraine], Ria Novosti, March 3, 2022.
7 The Priapus complex is named after a Roman god who was cursed with an enormous phallus.
8 Vladimir A. Lefebvre, *Algebra of Conscious* (Dordrecht, Netherlands, 2001).
9 Lefebvre, p. 23.
10 Lefebvre, p. 21.

Chapter 7

Transcorruption
Russian Boundlessness and Shadow Aspects of European Civilization

Dmitry Kotenko

The main ideas for this chapter emerged in the capital of what is still the largest country on our planet, in the Hero City of Moscow, and were first discussed in Frankfurt am Main, the main financial center of Continental Europe. I believe that city was a very appropriate place to formulate a story about the modern phenomenon of *transcorruption*.

I have decided to use this term to define processes that I observe in Russia: Transcorruption covers not only local corruption, but also transnational cooperation in hiding stolen money. In expert estimates, the amount of money Russia loses through corruption yearly is already comparable to its annual budget.[1] The corrupt Russian political establishment understands these problems and the risks it has created. It is afraid of its own country, however, and prefer to keep its funds in the West: in the United States, the EU, and Switzerland.

Thus, Russia and the West are very closely connected. Despite the feeling that a new Iron Curtain is about to fall, the West is a very good "helper" for Russia when it wants to hide stolen money. What is going on between the West and the East nowadays? How can we interpret this strange and painful dream that is not going to end, and how can we respond as individuals?

I have decided to try to find some landmarks in this dark and unexplored area. Given the considerable difficulties that prevent me from traveling, I would like to underline the preliminary nature of my research. I have tried to bring together my observations and ideas and present them for your consideration. I hope to draw attention to certain realities that I feel are extremely significant for understanding everyday life in Russia.

In the Soviet Union, any research paper had to have a quote from Lenin. Otherwise, the work would not be considered scientific. I observe something similar in the Jungian community regarding Jung's quotations, although I would like to believe that, in the case of Jung, we develop his ideas and do not exploit his past.

His main idea, which inspired me to prepare this research, can be found in his last book, still of relevance today, *Man and His Symbols*.

If, for a moment, we regard mankind as one individual, we see that the human race is like a person carried away by unconscious powers; and the human race

DOI: 10.4324/9781032695143-10

also likes to keep certain problems tucked away in separate drawers. But this is why we should give a great deal of consideration to what we are doing, for mankind is now threatened by self-created and deadly dangers that are growing beyond our control. Our world is, so to speak, dissociated like a neurotic, with the Iron Curtain marking the symbolic line of division. Western man, becoming aware of the aggressive will to power of the East, sees himself forced to take extraordinary measures of defense, at the same time as he prides himself on his virtue and good intentions.

What he fails to see is that it is his own vices, which he has covered up by good international manners, that are thrown back in his face by the communist world, shamelessly and methodically. What the West has tolerated, but secretly and with a slight sense of shame (the diplomatic lie, systematic deception, veiled threats), comes back into the open and in full measure from the East and ties us up in neurotic knots. It is the face of his own evil shadow that grins at Western man from the other side of the Iron Curtain.[2]

There is no more Iron Curtain between the West and Russia: I can go to Europe, but not so easily—I need to get a visa first. However, the idea of an Iron Curtain or an associated attitude is still alive in the collective unconscious, and I can feel something iron between the West and Russia.

Following Jung, I tried to find some vivid examples of how the West and Russia are shadowing each other. I did not have to go far—I found gays and the Christian Church.

In the West, we witness a process of desacralization as churches are turned into offices, shops, or apartments or are simply demolished. A strikingly symbolic example was the demolition of a nineteenth-century Catholic church in a village in western Germany to make way for a coal mine.[3]

At the same time, in Russia, there is unprecedented construction of new churches. The patriarchate of the Russian Orthodox Church reports that, in 2017, some 1,500 new churches were opened. It means that three new churches were opened every day![4]

In the West, every large city holds a gay pride parade, whereas, in Russia, a ban on "gay propaganda" has been established by law.

Thus, if we assume that we are parts of a single individual, and Russia is the shadow of the West, we can understand each other better by exploring our shadow aspects and complexes. In this chapter, I focus on two very dominant Russian cultural complexes that are manifested in relations with the West.

Boundlessness

I named the first one *boundlessness*. Boundlessness is something that does not have borders and does not want to have any limits. What does a person feel when they are close to something boundless? Russian philosopher Nikolay Berdyaev said that Russia's boundlessness is a key determiner of the soul of the Russian people.[5]

Russian psychology includes both the boundlessness of the Russian state and the boundlessness of Russian fields. This infinitude makes Russians amorphous and chaotic. It is notable that, in 2016, Russian President Vladimir Putin said that Russia's border does not end anywhere.[6]

Russia's geographical boundlessness forms part of the Russian soul and greatly influences it. Russia's boundless territory represents a geography of the Russian soul. Russians have neither the narrowness inherent in Europeans, who concentrate their energy in a way that affects the soul, nor European prudence, the ability to manage territory and time and the intensity of culture.

The potent influence of boundlessness over the Russian soul gives rise to a raft of distinct Russian features and flaws: Russian laziness, carelessness, lack of initiative, lack of a sense of responsibility, suppressed energy, and extensity. Vast Russian territories require submission and sacrifice. At the same time, faith in miracles and in Mother Russia is far too strong. It is emblematic that, in the twentieth century, the word *Fatherland* was superseded by the word *Motherland* when expressing the concept of homeland in Russia. Russia's image has ultimately dissolved into the archetype of the Great Mother.

Russia blatantly flaunts its archaic and chaotic power, its messed-up laws. The Father has been toppled in Russia; he is befuddled and overshadowed. The rule of the Father has been replaced by the rule of the Mother: amorphous, dark, and hopeless. Russia is ruled by corruption. Russia's life is that of perpetual suffering and sacrifices to the archaic forces. The men who are holding power in the country are only imitating the Father; in fact, they are just menials of the ancient chthonian energy of chaos.

An open manifestation of the complex of Russian boundlessness happened in 2014, with the annexation of Crimea, as it is referred to in the West. The term used in Russia is "the reunification of Crimea with the Russian Federation."

What happens inside this complex of boundlessness? What archetypal forces feed this Russian complex? What does this terrible power look like?

What comes to my mind is the awe-inspiring statue, *The Motherland Calls*, in Volgograd (Figure 7.1). This colossal sculpture was completed in 1967; it embodies a part of the collective spirit frozen in concrete. What a powerful fusion of two archetypal energies—the energy of the Great Mother and the energy of the Warrior.

This Mother not only calls on her sons to fight the enemy, she herself is ready to cut off heads with a heavy sword. With her huge feeding breasts that attract attention to her nipples and her wide fertile hips, she can give birth to many. A huge sword in the right hand is ready to destroy any who challenge or threaten her. Eros and Thanatos are united in one image and pose a great danger to the bearers of this collective reality.

The Warrior is responsible for the establishment of precise boundaries. The Mother, on the contrary, is responsible for chaos. Jung compared Mother to the sea, and the sea is boundless.[7] The Mother holding a sword in her hand is a boundless militant.

Figure 7.1 The Motherland Calls. The compositional center of the monument ensemble *Heroes of the Battle of Stalingrad* on Mamayev Kurgan in Volgograd, Russia (Photo Creative Commons CC0)

The breasts and the phallus (the sword) have united in one image. The phallic female Mother is a collective female image, a symbol of a huge archetypal force, impossible to resist.

It is somewhat synchronistic that, in the Soviet era, images of the Motherland with a bare sword were also erected in Kyiv and Tbilisi, as nowadays Russia has border conflicts with both Ukraine and Georgia.

A Mother-Warrior raises her sons to do battle. She needs a war. She is a mother-protector and a mother-aggressor at the same time.

Look at her face and her pose. Her look is terrifying. I want to hide from a mother like this. This idea is reflected in a piece of poetry by a contemporary Russian poet, Vera Pavlova:

Доченьку бьёт и сыночка
лупит тяжёлой рукою
родина—мать-одиночка.
Да и кто уживётся с такою?

She beats her daughter and her son,
She strikes with a heavy hand,
Motherland—a single mother.
Who will be able to get along with her?[8]

Now let us look at Europe. In my opinion, boundlessness is an important complex that is in a shadow state in the European unconscious. Possibly, it manifests itself in modern postcolonial politics. For example, in Italy, African refugees are being exploited as cheap farm labor. If we trace the history of Italian aggression in Africa in the twentieth century, we will see that this is just a shadow way of a new colonization—using African human resources.[9]

The idea of boundlessness or the lack of borders is partly replicated in the concept of the European Union, whereby citizens of EU member states can move and work freely within the territory of the Union. But, as recent events show, not all Europeans can withstand the stress created by the lack of borders. One of the main populist slogans and conditions of Brexit was the idea of giving the United Kingdom control over its borders.[10]

So, Mother Russia is chaotic and boundless. The chthonic energy of chaos could be limited by the energy of the Father—the Law—but in Russia the Law does not work. Besides, how terrible must the Father be to be able to stay close to such a Mother? Hence the powerful longing for the Father in Russian society. It seems incredible, but there are people today who are ready to celebrate Stalin's birthday— the Reds come to his grave with flowers. Those who wish Stalin to burn in hell also come. However, they—unlike the fans of the mustached leader—get detained by the police.[11]

On the one hand, Stalin could be a figure that represents the archetype of the Great Father. But, on the other, he is not a good Father; he has no idea or regard for any law other than his own.

Lawlessness

In order to understand the reasons behind Russians' peculiar attitude to the Law, we must look into the origins of Russian ideology. *Sermon on Law and Grace*, written by Hilarion of Kiev (1051–1054), the first Russian metropolitan, is an outstanding piece of verbal art.[12] One of Metropolitan Hilarion's main ideas is the Idea of Grace, which he sets against the Law. This idea lies at the very core of Russian Orthodoxy.

It was first put forward immediately after the Baptism of Rus. The Idea of Grace separated Russian Orthodoxy from Byzantine Orthodoxy and created a unique Russian worldview. In essence, the entire Russian culture is based on that work by Metropolitan Hilarion. Russian philosophy, Russian literature, and Russian poetry can be traced back to the *Sermon on Law and Grace*.

What Does the Idea of Grace Actually Mean?

The Sermon on Law and Grace presents the Grace of the New Testament as surpassing and replacing the Law of the Old Testament. Hilarion emphasizes that the Law came first, and then came Grace, just as Ishmael came before Isaac. He then explains that the Gospel spreads over the whole Earth, whereas the "lake of the Law" has dried.

The New Testament invites all people to eternity. The Old Testament was only for the Jewish people; the New Testament has worldwide distribution.

There is one very important detail: The Law of the Old Testament comes from God and is holy. But the Law is given to humans, and humans understand that they cannot be saved by the Law.

Jesus came and said, however, "With men this is impossible, but with God all things are possible" (Matthew 19:26). Christ brings the possibility of granting humans Grace and salvation—that is the main meaning of his coming.

Rejection of the critical role of the Law in salvation, on the one hand, and the triumph of Grace over the Law, on the other hand, form the basis of the Russian attitude to the Law. Law is secondary.

The conflict of the Law and Grace in the collective Russian soul has found a symbolic reflection in Andrey Zvyagintsev's film *Leviathan*, released in 2014.[13] A house that was built in full conformity with the Law is demolished only to be replaced with a church. The lawful owner of the house and of the land loses a legal battle. Grace wins over the Law. If you want to feel the toughness of the Russian way of living, you are welcome to watch this unnerving movie.

In northern transepts of Russian churches, one can often spot an image of the Penitent Thief (Figure 7.2), also known as the Good Thief. This is an important image for the Russian soul. The first person to whom Christ said, "Today you will be with me in Paradise," was a robber (Luke 23:43). Based on profound ancient Russian apocrypha, "Passions of Christ," this robber was, in fact, a milk brother of Christ. When the holy family fled to Egypt with the gifts of the Magi, they were robbed by a gang of robbers. But the leader of the bandits had a sick wife and a baby the same age as Christ, and the Virgin Mary breastfed the baby. Eventually, that baby was the robber who was on the cross next to Jesus Christ.[14]

This is a very touching story, which offers a deep reflection of the Russian outlook. The main cathedral in the Moscow Kremlin is dedicated to the Dormition of the Theotokos, commemorating the Assumption of the Virgin Mary. The Virgin Mary is the patroness of Russia; she feeds the sinful children of the Russian land with her milk. The salvation of the Russian soul has been predetermined. A Russian can, therefore, sin and expect to receive Grace, just like the Good Thief could obtain it.

There is, in fact, a profound difference between the attitude of Russia and that of the West: The way to salvation is Grace, not the Law. Robbers in Russia are often romanticized and idealized.

Let us look at a manifestation of this complex: Since 1998, the European Court of Human Rights (ECHR) has collected almost EUR 200 million in damages from the Russian Federation. Most of them were paid for torture, violations of the rights to a fair trial, freedom, and personal inviolability. In 2017, Russia became the number one state in Europe in terms of the amount of just satisfaction payments awarded by the ECHR.[15]

Is the Law present in the West? Is the Father with his Law still strong in the West, or is there a devaluation of his power underway?

Figure 7.2 Icon of the Penitent Thief

Russia is like a blind child trying to find the Father figure and suffering from its absence. The West, in contrast, is going the way of rejecting the Father, step by step. This process is so intense that, now, millions of Muslims, with their strong, declared restrictions and rules, need to be in Europe to support the falling Father figure. The profound significance behind this migration can be viewed as a deliberate effort to restore a patriarchal system. Within Muslim communities, there exists a deeply rooted set of values emphasizing the importance of paternal influence. I consider this an unconscious desire that propels these people toward Europe. Their arrival can be seen as a compensation for the significant devaluation of the patriarchal structure and diminishing Father figure.

How Can We Deal with Transcorruption and the Forces That Feed It?

The crimes committed by a modern, corrupt Russia would not have been possible without an ideal Western financial safe haven. Who are the real beneficiaries of the flight of corruption-fueled capital from the world's richest country? The West benefits greatly from the empire of chaos in Russia. And these are not just financial benefits: Russia allows Europe to see a reflection of the dark and inconvenient part of European civilization.

Our governments are deploying against us the latest state-of-the-art information weapons, awakening us to uncontrollable life archetypes that were previously sleeping deep in our souls. How do we deal with these energies? How can we digest them? Our future—if we still have a future—depends on these answers.

I would like to share with you my experience of finding answers to these questions. My unconscious helped me in this search. One night, when I was writing this chapter, I had a dream in which a voice told me that the full title of the novel by the Nobel-winning author Boris Pasternak is not *Doctor Zhivago*, but *Doctor Zhivago: Life under Black Square*.[16] Indeed, my dream inspired my own adaption of the *Black Square* by Kazimir Malevich (Figure 7.3).

There was a rather unexpected combination of symbols in my dream. Doctor Zhivago's story is very symbolic in itself, as every character in that book means something general, more than just personal—something collective. Doctor Zhivago dies in Moscow, Russia, without seeing his wife and children, who were forced to emigrate to France to escape the Red Terror. The Iron Curtain dropped, and the doctor could not leave Russia.[17] It appears that something similar has happened and is happening with Russia and the West: like a separation of husband and wife. It can mean something like a disruption in the flow of libido. I can compare the flow of libido to the flow of a river: If there is a block, the river will find another way to seep through. Similarly,

Figure 7.3 Dreaming of Black Square, acrylic and watercolor on paper, 2023

now, the West and Russia do not have a straight way for the libido to flow, so this energy has found another way—corruption—as a shadow way of being in contact.

The egoistic statements of our collective conscious do not allow for a way to communicate, so this work is being done by the collective unconscious through a shadow movement of funds—transcorruption.

In this case, in my dream, two powerful symbolic creations were combined: The first is the story about a disruption in relationships, and the second is *Black Square*. And I realized that this painting is really a very good symbol of the Russian mood. Something that I feel as hopeless. Its roots extend far back into the past: blackness. In alchemy, the color black symbolizes the nigredo stage of transformation. But it is not just a color; it is a deep, black abyss.

Malevich saw in his *Black Square* a figurative expression of the victory of active human creativity over the passive form of nature: the black square instead of the solar circle. The way the painting used to be exhibited also had an important symbolic meaning. *Black Square* hung in the most prominent place, in the so-called red corner, where Russians usually place religious icons.

Yet, for alchemists, the nigredo was a cause not for dismay but for rejoicing. It was the conjunction with psyche's unlimited power in which the golden embryo of Self could be conceived.

Perhaps, transcorruption could be a manifestation of the depressive stage of transmutation, so-called nigredo. If so, based on alchemical processes, the next stage should be albedo, the white one. Reaching this stage requires energy. Money is energy. Corruption is always about the shadow movement of money and funds.

Figure 7.4 Dreaming of Suprematist Composition: White on White, acrylic and watercolor on paper, 2023

Perhaps, unconsciously, we warm up our relations in order to move to the next stage of transformation.

As an omen of this, there is another Malevich square—*Suprematist Composition: White on White* (Figure 7.4), which inspired me to paint another adaptation.

We need each other as parts of a single whole in order to get through the transformation. But today, with obvious clarity, there arises the question of the price of this transformation, which is passing in the shadow mode. Are we ready to continue to pay higher interest rates for servicing shadow capital, the hidden resource of the collective psyche? Or will the transition of these processes from the shadow allow us—with fewer losses—to move to a new level of interaction and integration of the still hostile parts of the collective psyche?

Addendum: War Statement

The modern conflict between Russia and Ukraine vividly demonstrates the manifestation of the two Russian cultural complexes—lawlessness and boundlessness. The illegal seizure of the territory of Ukraine and the commission of unmentionable crimes in the occupied territories exemplify these complexes in the most concrete and horrific way.

During the twentieth century, in Russia, the manifestation of the lawlessness complex showed monstrous depth. Russia remains unable to come to its senses and cannot comprehend the crimes that have occurred. The traumatized collective psyche of the Russian people continues to gain bloody momentum in the twenty-first century. Unhealed trauma further activates the complexes, and it requires new victims.

For Russia, the year 2014 initiated a new, exact countdown for the repetition of the traumatic events of a hundred years ago: the beginning of World War I and, coming immediately after that, the bloody revolutionary events and civil war in Russia until 1924. All the inhabitants of Russia, and eastern Ukraine as well, whether they realize it or not, are taking part in an anniversary reaction.[18]

The need for Grace is the need for Divine Love. The lack of love is what provokes the activation of the lawlessness complex. The collective Russian psyche is in dire need of the return of the drowned part of its soul. The legend that most fully describes the plight of the collective Russian psyche is the legend of Kitezh-grad.[19] This is a legend about the creation and existence of a secret city that went to the bottom of a sacred lake—as the fulfillment of the prayers of the inhabitants of the city—as a way of escaping desecration by the invading enemy.

One way of thinking about the legend is that Kitezh-grad is a sacred place that went underwater, into the unconscious, from the world of consciousness. As the ego structure above is flooded, there is a Self-structure immersed below in the unconscious. Reconnection with the submerged sacred city below requires both the confidence that such a sacred place exists in the collective psyche and the Grace of God.

Kitezh-grad can also be thought of as an image of collective trauma and as an image of the gateway to the world of the dead. Perhaps the collective Russian soul wants to find a way there to be united with its lost sacred part. One of the features of the boundlessness complex is that it offers the promise of the ability to overcome any boundaries, including the boundaries that separate the world of the living from the world of the dead. In the legend, only those who have a pure heart can find their way there. Another possible resolution of the crisis in the legend is through the apocalypse. Perhaps this is another explanation for the attraction of the Russian soul to collective psychoses such as revolutions and wars: Through collective transformations, there is a chance to undergo personal changes as well.

Russia is the largest state in the world. Does Russia need additional land? The reasonable answer is obviously no. But, on an unconscious level, the answer is "Yes." What does Russia need? Why are we now witnessing this war, shamefacedly labeled in Russia "a special military operation"? Boundlessness can be interpreted as a rush to universal unity and could be considered a goal of the collective Self—the internal search for the lost part of the collective soul.

Perhaps the endless acquisition of new lands and citizens (whether they are living or dead does not matter) might fill some important internal need. What is missing? What feeds the unstoppable hunger to acquire?

Russia hungers to annex the land of Ukraine, but the main goal is the Holy City of Kyiv. Kyiv becomes the object of collective projections of the Self—not unlike the legend of Kitezh. Kyiv is a Russian Jerusalem. For a Russian person, Kyiv is the Mother of Russian cities: a Holy Mother. And Russians must not allow their own Mother to drown in the sinful liberal waters of the West. And who is Russia without a Mother? An orphan. Russia's untreated collective orphanhood provokes a blazing aggressive reaction. Unfortunately, the search and struggle for the "Kyiv heritage" turned into a struggle between Russia and Ukraine, which once again emphasizes the uniqueness of Kyiv as a sacred center.

The activation of the lawlessness and boundlessness complexes is initiated by both the reenactment of old trauma and the wish to heal centuries of suffering. However, the old and new trauma only add to the ongoing identity crisis of a long-traumatized people. In that context, the modern conflict between Russia and Ukraine is another effort by Russia to redefine its identity by once again diving into the lawlessness and boundlessness cultural complexes that have resulted in so many bloodbaths over the centuries. Russia's boundlessness and lawlessness allow it to dive into another destructive adventure in which Russia seeks to consolidate a national identity for the Russian people, who, in fact, represent more than a hundred different nationalities that have been dissolved into the physical territory of the Russian Federation.

Notes

1 J. Suntsova, "Question of the Day: What Is the Real Corruption in Russia?" *Novye Izvestia*, July 4, 2018, https://newizv.ru/news/politics/04-07-2018/vopros-dnya-kakova-zhe-realnaya-korruptsiya-v-rossii

2 C. G. Jung, *Man and His Symbols* (New York: Doubleday, 1988), p. 85.

3 Staff Reporter, "Historic German Church Demolished by Mining Company," *Catholic Herald*, January 11, 2018, https://catholicherald.co.uk/historic-german-church-demolished-by-mining-company/#:~:text=St%20Lambertus%20church%2C%20known%20locally,and%20relocated%20seven%20miles%20away

4 "The ROC Annually Opens up to One and a Half Thousand New Churches, the Patriarch Said," *RIA*, December 5, 2017, https://ria.ru/religion/20171205/1510266107.html.

5 Nicholas A. Berdyaev, *The Fate of Russia. Experiments into the Psychology of War and Nationality* (Moscow: G.A. Lehman and S.A. Sakharov, 1918).

6 "Vladimir Putin: Russia's Border 'Doesn't End Anywhere,'" *BBC News*, November 24, 2016, www.bbc.com/news/av/world-europe-38099842/vladimir-putin-russia-s-border-doesn-t-end-anywhere

7 C. G. Jung and Carl Kerényi, *Essays on a Science of Mythology* (New York: Bollingen Foundation, 1949), p. 96.

8 Vera A. Pavlova, *Izbrannyj* (Moscow: "E," 2018). By permission of Vera A. Pavlova. Translation by author.

9 "Refugees in Italy as Europe's New Slaves," *Deutsche Welle*, www.dw.com/en/refugees-in-italy-as-europes-new-slaves/av-41659725 (accessed October 20, 2018).

10 Jim Pickard and Sarah Gordon, "Theresa May Says Brexit Deal Will Give UK 'Control over Our Borders,'" *Financial Times*, November 19, 2018, www.ft.com/content/dcc d97a4-ebed-11e8-89c8-d36339d835c0

11 Alya Ponomareva, "To Stalin—with Flowers and Damnation," Radio Svoboda, December 21, 2016, www.svoboda.org/a/28189466.html

12 Simon Franklin, "Ilarion, 'Sermon on Law and Grace,'" in *Sermons and Rhetoric of Kievan Rus,'* Vol. 5 of the Harvard Library of Early Ukrainian Literature (Cambridge: Harvard University Press, 1991). A metropolitan is a bishop having authority over the bishops of a province, in particular (in Orthodox churches) one ranking above archbishop and below patriarch.

13 *Leviathan*, directed by Andrey Zvyagintsev, Non-Stop Production, 2018.

14 O. A. Savelieva, "The Apocryphal Tale 'The Passions of the Christ': Some Questions of Structure and Poetics," *Problems of Historical Poetics* 3 (1994), http://poetica.pro/journal/article.php?id=2375

15 "Russia Becomes the Number One State in Europe in Terms of Damages Awarded by the ECHR," *ПРАВОRU*, April 5, 2018, https:// pravo.ru/news/201577

16 Boris L. Pasternak, *Doctor Zhivago* (New York: Pantheon, 1958).

17 Ibid.

18 Psychological literature calls it the *anniversary reaction* and defines it as an individual's response to unresolved grief resulting from significant losses. The anniversary reaction can involve several days or even weeks of anxiety, anger, nightmares, flashbacks, depression, or fear.

19 Wikipedia, s.v. "Kitezh," last updated January 21, 2023, 10:37 UTC, https://en.wikipedia.org/wiki/Kitezh

Chapter 8

Perseus

A Myth for Our Times

Viktoriya Roslik

War's destruction and trauma are evil. War is a scar for life that is never forgotten. However, it also provides an opportunity for people to unite, awakening kindness and compassion toward each other. Many countries and people offer those of us in Ukraine help, support, and sympathy.

Mythical stories and rituals resonate in us today, providing depth in the presence of timeless reality. They tell us how to endure and how to understand grief and sorrow. There is never a time or myth where life is possible without suffering. Myth serves our consciousness, offering us the necessary images and various survival strategies—compromise, cunning, daring, courage—to shape a motivating spirit.

One of the most expressive mythological figures, which is an integral part of any myth, is the hero archetype. The hero figure is most vividly represented in Greek mythology. One of the best-known and most iconic heroes of ancient Greece is Perseus.

Many myths of Perseus have been passed down to us, telling of his greatest deeds, such as his victory over the Gorgon Medusa and the rescue of Andromeda. The Medusa complex is always present in wars, where the human spirit is frozen and sacrificed to "petrified ideas." The "war Gorgon" kills before contact and compromise can occur. This psychopathic indifference to others leads to violence in various forms. This complex can affect entire generations, including state systems where human life has no value. And, like any complex, it can stem from trauma.

Medusa was once a beautiful woman who was charmed by Poseidon. When Medusa rejects Poseidon, he forces himself upon her in the temple of Athena. Poseidon's affect is so strong that it cannot be controlled by the ego, existing in the inner world as uncontrollable rage capable of destroying everything. Athena, as punishment for desecrating her temple, endows Medusa with the horrifying power to turn all living things to stone with her gaze, imprisoning all femininity in the chains of terror. This is how trauma can make us stonelike, freezing our ability to love and show compassion.

Athena, as a goddess-virgin and symbol of wisdom, represents a facet of femininity in the psyche that does not allow for sensual spontaneity or emotional freedom. She was born from Zeus's head and was fated to be his daughter and uphold the patriarchal world. Perhaps Athena's suppressed energy is that of the Gorgon,

DOI: 10.4324/9781032695143-11

as her own traumatic birth did not allow her to receive the gifts of the mother, the primal source that grants the blessings of sensual femininity.

In Greek mythology, the hero Perseus's feat is directly tied to the killing of the Gorgon Medusa. It would be good if we could find our own Perseus within and equip him with the necessary tools to sever the terrifying head of Medusa that causes us to suffer, freezing our emotions. The hero needs help in overcoming his fears, to gain courage, to accept challenges, and to gather all his strength of spirit. Hermes, Athena, and the nymphs provide the necessary support for the hero.

Hermes, the god of liminality and luck, gives Perseus the sword of consciousness, enabling him to navigate life more consciously and to determine his stance toward whatever he faces.

Athena gives Perseus a shield so he can protect himself and maintain a respectful distance from archetypal forces. We too can develop an indirect relationship to archetypal forces through images, so as not to be consumed by them. Thanks to Athena's shield providing Perseus with essential distance and protection, he manages to decapitate Medusa.

From the nymphs, Perseus receives the helmet of the ruler of the underworld, Hades, which allows him to be present yet invisible in times of danger. From them, he also receives winged sandals that give him the ability to fly or access to the spiritual dimension. And finally, he receives from them a bag in which he must put Medusa's head in order to hold and contain such shadowy forces.

From the body of the beheaded Gorgon Medusa, both the winged horse Pegasus and his brother, the warrior Chrysaor, owner of the golden sword, are born. Pegasus becomes a symbol of victory of the spiritual over the material, and the golden sword becomes a symbol of the divine hidden in the human being. This is how the living, but imprisoned, spiritual energy is freed.

Returning home, Perseus frees Andromeda, who has been chained to a rock by a sea monster. She is a chaste bride, and her virginity signifies something untouched, which is the foundation of wholeness. Thus, the hero Perseus awakens the soul that was imprisoned in the unconscious. Andromeda is the true treasure that Perseus brings home. She is the anima—the soul that has the potential to stimulate life.

This is an incredibly rich myth about the transformation of death into rebirth, evil into good. It can awaken us to the wisdom of life, its suffering, and show us the symbolic keys to our spiritual potential.

Currently, in Ukraine, there are many real earthly heroes who return and defend our lands, perform incredible acts of bravery every day, and are willing to sacrifice themselves for the sake of saving their brothers and sisters, all of us. Most myths tell of a heroic transformation of consciousness, when we stop thinking only about ourselves and our own existence and are capable of acts for the sake of someone or something else. And today, we can observe such a heroic transformation of men and women who risk their lives for something greater than themselves, and many have voluntarily chosen such a fate.

Today, more than ever, we understand Bertolt Brecht's phrase from the play *Life of Galileo*: "Unhappy is the land that needs heroes," referring to the political situation.[1] Our heroes are our strength, our pride, and our pain.

A very important topic is the hero's shadow. In his book *Enemy, Cripple, & Beggar: Shadows in the Hero's Path*, Erel Shalit writes that a hero without a shadow is like an ego without a soul.[2] The shadow is the lifeblood of the hero's soul. If he were only virtuous, he could not be a hero. And not being aware of his shadow can lead to devastating pain. Joseph Campbell writes, in *The Hero with a Thousand Faces*, "The hero of yesterday becomes the tyrant of tomorrow, unless he crucifies himself today."[3] So, when returning from war, when the mission is complete, it is important for the hero to leave all the heroism on the battlefield. Otherwise, the warrior's energy can be destructive in peacetime.

In the myth of Perseus, the hero returns with treasure, with that part of feminine sensuality that nourishes the soul and revives life. This not an easy task for a country at war, but a very important one, so that our country, Ukraine, can bring something new into the world—changes that would strengthen and enrich our country. Perhaps our compassion, respect, and understanding of the consequences of war for the psyche of our earthly heroes can also be among the first steps in healing their souls.

In Ukraine, there are national mythological heroes who are seen as a source of strength, support, and inspiration during challenging times. Foremost among them are the Zaporozhian Cossacks. It is from the period of the Zaporozhian Cossacks that Ukrainian identity emerged. Generations were raised on the legends of Cossack heroes. These heroes were both real individuals who sacrificed their lives while fighting for their land and also collective representations of warrior Cossacks, among whom Mamay is one such figure.

Cossack Mamay is a collective image of a national hero of Ukraine about whom legends and various tales were told. He is a symbol of courage, strength, and love for freedom, an embodiment of the image of a defender of Ukraine. This figure was especially common in Ukraine in the eighteenth and nineteenth centuries. Paintings of Mamay often hang in Ukrainian homes alongside icons. They do not bear the names of the painters, as there are too many of them, and this phenomenon can rightfully be called "folk painting."[4]

In paintings featuring the Cossack Mamay, certain objects are always depicted: an oak tree, a horse, a spear, a pipe, and a *bandura* (or *kobza*, a stringed folk instrument), a cup and a hat, and weapons. The oak tree represents kinship, the tree of life and vitality. The horse is the Cossack's best friend and companion, both in peace and in war. The horse is a symbol of freedom, loyalty, and self-sacrifice. The spear, as well as the cup or jug, remind us of the fleeting nature of life and the daily threats that awaited the Cossack. Spears were placed at burial sites, whereas cups and jugs were "taken from the other world." They are symbols of fate. Sabers are symbols of victory.

In paintings, the Cossack does not hold weapons in his hands, but he does not have them far away either. Thus, if necessary, the peaceful Cossack can quickly defend himself. And, as a rule, our hero is depicted sitting in a Buddhist pose. It is amazing that we most often catch a glimpse of this famous hero at rest rather than in a typical battle scene. He looks calm, relaxed, and a bit dreamy. His inner strength is revealed in peace, not in action. Perhaps here lies a deeper perception and understanding of the world and self-awareness.

Mamay is a traveler, a warrior, a storyteller, and a sorcerer (in Cossack culture, this was called a *characternik*) as well as a philosopher. He appeared as a hero when other Zaporozhian Cossacks needed his help, and he could transform himself into an animal, stop bleeding and heal wounds, catch bullets with his bare hands, walk on water and fire, become invisible, and instill panic in his enemies. Another important aspect of his character is his sensitivity to beauty, emotional depth, and delicate lyricism. It's no wonder that most of his paintings feature a *bandura* or *kobza*. The bandura highlights Mamay's poetic nature and aestheticism. The bandura reveals his emotional movements, his thoughts, and his weary sorrow.

The sound of strings doesn't always bring joy or inspire heroic deeds; it can also be a mourning for those who have left this fleeting world, a call to remember brothers-in-arms who fell in the fight for independence. Mamay embodies both masculine and feminine qualities.

I am a philosopher, but also a warrior. I am free, for here is my weapon and here is my horse. I am relaxed, or at least appear to be. I think my own thoughts, I smoke, I rest, and if you are my friend—sit beside me, take a bottle, drink and smoke. I will play the bandura, and you can sing if you wish. But if you are not my friend, then I have a spear, sword, and pistol for you. And a tree on which to hang you. Don't provoke me, for you won't like the consequences. Just don't provoke me.[5]

In his book *The Power of Myth*, Joseph Campbell describes how an Indian political book states that a ruler must hold a weapon of war, a large stick, in one hand and a song calling for peace and joint action in the other.[6] And this description, in my opinion, resembles our Ukrainian hero Mamay, who was a warrior-characternik of the *Zaporozhian Sich*.

The Zaporozhian Sich was founded in the sixteenth and seventeenth centuries on the islands of the Dnipro River and became a place where Zaporozhian Cossacks united and enjoyed autonomy from the Polish-Lithuanian and Moscow authorities. The Zaporozhian Sich can rightfully be considered the first political entity on the territory of Ukraine, as it exhibited all the features of a republic. It was independent and had a constitution, and all European countries attempted to establish diplomatic relations with it.

The Zaporozhian Cossacks can be said to be the soul of Ukraine; their strength lay in uniting many peoples and respecting different cultures and languages. People from different countries came to learn from them not only military skills but also how they wisely managed their own affairs internally. Despite their harsh nature, the Zaporozhian Cossacks lived by the principles of complete democracy. All important decisions were made solely through general voting.

The Cossacks always set out on their expeditions with their right foot first, demonstrating that they were going to do what was right. Only those who had passed all the previous tests and were initiated into the Cossacks could wear the "herring" on their head, which was twisted behind their left ear.[7]

The secret weapons of the Zaporozhian Sich were the characterniks, among whom was Mamay. They possessed supernatural abilities. The most remarkable and unusual feature of the characterniks was their invulnerability to bullets and sabers. Characterniks could feel when a bullet was flying toward them—their necks would become cold—and that way they could easily avoid being shot. Characterniks were also skilled at finding treasures, healing wounds, bringing the dead back to life, and casting spells on enemies. If they needed to hide from pursuers for tactical purposes, the Cossacks would guard themselves with spears and enter a special psycho-energetic state. The enemy, mistaking them for reeds, would pass by them. They developed a special technique called *Cossack salvation* that had a unique psychological effect on the enemy. One of the well-known, real heroes of the Zaporozhian Sich was Ukrainian Cossack Ivan Sirko—a military commander who never lost a battle in which he took part. He won sixty-five battles and was elected *Koshevoy Otaman* (chief officer) twelve times. He was also a characternik warrior.

The constitution, proclaimed on April 16, 1710, between Hetman Pylyp Orlyk, the Cossack leadership, and the Cossacks of the Zaporozhian Sich is considered one of the earliest written constitutions in Europe. It laid the foundation for democratic principles and a civic system. Despite its historical significance, the constitution of Pylyp Orlyk was invalidated by the Russian Empire and had limited practical application. Nevertheless, it left a lasting impact on the political thought of its time and became a symbol of the Ukrainian aspiration for freedom and democracy.

Certainly, in real life, the Cossacks had plenty of room for adventure. However, they also had a violent side to them, one that doesn't quite fit the romanticized image. Metaphorically, Cossacks can be referred to as *steppe pirates*. What's important to note, though, is that such an organization was exceptionally effective from a military perspective. Unfortunately, in 1792, the Zaporozhian Sich was dissolved by Catherine II. Nonetheless, the spirit of the Zaporozhian Cossacks can still be an inspiration for our country today. It was the Cossack traditions that ultimately shaped the Ukrainian identity, sowing the seeds of freedom, democracy, and self-defense within it. I would like to conclude my essay with a performance by a choir of bandura players. In Lviv, 407 bandura players performed a piece from Taras Shevchenko's *Kobzar*; the bandura symbolizes the lives of the unconquered, who lived and died with dignity, preserving their values. You can listen to it on YouTube at https://www.youtube.com/watch?v=iKA_FXZ7zzY.[8]

Addendum: An Exchange between Viktoriya Roslik and Jörg Rasche about the Need for Heroes in Times of War

Jörg to Vikoriya, August 22, 2023

Dear Viktoriya,

Thank you for your chapter and permission to include it in our book.

I have some questions regarding the history of Ukraine as it is important that we state it as accurately as possible. You write that the Zaporozhian Cossacks established the first Ukrainian state:

> The Zaporozhian Sich can rightfully be considered the first political entity on the territory of Ukraine [. . .] The constitution, proclaimed on April 16, 1710, between Hetman Pylyp Orlyk, the Cossack leadership, and the Cossacks of the Zaporozhian Sich is considered one of the earliest written constitutions in Europe. It laid the foundation for democratic principles and a civic system.

As far as I know, the Kyivan Rus was the first state on Ukraine territory. It was a feudal kingdom, and it also marks the origin of the Orthodox Church in Ukraine after 988 CE. The Orthodox Church was established on Russian territory later. Kyiv became a Holy City, the "Orthodox Jerusalem"; it was also recognized as such for Russians. I'd like to know more about the history of the Cossacks. As with the cultural complexes of other European countries, each nation always has a foundation myth. They trace their cultural identity backward to mythological heroes, like Aeneas and Romulus for Rome; Cech, Lev, and Rus for the Slavic people; or Krak for the Polish state of Krakow. Do the Ukrainians today regard Mamay as a founding hero of their culture?

The question is most important because in times of war nationalistic narratives resurge or are reborn. Mythic heroes and mythic enemies (usually the neighbor) emerge as symbols for the collective Self and its antagonist. In Hitler's Germany we had such a revival of these nationalistic narratives, and we Germans are, as we say, "burned children" regarding any kind of mythological heroism. Can you tell me more about the role of the mythic Ukrainian hero today? I asked a Ukraine friend this question years ago and he said: "I am not a nationalist; I am a patriot."

As you know, there were some Cossack armies serving the Tsars. For example, they conquered Siberia for the Russian empire. So, they were agents of the so-called inner colonization of Russia. Am I right? The Cossacks of Crimea suffered under Stalin; are they a different people?

Myths, be it Mamay or Medusa and Andromeda, are fascinating. There is never a single reductive "explanation." They show images and stories about archetypal patterns in our life—and so also in our collective life. For our study of cultural complexes, it is helpful to check their meaning in each specific historical situation, as much as possible. Why do some myths come alive again? For what reason? What do we project into them? Who tells the story? And how do they influence our thinking and feeling? I hope I have not asked too many questions and expressed too many different ideas. Your paper is most stimulating to me and that is undoubtedly the best one can say about a text!

Warmest,
Jörg (Berlin)

Viktoriya to Jörg, August 26, 2023

Dear Jörg

I hope this email finds you well.

First, I would like to address the topic of Germany and the mythical heroism that makes contemporary Germans feel like "burnt children" when it comes to such identifications. It seems to me that the situation you describe is quite different from our situation in Ukraine, if I understand you correctly. We are a country that has been attacked, and the spirit of our mythical figures holds significant importance for us in these times. It is this spirit upon which we rely as we navigate the survival of our people, our lands, and our independence. The spirit is not based on a notion of conquest. Our focus is on defending our territories, not aggressive ambitions.

At the onset of the war, our entire nation, from young to old, sang the song: "Oh, the Red Viburnum in the Meadow . . ." During World War I, this song served as the anthem for Ukrainian Sich riflemen who fought within the Austro-Hungarian Empire's army against Russia. This anthem provided us solace in the initial months, bolstering our spirit. Although it is seldom heard now, we persist in seeking resources that help us confront helplessness and despair and fortify our resilience. In my view, Mamay becomes an important carrier of the hero archetype in our current situation. It was the Cossack traditions that essentially shaped the Ukrainian ethnicity, instilling seeds of freedom, democracy, and self-defense within it. Of course, there is always a shadow aspect, if that's what you are referring to. Metaphorically, one could even call the Cossacks *steppe pirates*. Indeed, these people had many adventurous tales, but there was also much violence, which doesn't align well with Romanticism. However, what's crucial is that this organization was remarkably effective militarily. I believe our present focus should be on surviving and enduring. A time for analysis and reflection will come when resources are more abundant, and peace prevails.

Although I am not a historian, I'll try to address your questions.

The first state within the boundaries of modern Ukraine (as you rightly pointed out) was Kyivan Rus. It emerged in the ninth century and endured until the beginning of the thirteenth century when the Mongol-Tatars conquered much of Eastern Europe. The Baptism of Rus took place on July 28, 988 CE, a significant event associated with Prince Volodymyr. Although Kyivan Rus is not a direct precursor to modern Ukraine, it holds great significance as one of the earliest states to form on this territory, influencing the development of Ukrainian national consciousness and culture.

The earliest recorded mentions of Ukraine, specifically by that name, are linked to the Zaporozhian Sich. The Zaporozhian Sich can be considered a precursor to the Ukrainian state, as it was more of a civic and military alliance among Cossacks inhabiting historical Ukrainian territories. Established in the sixteenth and seventeenth centuries on the islands of the Dnipro River, the Sich became a place where Zaporizhian Cossacks united and enjoyed autonomy from Polish-Lithuanian and Moscow authorities. Although the Sich had its organizational structure and way of life, it did not qualify as a fully fledged state. It is in the period of the Zaporozhian Cossacks (specifically the Zaporozhian Cossacks because there were Cossacks not only in the Zaporizhzhia region) that Ukrainian identity began, and generations were raised on Cossack heroes. They were real heroes who gave their lives fighting for their land, and there were collective images of Cossack warriors, one of whom was Mamay.

Pylyp Orlyk's constitution, also known as the Treaties and Resolutions of the Rights and Freedoms of the Zaporozhian Army, was proclaimed on April 16, 1710. This constitution is recognized as one of the first written constitutions in Europe, establishing the foundations of democratic principles and societal organization. Despite its historical significance, Pylyp Orlyk's constitution was invalidated by the Russian Empire and didn't see substantial practical use. Nevertheless, it left an imprint on the political thought of the time and became a symbol of aspirations for freedom and democracy.

In 1654, Bohdan Khmelnytsky signed the Treaty of Pereyaslav, establishing a protectorate with the Russian Tsar. Clearly, the various Russian Tsars sought to utilize the military experience of the Cossacks for their own purposes, summoning Cossacks from Ukraine, Don, and northern Kazakhstan for military campaigns. Regarding the conquest of Siberia, it was an expedition led by Don Cossack Yermak in 1581–1585 that aimed to subdue Siberia. Yermak's army consisted of diverse groups, including Cossacks, soldiers from different regions of Russia, and local Siberian tribes. Additionally, discontented Tatars joined Yermak's forces as they were unhappy with Mongol rule. Yermak's army was composed of around 540–600 individuals.

The Zaporizhian Sich was disbanded in 1775 by order of Empress Catherine II. Stalin's repressions in Crimea were directed not at the Cossacks (as they no longer existed), but against the Crimean Tatars.

This is, of course, a concise overview of Ukrainian history. Please let me know if any questions remain open. And thank you for adding an interesting addition to the myth of Andromeda.

Wishing you all the best and sending my warm regards,
Vikoriya

Jörg to Vikoriya, August 28, 2023

Dear Vikoriya,

Thank you so much for your clarification!

First: I understand very well that your people need heroic symbols in your existential fight for freedom and identity. So please excuse my insensitive wording about the "burnt children." We Germans still must struggle with the fact that the Nazis took over and perverted nearly all positive representatives of our German old culture for their racist and fascist manipulation. To be conscious of and suspicious about the manipulation of myths and symbols for political purposes has now become a basic element of our German feeling or cultural complex. Putin's totalitarian disinformation and manipulative system show today to what extent people can be brainwashed into a collective anesthesia, amnesia, and ignorance regarding the crimes of their soldiers and politicians. The suffering of their declared "enemies" concerns me. Of course, we in the West are also subject to the manipulations of propaganda from many different sources. . .

To edit a Jungian book about an ongoing war is an impossible task. Under usual conditions I can't imagine a "Jungian on a battlefield." C. G. Jung was a pacifist, to the extent that he tried to craft arrangements with the Nazis to safeguard psychotherapy in the Third Reich. When I told my German colleagues about what I was hearing in Kyiv about the suffering and heroism of Jungian colleagues in Zaporizhzhia from 2015 to 2019 they didn't believe me. It was as if we were living in two different worlds. Of necessity, our book will have to show a condensed overview of cultural complexes in Europe now. But at least we can speak directly of the disinformation, manipulation, and barbaric violence that Ukraine is experiencing in its existential fight against an unscrupulous regime.

Your paper on the Zaporozhian Sich and Mamay will be a central statement in our book. We and our readers are not so well informed about Eastern European history. We know mostly the Russian version, if any version at all. I am especially moved by your evolving "this spirit upon which we rely as we navigate the survival of our people, our lands, and our independence." And later, you correctly note: "A time for analysis and reflection will come when resources are more abundant, and peace prevails." In a way, this shows exactly the dilemma we face in putting this book together. We are all right in the middle of it right now.

I wish you, your family and friends, and the men and women who are fighting so bravely in this horrific war all my best!

Warmest,
Jörg (Berlin)

Notes

1 Bertolt Brecht, *Life of Galileo* (1939), sc. 13.
2 Erel Shalit, *Enemy, Cripple, & Beggar: Shadows in the Hero's Path* (Fisher King Press, 2008).
3 Joseph Campbell, *The Hero with a Thousand Faces* (Princeton: Princeton University Press, 1949), p. 353.
4 For a gallery of paintings of Mamay, see https://en.wikipedia.org/wiki/Cossack_Mamay
5 The direct speech in Mamay's case refers to inscriptions on paintings or objects where Mamay was depicted. Unfortunately, most of the paintings featuring Mamay do not have identified authors, and it is unclear who wrote the poetry or the text accompanying them. For example, there are inscriptions under paintings depicting Cossack Mamay in certain regions of Ukraine that read: "Why are you staring at me? Can't you guess where I come from and what my name is? You know nothing! I have more than one name, and there are many," or, under many paintings, you can find short texts such as: "I am Cossack Mamay, do not occupy me," or "I envy no one—neither the lords nor

the tsar. I thank my holy God for everything! Although I am not famous by title, I lead a cheerful life and will never be lost." This is a form of folk art, and, unfortunately, the authors remain unknown.

6 Joseph Campbell, *The Power of Myth*, with Bill Moyers, ed. Betty Sue Flowers (New York: Anchor Books, 1991).

7 For a photo of the Cossack herring, see www.pinterest.com/pin/cossack-hair-wig-or-herring-royalty-free-stock-photo--333970128624787652/

8 "Breaking the Record with a One-Hour Bandura Performance," Lviv, Ukraine, March 9, 2019, Studio 4, https://youtu.be/iKA_FXZ7zzY

Chapter 9

Inside the Russian Complex

Natalia Pavlikova

It is important to view any global crisis—both political and psychological—in a historical context and in the context of the interactions between different countries, not just those countries that are directly involved in the crisis. In this chapter, I am focusing on describing my vision of what is happening in the collective mental field of Russian citizens since February 24, 2022, a date that has overturned for many their ideas about themselves, their country, the world, and life in general.

This text represents only my personal reflections on the processes taking place in Russia since February 24, 2022, and some ideas about what led to these events. I hope that this text might begin a dialogue in which it will be possible to share our visions and understandings of what is happening in the world, to enrich each other's picture of the world rather than to argue about it.

Since February 24, 2022, these questions, among many others, have been raised in my office: Is it possible to remain a citizen of one's country and not obey the orders of the country's leadership? Is it possible to remain a human being by picking up a weapon to use against one's neighbor? Is it possible to respect those who flee in a panic, leaving women and elderly relatives in a country where moral horror is taking place?

For the first time in many years, we are forced to face vital collective and personal questions and make meaningful decisions about ourselves and those around us. Yet not everyone turns out to be ready to confront their real values, their real fears and desires. Some still want to hide behind the collective, behind someone who will take responsibility for those important decisions that each of us needs to make. It can be hard to find your individual attitude in the midst of such powerful collective forces. And, for the individual, it can be hard to see the scale of what is happening in the movement of the collective masses. At such times it is important to hold both poles in consciousness—the collective/archetypal and the individual level of the ego. Only by holding the tension between these poles, without merging with either one of them, can a possible solution emerge that will satisfy the needs of both.

I keep waiting for a symbol to emerge at the collective level that will unite these poles, rather than mingle them together. So far, there isn't one. So far, the world is falling apart more and more. Hopefully, this phase will inevitably be

DOI: 10.4324/9781032695143-12

replaced by a next phase that seeks integration. Since February 24, 2022, I feel as if we are living in a world of a million truths. Working with clients, meeting with colleagues, talking with friends, hearing the news channels, reading political reviews, I see that many people, trying to protect their own mental safety, construct explanatory concepts within which they can continue to feel human without losing respect for themselves, often disregarding the principle of reality. No facts or arguments that describe a picture of the world different from their own are accepted or considered. Within each constructed worldview, everything looks very logical and consistent.

The USSR and the Historical Roots of the Cultural Complex

The crisis that has been created by the conflict with Ukraine has stirred up underlying processes on which the national and civic identity of Russians has been built. Russian identity is based on many different ethnic components that have been fused together for many decades and many generations. The post-Soviet space is inhabited by people whose ethnicity is not limited to their Russian citizenship. Many of my clients and colleagues are of multiple ethnicities. The declared ethnic policies of the former Soviet Union, which had united 15 republics and 127 ethnic groups under its roof, were aimed not only at maintaining the ethnic identity of each of the republics but also at mixing these ethnic groups together.

Ethnic Identity and Language

The first policy, designed to maintain ethnic identity, focused on teaching the language of the main ethnic group of each Soviet republic. In addition to learning Russian as the official state language, this second language was to be taught in schools and universities. The Russian language was the common language that gave the inhabitants of different regions an opportunity to understand each other and communicate in one language.

It is easy to encounter criticism of the language policy of the USSR in that not all peoples from the different regions were able to learn their native language, and not all regions were taught in their native language. Knowledge of the Russian language was often more prestigious, and thus it was used more often. It depended on people on the ground in specific regions and on how they carried out the orders sent down from above. It also depended on family values, on how parents presented national differences to their children. For example, in the Kazakh cities, the educated spoke Russian, and they taught their children, even ethnic Kazakhs, to speak Russian only. And this happened despite the fact that each republic had its own press organs, which published newspapers and magazines in the local language, and its own radio and TV channels, which also broadcast in the local languages. All official documents (passports, birth certificates, and so on) were in two languages.

The state system was designed to support the learning of the language of the republic, which was a part of the USSR. The opportunity to learn and maintain one's culture was always declared on a collective level. The fact that this mandate was not fulfilled was less about the policy itself than the people of each region. If parents did not insist, did not teach, did not pay attention to the quality of teaching of the native language at school, it was not the fault of the state, but of the people themselves, who turned a blind eye to what was happening in their particular lives. Language is a means of communication in which people must invest time and energy. Learning a language is always hard work.

Ethnic Mix

The second policy, aimed at mixing different ethnic groups, was to send people who received higher education to work in different regions, depending on where their specialty was in demand. Labor migration was a way of accomplishing ethnic mixing. In addition, students from different regions came to study at various institutions of higher education and, during their studies and following graduation, they entered into interethnic marriages. During the time of the Soviet Union, there were all-USSR construction projects. Important industrial state facilities were built, and people came from all over the USSR to work on them, which also led to a mix of nations. During World War II, most of the western and central populations of the USSR were evacuated to the Urals, Kazakhstan, and the Central Asian republics, which also resulted in mixed cultures. A shadowy process of ethnic identity blurring was the bloody, forced deportations of millions of peoples, such as those in the Caucasian republics, where their populations fell under various kinds of political suspicion in the eyes of the authorities.

When I was a child, I used to spend summers with my mother's relatives in Samarkand. Tatar, Russian, Ukrainian, Armenian, and Jewish families lived in one courtyard, and all of them spoke Russian with each other. Some of them were in Samarkand before the revolution; some were evacuated during World War II; some were exiles. In Moscow, I was also immersed in a multiethnic culture. My peers were not much concerned with clarifying each other's ethnicity. I felt "Soviet" and was proud of it. Thus, throughout the existence of the USSR, there were two multidirectional tendencies, one of which sought to maintain ethnic identity and the other of which worked to blend ethnic boundaries and create a single identity for the Soviet person—the *homo sovieticus*.

This national policy of the USSR was the heir to the national policy of the old Russian Empire under the tsars, which united vast territories within its borders for several centuries. Russia's imperial policy still raises many questions and controversies. The Russian Empire did not develop the way empires did in France, England, or other European empires. It developed inland, attaching neighboring lands to itself rather than those beyond the seas. Not all lands, however, were attached during war. Georgia, for example, asked for help and protection from the Russian throne to avoid absorption by the Ottomans and Persia. In the process of being incorporated into the Russian Empire, the new lands retained their ethnic and religious features. Russia incorporated them, but did not change their identity. On the one hand, the new territories were obliged to benefit the treasury (pay taxes). On the other hand, in exchange for protecting their borders and interests, separating from the Russian Empire was forbidden. In some annexed territories, living conditions were many times better than in the central regions. For example, there was no serfdom in the periphery. As industrialization and capitalist tendencies developed in the nineteenth century, the imperial policy of Russia came under strong criticism from its educated citizens, of which Lenin's own rhetoric was a product. He accused the Russian Empire of the brutal exploitation of the incorporated territories. And this was one of the factors that led to the revolution.

Regression

In my opinion, the Soviet Union managed for a short period to incarnate the idea of international rather than transnational values. The USSR sought to form people's identity based on the highest bar of the social system, the civilizational system. Historical forms of human community begin with the family, then comes the kin, then the tribe, then the ethnos, then the people, the nation, and then the civilization. Soviet identity assumed identification with the most developed, most socially complex standing at the top of the hierarchy of identity—belonging to a civilization that allowed different nations, peoples, ethnic groups, and tribes to live in peace, where everyone had equal rights under the constitution. Each higher level organized, ranked, and brought peace to the lower ones. The head of a socially complex system, comparable to the USSR, had the responsibility to respect, to welcome, to treat courteously, to resolve conflicts, and to organize peace among all its parts, so as to avoid splits.

During the years of the USSR's existence, all the nations were so intermingled with each other that it was difficult to find a single region where only "natives" remained by the beginning of the 1990s. The collapse of the Soviet Union along national and political lines in many of the former republics deeply wounded the civilizational fabric of Soviet identity. Many republics broke off from the "civilization state" of the USSR and began to build their own national and ethnic states. In my opinion, these old/new republics were built on a lower level of social identity. There was a regression in social development. The pain of this destruction was driven out of consciousness and explained away with political and economic rationalizations. In the 1990s, the structure of the USSR—which had given a sense of belonging to a powerful state in which everyone could see their own projections of Shadow, Self, Defender, Persecutor, Great Mother, Great Father, and so on—was destroyed.

It was not only the state structure (*russification*) of the country that was destroyed in the 1990s. The ethical structure of the country dissolved, and suppressed shadow energies were unleashed. Power was assumed by people who were physically strong, who were greedy for profit, and who had no capacity for empathy or large-scale vision. The removal of the state security services' control over these shadow forces led to powerful changes in the political order not only of Russia, but also of several other post-Soviet republics.

Some people living in different post-Soviet republics still have nostalgia for the USSR. I need to understand the reasons for and cause of the emergence and disappearance of the USSR. And, with the crumbling of the USSR, what kind of generation is growing up today, and what basic experiences are forming its foundations?

Heroes

The USSR was full of stories of people who became heroes in different professional and social fields. The USSR greatly encouraged the development of the heroic scenario in people. The Soviet Hero did not serve an individual scenario, but a collective one, sacrificing his or her personal interests to the needs and demands of the state. The Soviet cultural complex was built under conditions where no individual exists without the collective, and no collective exists without the individual. Following that model, the individual and the collective together still make a strong, ideal pair within the cultural layer of post-Soviet people. However, the specific dynamic of this pairing changes from generation to generation.

My parents belong to the generation that was raised by the heroes of World War II. And their parents were raised by the heroes of the Russian Revolution and the Civil War. They set themselves the goal of achieving mastery in what they chose to do. They devoted their time to grueling training and self-discipline. Their capacity for self-regulation and goal-setting was admirable. But these abilities worked only for as long as they were supported at the collective level. Once the USSR collapsed, the current generation failed to foster the same principles and passion in their own children. The Soviet generation, which believed so much in these ideals of perfection and humanism, could not pass this belief on to their children and grandchildren.

The collapse of the Soviet Union led to an individualistic way of surviving. It became more important to respect boundaries, both others' and your own. The environment fostered the separation of people. In my building, for example, neighbors rarely greet each other, even if they have lived together in the same building for a long time. In my country, a sense of community and a sense of collective identity have been lost. Our level of ordinary human culture has declined dramatically. Without raising the level of education, without tutoring, the capacity for moral and critical examination of reality and what is going on around us began to be diminished. Our own humanity and capacity for empathy began to be lost.

When the principle of "it's not my funeral" rules everyday consciousness, it is easy to take advantage of the suppressed need for solidarity by calling for patriotism. And some Russians are now actively uniting in this patriotic impulse, largely constructed by state propaganda. The patriotic attitude is also reinforced by the negative attitudes displayed by foreigners toward Russians.

Here, too, the levels of the collective and the individual get mixed up with one another. The sanctions imposed on Russia belong to the collective level of the state. But they are perceived by many citizens as a personal attack—that is, as an individual humiliation. And, somewhat paradoxically, this works to strengthen the sense of community and patriotism. But what kind of patriotism can there be in a people who do not have a conscious collective identity and solidarity, a people who do not experience the joy of being together? And then, what kind of collective guilt can there be over actions taken by the state if there is no collective with which to consciously identify?

Re-archaization

Contemporary Russian patriotism is a re-archaization of communality and collective responsibility.[1] The current unification under the banner of patriotism has not reached a new level of bonding, but has repeated and regressed to an old "peasantism," which is what previously stalled the development of Russia in general. The peasant mentality and community persisted after the abolition of serfdom and prevented a transition from peasantism to farming.[2]

Perhaps what is happening now is a "message" to all of us that it is time for a more genuine coming together? A coming together, not against anyone, but with each other, because we are human beings. We are alive. We are all mortal. We are all very vulnerable, and everyone's life is very fragile. And we can all let love and care for each other in. Not because someone forces us to do it, not because we hear it from the outside, but because that impulse is there inside. We are united with each other, not on the principle of belonging to this or that state or ethnicity, but on the principle that we are alive and belong to the world of the living on this planet.

It is possible that we in Russia are now facing a hard and long period of "rotting," the alchemical nigredo, in the process of which we can reunite with each other, no matter what ideas the other may hold. If we can withstand the "rotting nigredo," perhaps we can start talking about taking and living both our collective guilt and our collective responsibility.

In the alchemical cauldron of permanent revolution, the early leaders of the USSR wanted to melt away all social and class distinctions and create a new human being worthy of a communist, bright future—a dangerous utopia. What was hovering as a philosophical idea in Europe was realized in the USSR. In fact, it was a violent and bloody realization everywhere. If we were to evaluate that historical period in terms of modern humanistic values, we would see that the situation in most European countries was no less bloody or brutal. And these humanistic values emerged only after a painful journey through the catastrophes of the twentieth century.

The early twentieth century began with World War I. Europe was drowning in the blood that resulted from the release of the beast from the depths of the unconscious. These layers of the unconscious had until then been controlled and held together by religion and the state, modern civilization, collective laws and rituals. The old laws and rules had collapsed, and the new ones that emerged could not cope with the shadow energies that had infiltrated consciousness. The individual ego, boosted by scientific and technological advances, proved to be no stronger in the face of the collective-level shadow than the ego of the human tribe of traditional cultures.

In my view, the inflation of the individual from countries with advanced science has led to today's crisis, in which the undeveloped moral part and feeling function are unable to cope with that influx of shadow from the collective archaic level, the defenses against which were removed in the twentieth century. Religion and collective rituals helped us build defenses against the shadow, to set directions for development. Then, individuals found themselves alone, not only with enormous potential, but also with enormous shadow. The destruction of many important collective rituals occurred before the emergence of the individual's capacity to recognize and resist the shadow. It was important to direct the energy released in consciousness toward collective goals, which was exactly what Soviet ideologues did. But their resistance to the shadow side of this energy on a personal level was also neglected. The shadow of power swallowed them up, and they failed to build new boundaries and rituals to deal with shadow energies of a new scale and power, which came to the surface in the 1990s.

There was a commitment on the level of external accessibility to all the resources the modern world had to offer without conscious consideration of people's inner abilities and capacities to digest and assimilate these resources. This lack of consideration of internal realities led, among other things, to paranoia and repression on the shadow level. On the level of the state Persona, schools, factories, and a free medical system to help everyone were built. But we did not consider the inner world of humans and their shadow sides, in the face of which we were powerless at the end of the twentieth century.

The Luciferian Light and the Loss of Feeling

In my view, humanity as a whole was held captive in the twentieth century by the Luciferian light of consciousness. On the one hand, class boundaries were erased; on the other hand, in response, European countries erased borders in World Wars I and II. Nations were literally erased from the face of the Earth, as in the Jewish genocide.

The international becomes transnational before it can be fulfilled at the level of fostering respect for the Otherness of the other. For example, in my childhood we had many different juices, milk products, vegetables, and fruits that came from different countries. There was a wide international market with many choices, each bearing their own local name. Now, we have almost the same names of food products from all over the world. However, transnational companies swallowed all the local ones with their unique names. The rate of development of the rational mind has exceeded by many times the rate of development of the soul and the ability to make moral judgments. Thinking has overtaken the development of feeling. The imbalance in the rational axis of mental functions has led to a compensatory outburst of sensory and intuition development and irrational functions. But they are definitely not capable of solving the moral problems that have confronted humans since the end of the nineteenth century.

In the USSR, very good values were declared—family, education, culture, health, sports, and human dignity (and, in contemporary Russia, there are many programs aimed at these values). Of course, many of the declared values were violated. But these values enabled inner growth and the desire for this inner growth. If you were a pilot, then you would be the best pilot; if you were a salesperson, then the best salesperson; if you were a teacher, then the best; and so on. And not only for the money, but also for the respect of others. This made it possible to go beyond the material ego in which only material urges prevailed—more money, more material needs satisfied, a bigger house, a more expensive car, more gold, and so on. In a sense, this was a starting point for building a link between the collective and the individual, between the ego and the self.

With the collapse of the USSR, the situation changed. People began to strive more for external values, for making more money. After the collapse of the USSR, we did not evolve to higher values, but regressed to more primitive and archaic levels of existence, where the tasks of inner growth are not set at the collective level but are given to each individual to figure out.

Loss of Spirit and Commitment

Money and material goods cannot become the only reality to live for. In Russia, the opinion is that we have sacrificed our exploration of space in order to satisfy our domestic needs. Space exploration in the Soviet Union was seen as something that had no pragmatic meaning, only a romantic one. Today we all have cellphones and internet access, but we still haven't begun to fly to other planets, as our ancestors in the USSR dreamed of doing. And these dreams do not seem to be the dreams of the modern generation at all. The ability to dream and fantasize has begun to revolve around more pragmatic things. In the struggle between body and spirit, so far, the body is winning. The spirit has stopped getting stronger in recent decades, although the needs of the body have been strengthened quite substantially by the latest technology.

The generation that beautifully strengthened its spirit in the Soviet Union was not able to help strengthen the spirit of the next generation. This is likely because the path of strengthening their own spirit was not automatic. The power of their spirit, the energy of their animus, served the Great Mother rather than their individual needs.

For all the criticism of the USSR, it seems to me that it is important to note that many Russians took seriously the humanistic values proclaimed by the Soviet

Union and tried to implement them in reality. For example, since the nineteenth-century Russian Empire, illiteracy has been fought and conquered. Soviet historian Natan Eidelman describes the situation with education in this way:

> In the 1860s a number of reforms were carried out in the Russian Empire, one of which was in the field of education. Those years saw an increase in the number of literate people in the Russian Empire from 6% in the 1860s to 25–30% by the time of the revolution in 1917. In the 1860s the growth of literacy was due to the fact that the zemstvo, elected councils established in Tsarist Russia to administer local affairs after the abolition of serfdom, made enormous personal efforts to educate the people who had gained their freedom from serfdom. Educated people in the 19th century went about eradicating ignorance among the masses.[3]

But, in Soviet times, the situation had already changed greatly:

> [A]t the Russian Language Department, a large percentage of the students, especially female students, are graduates of rural schools, sent from there with a special referral, which obliged them to return to their native land as teachers after graduation from the Pedagogical Institute: "We give these girls a quiz, and they make 7–10 mistakes; without a referral from the outback they certainly would not have been accepted. And we enroll them, and a few years later they return to their native villages, making 3–4 mistakes in their quizzes."[4]

With the collapse of the Soviet Union, some of the gains in the educational field were lost. And this occurred not only in some distant regions where there were low levels of literacy originally, but even among the editors in central publishing houses. Previously, it was possible to read newspapers and books and be sure that the grammar and spelling of what was written were correct, but nowadays, in modern Russia, a publication that pleases the eye with an absence of errors is rare.

Another of the achievements of the Soviet Union was the availability of medicine, which over time has also degenerated. Now, even in medicine, the Persona's component of the profession is supported more than the Self component. There used to be a collective ideal maintained at the societal level that a physician had to become the personification of a true healer. This ideal was supported on a collective level in cinema and in literature. A humanistic goal was upheld for the profession. Now, on the collective level, the profession is more often a means to an external goal, that of making money.

Modern society does not build a path to Self at the professional level. Medicine, education, and other professional fields have been turned into service industries, making everyone into salespeople and managers who help companies make money and run successful businesses.

The Archaic Form of Government

What is happening now in Ukraine has its roots in processes that were frozen in place in Russia in the 1990s. No matter how we feel about the collapsed and replaced Soviet Union or USSR, it is still "embedded" in many of us. There is something important about this remaining unconscious identity. And this importance is not about statehood, not about politics, but about something bigger, lying somewhere in the deeper depths of the psyche. The statehood of all post-Soviet countries bears the legacy of the Horde form of government, a military–administrative association based on the Mongol Empire.[5]

The collapse of the USSR and withdrawal from the shared sociopolitical space that formed the identity of the citizens of the USSR have not been grieved at the collective level. This lack of grief still keeps Soviet natives locked in an unconscious identification with the old USSR. Deep feeling is locked away in this unconscious identification from which there has not been a psychological and emotional separation. This can be seen now in the aggression-charged relationships in the intolerable conflict between the Russian Federation and Ukraine.

The difficulty in understanding and going through the process of separation from identification with the previous USSR affects the perception of current events not only within Russia and Ukraine, but also in Western countries. Similarly, historical events are now being viewed through the prism of multiple projections. For example, in Russia, we were taught that the USSR had won World War II. Now we are told that it is the United States that won that war, and that the USSR just played a secondary role. Another example is the Holodomor, a famine that took place in all the southern regions of the USSR, not just in Ukraine. The role of Stalin has been rewritten several times in totally different ways. He is portrayed by some as a savior and by others as a destroyer of the nation.

Before our eyes, the history of the twentieth century is being rewritten, and new meanings and values are being given to historical events and persons. And this is not the first time such a rewriting of history has occurred in the world. On the one hand, the current crisis has led to a great wave of interest in Russian history in my country. People have become much more interested in historical events, looking for their roots and connections. Some contemporary Russian writers have refocused on working with historical themes in their writing. On the other hand, there is a unification of the interpretation of historical events to solve exclusively ideological tasks. I see a similar trend in Western society.

Seeing Russia through Western Eyes

Since the eighteenth century, the history of Russia has been seen through the prism of Western thought and terminology. And this is a very interesting phenomenon. Alexander Etkind writes that, starting with Radishchev's *Journey from St. Petersburg to Moscow*, published in 1790, the view of Russian history has been influenced by the Western world. Etkind's *Internal Colonization: Russia's Imperial Experience*, published in 2011, gives a radically new reading of Russia's cultural history.[6] He traces how the Russian Empire conquered foreign territories and domesticated its own heartlands, thereby colonizing many peoples, Russians included. This vision of colonization as simultaneously internal and external, colonizing one's own people as well as others, is crucial for scholars of empire, colonialism, and globalization. Radishchev is already beginning to look at the people and events around him as if through the "eyes" of a European, alienating himself from his country and introducing an "outside observer." Here are a few examples.

The imposition of an imprint of the Western point of view is in Radishchev's speculations that Peter I began, in 1698, to shave beards and actually tax men with beards *as part of an effort to bring Russian society in line with Western European models*. To enforce his ban on beards, the tsar empowered police to shave forcibly and publicly those who refused to pay the tax.

I am reminded of the peoples of the Amazon who continue to live their original way of life and whose territories have been brutally exploited by Western civilization, which doesn't notice how, with its obsession to "carry the light" of new knowledge and technology, it destroys life. Not everyone on Earth wants to live in the light of Western civilization. And this reluctance does not prove that they are "uncivilized" and "savage." Although that is exactly how the Western world has seen them. The Western worldview does not allow for the freedom of life of the true Other. The life of the Other can only be understood in the language of Western thought. But these "Others" have their own language, which is no less valuable to them than the Western language is to the West.

In my opinion, it would be very valuable if the civilized world became *polyphonic* (rather than *cacophonic*, where there can also be many different voices, yet they lack inner harmony, connections, and roots). Russia has inherited all the projections that were associated with the USSR. The difference between Russia and the Soviet Union is not fully considered.

Even among Russian psychologists, there are stories now where "specialists" force their students or clients and others who are dependent on them to "recognize" the political position necessary for the "specialist" to continue working with them. It has become acceptable for the "specialist" to act as a dictator over his "subordinates." In Western culture, an orientation toward external adaptation to society is encouraged from an early age. Children are taught to compete, and the desire to be better than others is encouraged. I am now also noticing among my fellow psychologists the reinforcement of this vicious cycle of Western upbringing.

About the Archetype of the Great Mother in Russia

In addition to Russians seeing their own history through the eyes of Western attitudes and thought, the actual geographical position of Russia has put its imprint on the psyche of those living within Russian lands and their perception of the world. Most of the landmass lies between 50 and 70 degrees in the northern hemisphere. Within this territory, there are distinctly marked changes of the seasons. Mother

Nature shows the full range of her own nature—accepting and rejecting, nourishing and killing. She does so with great regularity, which can be integrated into the psychic rhythms of daily living. There are many proverbs and sayings in Russian that reflect this relationship with nature—for example, "Prepare the sleigh in the summer and the cart in the winter." To survive in a harsh climate, it is important not to forget, even during warm weather, that nature has a cruel and unchanging side, no matter what you do to subdue it. And this is mirrored in how the Great Mother archetype dwells in the Russian psyche and cultural complexes.

The vastness of the country also affects the formation of national character and can influence a feeling of personal vastness or smallness. The vastness of the country has contributed to a sense that one can always escape or relocate without losing a sense of national identity, remaining Russian. And it has contributed to a feeling of impunity and anonymity. Huge distances have also influenced the fact that people are aware of the size of their country but do not often travel outside their town, or village, or region. Those who can afford to are more likely to travel westward than around their own country. Russians can fantasize endlessly about the size of the country and the diversity of its peoples. And this fantasy of the hugeness of people and land has become part of how the Russian people habitually think of themselves.

Unlike Europe, Russian territory has always been dominated by rural settlements, not cities. Therefore, there was little expression of the bourgeoisie class, who were mostly city dwellers. And rural culture developed out of the more communal way of life of the peasants. In such a vast territory, it is extremely difficult to have one's own opinion, not to mention be heard by the system or Mother Nature. The Russian has no illusions about the possibility of being heard by the system. Rather, it is important to learn how to live within the system. Fitting into the system is the way to survive, rather than aspiring to rebuild or transform it. After all, it is impossible to rebuild in winter in the cold (except in times of climate change). One can only learn to build warm homes or find relatively safe ways to hibernate from the cold. The vast distances also lead to the fact that Russian people are ready to spit on the observance of laws (as happened with the observance of language rules in the republics of the USSR). The existence of a law does not guarantee its observance on the ground. And this attitude toward the law is very common in the Russian Federation among representatives of different social and ethnic groups.

The Dominance of the Great Mother, the Absence of a Solid Inner Father

Road traffic in Russia has some peculiarities that are rarely seen in Western countries. For example, in Moscow, all vehicles on the federal highway are often stopped owing to the fact that, at any given moment, high-ranking officials from the Kremlin will be traveling. And a person can spend more than an hour in such road closures, with no way to get to the side streets or to turn in the opposite direction. The picture, to those who are waiting on side streets, looks sad—the highway is completely empty, but the traffic police do not allow them to enter it. And such situations happen often in Moscow. Sometimes these delays are unpredictable. Other times they are predictable—when, for example, a leader of a foreign country comes to the capital for a meeting with our head of state. And then, on such days, people look for alternative routes to avoid being in the way of the heads of state and their accompanying cars. Or they don't use ground transportation. And no one grumbles. "Servants ride," as we sardonically refer to our leaders taking over the major roads for themselves in such incidents. Or the "Father of the People," the president, is escorted by a huge cortege of guards with blue blinkers. Yet the president acts like the Great Mother. Because, if he were a Great Father, he would respect the law, which is exactly what we do not see in this traffic situation. Laws for ordinary people turn out not to apply to people of stature. It is hard to do anything against someone who identifies with the Great Mother and uses the law for his personal interest rather than to protect public interests—all the more so when he is someone who, on a conscious collective level, is presented as the "Father of the People" but is actually acting on behalf of the Great Mother, luring his citizens into playing the role of hero, especially in the present time. Such heroes, lured on in the name of the Great Father but actually serving the Great Mother, are destined for a sad path—back to the mother's womb or to be emasculated.

With this cultural manifestation of the Great Mother archetype, the real Great Father in our collective cultural field can only be found within, not embodied in an external figure of power or a religious figure, for example. The Great Father in our culture can emerge only as an inner law, helping to order our own lives, to build a relationship with the Great Mother without fighting, without killing her, and without running away from her. It is difficult to keep the Father's order in her presence. It is difficult to contain both the Father and the Mother without identifying with one or the other while remaining an ordinary, simple human being, living in the ordinary, simple human dimension, equal to other human beings. But this is exactly what the Great Mother, who now possesses the collective psyche of Russia, needs—the emergence of the Great Father within common people. But the Great Father is scary and impossible to discover in oneself. It is easier to regress to the level of a resentful child and complain in irritation about the awful Mother than to build a connection with the Great Father within oneself. It seems easier to suck up to the Great Mother so as not to get in trouble with her, rather than to stop her by feeling a connection with the Great Father within. It is easier to submit completely to the service of her interests.

In Russia, only the one who is "married" to Russia is kept in power. In Russia, the tsar was anointed by God and betrothed to the Land. The tsar or, in the new history, the president is entrusted as a sacral figure with the care of the Land and the People. He is akin to the seasonal kings, the husbands of Isis, and of the kagans, who were also sacred figures. The respect given to the king belongs not to the individual but to the sacred King–Land pair, in which the chief figure is the Land, the Great Mother. And so, when war comes, the ethic of defending the motherland overrides the claim to the government.

It is not easy to write about what is happening to me now, here in Moscow. Russia's Great Mother has been aroused. It is almost impossible to loosen the Great Mother's hold on people in such situations. Trying to connect with the Great Father function in terms of knowledge, order, and law seems impossible when the historical dark depths of the Mother are in such ascendency. I see how people around me are suffering, losing the fragile connection to their inner Father, which had begun to take shape in the previous quiet years. For many, this connection has not had time to become internal, and they are unable to rely on it with confidence in the absence of external supports. This is especially difficult when one is inside the space of the Great Mother. But it also presents an opportunity to start asking oneself these questions: Who am I? Who am I if I am not just part of the Great Mother, not just part of my country? Can I think for myself in her presence, without being filled with fear or excitement or any other affect? Can I begin to rely on the Father, on a connection to the principles of law and order that have appeared within me? Contemporary Russian philosophers write that, for Western people, the important element in society is the law on which a democratic state is built. But, for Russian people, the notion of will, free will, and, hence, willfulness is more important. This echoes Islamic culture, in which everything is by the will of God, not by human will alone. In other words, the will within the Russian cultural complex is valued more than the law.

Aggression, Renewal, Civil War?

What scares me in all of this dark story is that questions of identity renewal always go hand in hand with civil war. The danger of a civil war in Russia has worried me before, right after the collapse of the USSR in the 1990s, and does so even more now. The level of aggression around us in Moscow is unbelievable. So far, it's only gaining momentum inside Moscow and in some other places; at the moment, the main outburst of aggression is taking place on the borders of the country, where a huge wound is being created to which all the "legalized" aggression from all sides is directed. But, when everything calms down on those borders (and it will happen eventually), all that aggression will come back into the country and will spread into Russian homes. Will we be able to process it here, to humanize it, to symbolize it? Will those who come back be able to wait calmly in traffic for the Servants to pass? Or will they no longer endure this unfair treatment under the law and show their power, directing it at the Servants? Will civil society itself be able to change by the time all these "special military operations" are over? Or will everything go back to the Great Mother's domain? Will we be able to stop waiting for the Great Father outside, projecting him onto one ruler or another, and finally locate him inside ourselves?

The Players in the Russia–Ukraine Conflict

There are many other countries involved in the conflict between Russia and Ukraine. There is a global geopolitical restructuring going on that stretches back to at least the eighteenth century. There have always been conflicts around the world, before World War I and after World War II. Today's conflict is different in its intensity because the main participant is a country that has nuclear weapons. That's why this conflict has engaged almost everyone in the West. And it also reflects the split in which we have become accustomed to living in recent years. There is the reality of the Western world in which everything is relatively comfortable and good. And there is another reality where there are wars going on that are far away from the West—in Neverland. These two realities coexist as if they are not in the same world: the world of people living in the West in peace and the world of all the other people, facing war, hunger, disease, and death. For eight years, the aggression erupting in Donetsk and Luhansk was "overlooked" by those who were not directly within those areas or in kinship or friendly relationships with them. It is as if this "little" war was taking place in Neverland. The world as a whole lived in denial of this "little war," and that denial has led to its inevitable return to the West, as if from somewhere else, some little-known, barbarian countries. About those "other" wars, most people in the Western world did not care and were not involved. Those wars were remote geographically and psychically. Even though there was some Western military involvement in that other world, it was sanctioned and did not raise questions among most civilians in Western countries. Then it began to concern all of us directly. It was no longer treated as if it were the same as Syria and Afghanistan.

I am against war and I am against splitting. I am for peace; I am for dialogue; I am for finding ways to build wholeness through acceptance and understanding the position of the other, through love and the search for opportunities for peaceful coexistence. But, in the midst of war, it is extremely difficult to understand what is going on. For example, I have clients whose relatives live both in the Donetsk Republic and in Ukraine. Those relatives living in Donetsk and Ukraine have a completely different picture of the same events. And my clients in Moscow find it extremely difficult to understand what is really going on there. But both sides evoke sympathy and love. At the same time, their relatives in Ukraine show much more distrust and rejection of my Russian clients.

In my experience of people in Russia who support the war in Ukraine, they are motivated by any one or combination of the following:

• They are very inflated in identifying themselves with some sort of cosmogonic myth in which there is war between "Earth" and "Heaven."
• They are gripped by primitive instincts that do not allow them to empathize, to sympathize with those who are under attack or hurt or dying.
• They are severely dissociated both from their own feelings and from the feelings of others.
• They lack the intellectual abilities to evaluate what is happening.

It takes a strong ego to maintain peaceful relations with those who do not share your opinion, who exhibit fundamentally different judgments, who live in different lands. In the mythologies of a cosmogonic war between Heaven and Earth, the gods (archetypal forces) do not care about mere mortals who participate in these wars without understanding what is behind them.[7] And these archetypal forces tempt mortals to fight for the gods, for the archetypal figures, for the collective polarities, forgetting about their own human nature, their human relations, and the limitations that all mortals have. Humans are seduced by the fantasy that the gods will make them the embodiment of ultimate truth if they join the battle on their side.

Overwhelmed by the Past

In looking at the conflict between Russia and Ukraine from a greater distance, it is a quite old confrontation between two powers. Some of the people project the good into one power, making the other power, respectively, the evil one, and the others project the opposite. In today's situation, this polarization is very visible. Another important theme, in my opinion, that can be seen in today's conflict is connected with the involvement of past generations in it, with the unresolved conflicts of the past. The stories of the grandfathers who fought in World War II are now actively resurfacing in the memory of the Russian people. In Russia, an immortal regiment has now been created for the May 9 Victory Day Parade, and it has marched every year since 2018. Its essence is that my contemporaries carry photos of their dead ancestors who fought in World War II and march with them in the ranks of the parade. The living and the dead mingle in those ranks. It's one thing when the living fight the living. It's another thing to fight with or against those dead who were left lying in the fields of World War II.

If you look at it symbolically, in this war, the people are enveloped by the past, by the archetypal energies of the ancestors, by the Otherworld. Until a secure boundary can be built between the living and the dead, between the human and the archetypal, between the individual and the collective, the war cannot be stopped. As soon as the archetypal collective energy of combat takes hold of us, we let this otherworldly force into us; we lose touch with ourselves, with the human within, and become possessed by the Prince of Darkness, the destructive energies of the long dead. And this can happen to a citizen of any nation. The Prince of Darkness, who stands at the head of the army of the dead, does not care.

I return again and again in my reflections to the fact that, since the beginning of the twentieth century, many tombs have been exposed and destroyed. This violates the legendary notion that these tombs protect this world from otherworldly evil. The tombs seal and secure the passage between "there" and "here," the living and the dead, good and evil. Can we, within ourselves, hold these seals intact, not letting evil break through in ourselves?

There is a Russian story about an Altai princess of the Ukok, a shamaness from the Ukok Plateau, a republic of Russia located in Southern Siberia. Around the fourth to third century BCE, she was buried along with her army and horses in one of the mounds of the eastern Altai. In the early 1990s, her burial site was found by archaeologists. They took her body to a Siberian city where it lay in the special laboratories of a scientific museum for almost twenty years. Local Altai shamans asked several times for the return of her remains because of their belief that she protected the passage between worlds. Eventually, her body was returned to the museum located near the site of her original burial.

The fate of the Ukok princess's burial site vividly describes what has happened in burial sites of ancient people all over the planet. We do not know why our ancestors buried certain people with such ritual attributes and honors. There is a theory that people buried in this way protected the Earth from the dark forces of the otherworldly realm. Since the end of the nineteenth century, so many graves have been destroyed by the piercing of boundaries by the Western mind. And many of the "seals" protecting this world from the dark forces of the Otherworld have been broken.

We can take these stories literally, but we can also take them symbolically. The rational masculine mind soared over the sensual feminine world of respect for ancestors and their traditions, and over the natural world. And this has led to the destructive consequences that we now face in our lives. It is very important for the world to reclaim the feminine and the natural in order to restore the balance that has been shaken. And this is not about literal feminism, but about respect for the planet and the lives of all its inhabitants who have ever lived on it. Having strengthened the spirit of the masculine, it is important to return to the soul, the feminine, the Anima Mundi.

What is happening in my country today has its roots far in the past. On the eve of the conflict, it was already obvious that the collective psyche in many different parts of the world was being overwhelmed by aggression and other primitive affects. And, unfortunately, there is still nothing to oppose this on the collective level. Resistance is possible only on the personal level—maintaining individual thinking and ethics, relying on one's own sensation and intuition. The ethical function, in terms of Jungian typology—the feeling function—has seriously "failed" us in recent years. It has been neglected everywhere. And now it is very much needed in order to preserve the human in oneself.

Modern society does not seem to give us the opportunity to cope with destruction and aggression in civilized ways. The reality of scientific progress and money-driven consumerism has largely opened the door to the shadow. If you have the means (monetary and technical), you can do anything. Morality is turned off by money and high technology. The silence of morality surrounds us on all sides. The yachts and gold toilets of high-ranking officials are terrible, not because of the shadow money spent on them, but because they corrupt the soul—and not only the soul of the owner of this luxury, but also that of those who envy it and begin to move in the direction of consumption. Western consumer culture is very conducive to such a movement toward the corruption of the soul. And this is where the words of the leader of my state, with which he criticizes the new morality of the West, particularly related to tolerance, sound poignantly. And these words of his unite around him those who are wounded by this attitude of Western culture.

If there are no effective, time-honored mechanisms for confronting the shadow in the collective consciousness, the individual psyche uses archaic ways of discharging tension. Unfortunately, this leads to outbursts of aggression at the collective level in the form of destructive aggression toward neighbors such as Ukraine.

Negative Projections onto and within Russians

We live in a time of unparalleled rapid change in both external and internal realities. I am amazed at how quickly all sorts of negative characteristics have been attributed to me and my Russian colleagues and compatriots. Literally a week after the invasion of Ukraine, all Russian citizens were equated to fascists and compared to the Germans of the 1940s. Excerpts from Jung's interview on May 11, 1945, in which he said that he would not work with Germans who did not admit their guilt for the actions of Nazi Germany, are often cited on the internet. Jung made his statement after the end of the war—not a week after it began. For me, the news of February 24, 2022, was as deafening and devastating as it was for the citizens of every other country. And I have as much influence over these actions as most other people. The only thing I can do is not to become inflamed with hatred for the people who spray this hatred around them. And go on working and living.

The fact that almost the entire Western world turned its back on the Russians in one week cannot be explained by the outbreak of hostilities in Ukraine alone. Russians became scapegoats overnight. It was as if the whole world was just waiting to see who would take on the role of fascists. And it was promptly projected onto all Russians, without regard to who was involved in what. I never once supported the war that was unleashed, although no one asked me. But, because of my background and residence, I found myself among those on whom a wave of hatred and accusations of fascism were unleashed. I cannot bear to read about my fellow citizens and colleagues encouraging anti-Russian measures in the world. I do not understand how psychological and psychotherapeutic societies can deny status and interrupt collegial relations with Russian colleagues simply because our troops are engaged in military action.

I am very grateful to the international professional Jungian community. So far we have managed to maintain our integrity. This is largely owing to the fact that we know each other personally. And membership has never been a mere formality to be paid for simply with hours of analysis and money for an exam. The training in analytic psychology places great emphasis on personal transformation, shadow integration, and individuation. Through training, analysts become familiar with both their shadow parts and collective processes. After studying and training, the ability to consciously retain one's own shadow sides within oneself without projecting them onto others emerges. The ability to distinguish collective from individual processes emerges. But, as today's events show, not all people have these abilities, and none of us has these abilities all the time. It pains me unbearably that our personal attitudes can bring even more pain into the world. Now, the shadow at both the personal and collective level reigns in much of the world and is rapidly destroying all that is personal and human. It is scary that, in the twenty-first century, it is so easy to deprive people of their human personality and draw them into a collective psychosis.

Currently, in the Russian collective field as well, there is a lot of splitting. Some people are gripped by the need for unity around patriotism, around saving everyone from Ukrainian Nazism and the approaching darkness, about which the state propaganda keeps screaming. Some people are gripped by the same need for unity, but expect the coming of darkness from our own government leaders. It is extremely difficult to accept the fact that one's own country is attacking a fraternal state without a good reason. Explanations are sought either in the pathological interests of third countries such as the United States and the countries of the European Union or in the pathological nature of the leader of one of the states involved in the conflict. The second option seems less realistic for those inside the Russian Federation because this option cannot explain the amount of hatred released in response to the Russians in the world.

Now, many are leaving the Russian Federation. Many people are breaking ties because of political disagreements in the family without going anywhere. The archetypal vortex of war has opened up and dragged ordinary people into resolving archetypal problems that have little to do with the individual level. The vortex centers on the collective level of the psyche, which includes the family, past generations, and even the dead and the gods. This is why I put great emphasis on learning about the history of the country and the history of client families. This history has enormous content and meaning. It allows individual clients to understand a bit more clearly their personal and collective past, perhaps even helping them to escape from the power of the past and the collective.

There is a clear tendency in the Russian cultural complex to unite all the different peoples and countries of the former Russian Empire and former USSR into a single whole. On the other hand, there has always been a distanced attitude in Russia toward the authorities, with a high level of distrust and an inability to take them seriously. The state apparatus has always been weak, whether in the Russian Empire, the USSR, or the Russian Federation. There have always been several different groups: those who live on the fringes of Russia but retain a sense of closeness to the authorities and those in power; those who live far away from the authorities (the runaways, exiles, those born in remote regions) and do not take the authorities seriously; and those who, because of poor education, can only submit to the representatives of any authority. The same thing is happening now. Those people who are against the government, but for the country, are forced to leave the Russian Federation. And those who remain are automatically perceived as being in support of the authorities, although the truth may be quite different from this appearance. Among those who remain in Russia, there are some who do not support the policies of the state. And, among those who have left, there are people with low social responsibility and morality. But also among those who stayed there are those who never chose or supported the government, but who have always been faithful to their roots and culture. In this, too, little has changed in the history of our country.

Finally, we need to find the strength to remain human and to remain respectful of one another, regardless of what the collective primitive archetypal forces want us to do. We need to find the strength to keep doing our jobs, to keep living, to keep loving, to keep supporting each other.

Notes

1 *Re-archaization* is a term that Eric Neumann used in *Depth Psychology and a New Ethic* to describe the return of the collective psyche to a more archaic state. See Eric Neuman, *Depth Psychology and a New Ethic* (Boston, Shambhala, 1990).
2 In *peasantism*, a peasant is given freedom to: "Pay Taxes to the governing Elites; Be responsible for his living expenses (pay rent, buy food); Die in wars when the Elites of his nation are involved in a conflict; Respect the borders drawn by the agreement of the world governing Elites; Be proud of his flag, language, religion, culture & superiority to other peasants." See *Urban Dictionary*, s.v. "peasantiam," www.urbandictionary.com/define.php?term=peasantism
3 Natan Eidelman, "Revoliutsiia sverkhu v Rossii" [Revolution from above in Russia] *Knowledge-Power Magazine* 10–12, 1988, and 1–3, 1989, p. 149.
4 Ibid.
5 The notion of the *Horde* form of government is based on the history of the Mongol Empire, which, by 1259, included a territory inhabited by many tribes, peoples, and nationalities that spoke different languages, were at very different levels of socioeconomic and cultural development, and had their own economic patterns, their own forms of life and their own skills. Neither economic nor cultural interests connected the heterogeneous and multilingual parts of the empire with one another. It was a typical military–administrative association. See Vadim V. Trepavlov, "The Takht Eli Khanate: The State System at the Twilight of the Golden Horde," *Remmm* 143: §§ 12, 13. https://doi.org/10.4000/remmm.11177
6 Alexander Etkind, *Internal Colonization: Russia's Imperial Experience* (Cambridge, UK: Polity, 2011).
7 See, for example, the cosmogonic war between sky forces and earth forces in the indigenous Khanty people of Russia. "Mythologies of the Mansi/Khanty People," Indigenous People's Literature, January 21, 2023, https://indigenouspeoplenet.wordpress.com/2023/01/01/mythologies-of-the-mansi-khanty-people/

Chapter 10

Archetypal Defenses of the Group Spirit in Russia and Ukraine

The Axes of Destruction

Thomas Singer

When confronted with the horrors of war in Ukraine or Syria or Iraq or Vietnam or Israel or Gaza, we try to figure out what is happening and why it is happening. We piece together the bits and pieces of stories and images that come to us from many different sources in order to create for ourselves a coherent narrative, knowing that at best we can only get a fragmentary glimpse of partial truths. Our abilities to explain are as limited as our comprehension of the seemingly endless and massive capacity of human beings to inflict pain, suffering, and death on one another. After considering all the studied explanations that contribute to the outbreak and conduct of war, we are still left with the sense that some inexorable process has been triggered, and that, once the conflict is ignited, it becomes increasingly difficult to halt it until it has run its course, almost like a fever.

Jung noted this when he wrote in his 1936 essay "Wotan":

> Archetypes are like riverbeds which dry up when the water deserts them, but which it can find again at any time. An archetype is like an old watercourse along which the water of life has flowed for centuries, digging a deep channel for itself. The longer it has flowed in this channel the more likely it is that sooner or later the water will return to its old bed. The life of the individual as a member of society and particularly as part of the State may be regulated like a canal, but the life of nations is a great rushing river which is utterly beyond human control . . . Thus the life of nations rolls on unchecked, without guidance, unconscious of where it is going, like a rock crashing down the side of a hill, until it is stopped by an obstacle stronger than itself. Political events move from one impasse to the next, like a torrent caught in gullies, creeks and marshes. All human control comes to an end when the individual is caught up in a mass movement. Then the archetypes begin to function, as happens also in the lives of individuals when they are confronted with situations that cannot be dealt with in any of the familiar ways.[1]

The focus of the collage I present in Figure 10.1 does not concern itself so much with the specific causes of the war in Ukraine, although specificity about who is responsible for what is always of great value when trying to understand

DOI: 10.4324/9781032695143-14

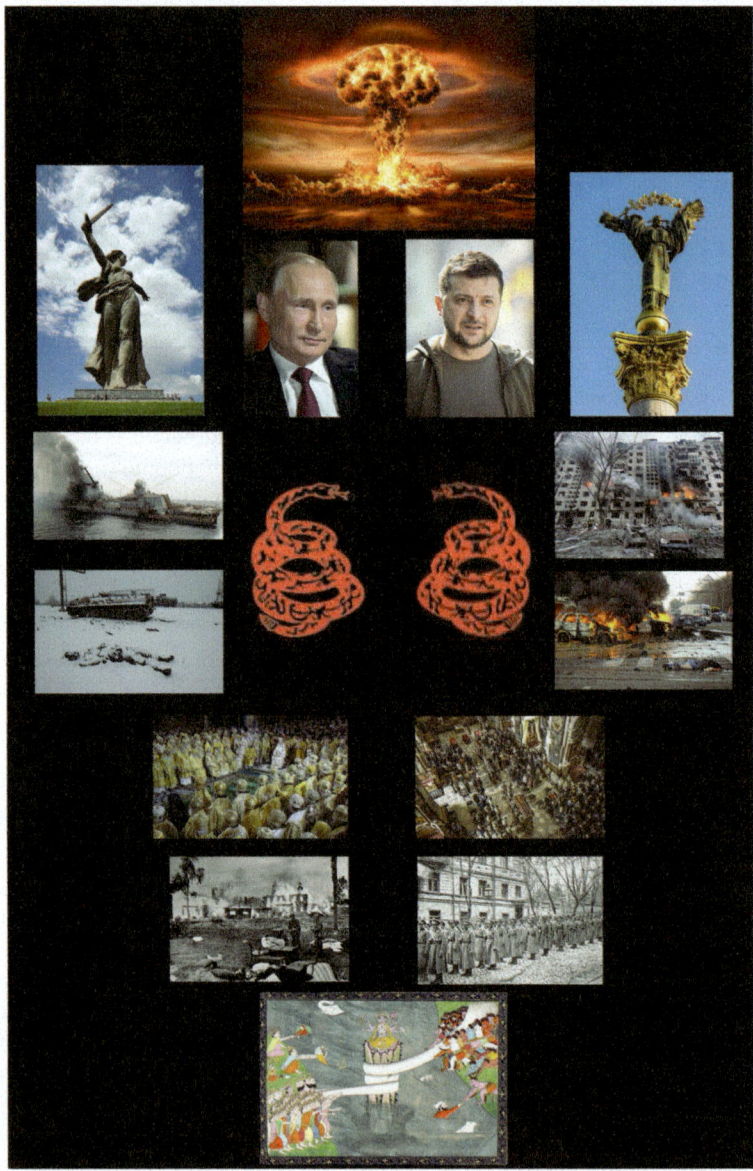

Figure 10.1 Archetypal Defenses of the Group Spirit of Russia and Ukraine, starting from top: **Image 10.1** Nuclear Blast; **Image 10.2** Vladimir Putin **Image 10.3** Volodymyr Zelensky; **Image 10.4** *The Motherland Calls*; **Image 10.5** *The Independence Monument*; **Image 10.6** Coiled Serpents; **Image 10.7** Russian Ship *Moskva*; **Image 10.8** Destruction of Ukrainian Homes; **Image 10.9** Body of Russian Soldier; **Image 10.10** Ukrainian Citizen Killed by Shelling; **Image 10.11** New Patriarch Kirill; **Image 10.12** Three Fallen Ukrainian Soldiers; **Image 10.13** Siege of Leningrad; **Image 10.14** Bolshevik Occupation of Ukraine; **Image 10.15.** *Gods and Demons Churning the Milk Ocean*

such fundamentally incomprehensible events. (The collages and images in this chapter can also be found on ARAS at https://aras.org/russiaandukraine.) Economic, geopolitical, sociological, psychological, and historical factors are all relevant and contributory. The stated causes for the war can be real, imagined, or manufactured, or all three—it doesn't seem to matter much once war breaks out. In presenting this collage my goal is to depict what happens when a war gets started, for whatever reason. At the core of this process, I imagine a basic dynamic in which the fundamental unifying vision or spirit of a country, often latent in the collective psyche, is touched and threatened. In the name of this unifying and threatened spirit, impersonal and potent defenses—sometimes hugely aggressive—are activated. This process taps into enormous collective emotion along with the willingness to make huge sacrifices, dormant in a society until its core spirit is imperiled and rallied. The suffering, violence, and destruction endured by citizens and soldiers alike are justified by participating in a shared belief and a unifying vision of the nation or the world.

In response to the threat—just as happens in a single-celled organism—the defensive response aims to protect the organism from annihilation. In this case, however, the organism is the nation-state. I call these defenses mobilized in defense of the nation "archetypal defenses of the group spirit" after the pioneering work of Donald Kalsched on the inner experience of individuals who are severely traumatized.[2] However, in the extension of Kalsched's model that I have proposed, the threat and trauma are not to the individual, what Kalsched calls "the personal spirit," but to the group as a whole and its "group spirit." The archetypal defenses that are mobilized to defend the threatened "group spirit" are primal and are as potent as, even identical with, the very forces that bind a group together in its identity. Once the "archetypal defenses of the group spirit" are triggered, the careening violence of whatever comes in the path of the "rock crashing down the side of a hill" seems independent of the specific causes that gave rise to the conflict.

In trying to select a set of images that illustrates this process, I find myself going back and forth between the wish to understand both the Russian and Ukrainian sides of the conflict and outrage at Putin's Russian invasion of Ukraine. But the psychological reality that I am trying to speak about objectively is about not so much who is responsible for the war in Ukraine, but what underlying processes come alive once propaganda and war machines get rolling on all sides. There is something autonomous and archetypically horrific that gets activated in the collective psyche in which all sides participate, no matter who is right or wrong, good or evil, perpetrator or victim. Even if it seems clear to most Westerners that Putin is wrong, perhaps evil, and certainly the perpetrator in this conflict, there is an important Russian side to the story, which I consider more in the commentary on *The Motherland Calls* under "Group Spirit."

I first began to explore the notion of "archetypal defenses of the group spirit" during the war between the United States and Al-Qaeda that followed the 9/11 bombings which ushered in the twenty-first century. I wrote two articles for the

San Francisco Jung Institute Library Journal, one in 2002 and the second in 2006. For the second article, Dyane Sherwood and Jacques Rutsky created a stunning collage (see https://aras.org/russiaandukraine) as a way of illustrating and bringing alive in symbolic imagery the notion of "archetypal defenses of the group spirit."[3]

The original collage demonstrates in image form how a true "axis of evil" is created in a horrifying dance of destruction, symbolized by the paired serpents, of the archetypal defenses facing off against one another when the sacred spirits of the group are attacked—symbolized in that image by the crescent and the mosque for Islam and by the candles of Western Christian and Jewish cultures. When core values are assaulted, as in the 9/11 attack on the United States or aggression by Western troops in Islamic lands, the archetypal defenses of the conflicting groups, "headed" by the figures of Bin Laden and Bush, generate the most terrible experience of mass and personal horror behind which lurks the ultimate symbol of modern destruction—the atomic bomb. Personal lives, cultural values, and archetypal forces collide and compete in the collective psyche.

When the Ukraine war with Russia erupted, I began to think again about that original collage and wondered what a contemporary version of it might look like. Using the original collage as a template, I soon realized that the circumstances of the two wars were quite different, and it would be foolish to try to make a new collage as an exact mirror image of the old one. At the same time, the underlying dynamics were similar with regard to the spirit of the group falling under threat and then attack, leading to the mobilization of ferocious defenses that result in horror and destruction. These defenses will use any strategy, device, manipulation, deceit, or brute power, including the fodder of human lives, to protect and preserve the ongoing life of the group.

Most creators of images do not like to tell their viewers what it is they are looking at. Artists much prefer that the creative process continue with the viewers bringing their own stories and interpretations to an image that can take on many different meanings. This is particularly true of symbolic images because it is in the very nature of a symbol to be multivalent and not to have a single meaning. In this case, however, because I am not an artist, I am going to upend that tradition and tell you what was on my mind in creating this collage. At one level, I have created a diagram of a very specific set of ideas, but it is my hope that the flesh-and-blood reality of the multidimensional idea becomes much more vivid and alive through the imagery. Of course, the viewer is encouraged to bring their own visions and interpretations to the collage as well.

Some Keys and Hints to the Design and Content
of *Archetypal Defenses of the Group Spirit in Russia and Ukraine*: The Axes of Destruction

Although the focus in this collage is on the conflict between Russia and Ukraine, its overarching theme is the notion that all groups, whether armed or not, are

Image 10.1 Nuclear Blast

psychologically "hard-wired" with archetypal defenses to protect their core spirit and being. This applies to nation-states as well as Republicans and Democrats, white racists, Black activists, anti-abortion Christians, pro-choice women and men—the list of groups threatened at the core of their being is endless.

The ultimate archetypal defense crafted by human ingenuity to date is the nuclear weapon. For this reason, the image of a nuclear blast (Image 10.1) is at the Satanic crown of these axes of destruction. The potential use of nuclear weapons has been in the foreground and background throughout the conflict between Russia and Ukraine. Noam Chomsky puts this hovering presence in the simplest terms possible in *The Dangerous Case of Donald Trump*:

> There are two huge dangers that the human species face. We are in a situation where we need to decide whether the species survives in any decent form. One is the rising danger of nuclear war, which is quite serious, and the other is environmental catastrophe.[4]

As I look at the collage as a whole, there are three intermingling axes of meaning that the images form. The first axis of images explores the relationships between the "spirit of the group" and the "archetypal defenses of the group spirit." The second, overlapping axis of images explores the relationships between archetypal, cultural, and individual levels of the psyche as it manifests in the world. The third axis of meaning only emerged near the end of creating the collage when consultation with colleagues led me to thinking of the collage in terms of "The Mythopoetic Imagination: *Gods and Demons Churn the Milk Ocean.*"

First Axis: Where the Spirit of the Group and the Archetypal Defenses of the Group Spirit Intersect

Group Spirit

As I formulate it, the group spirit is akin to what Jungians might call the *Self* of the group. The *group spirit* forms the ineffable core beliefs or sense of identity that binds people together. Nation-states have a group spirit, and their citizens often magically and unconsciously participate in it—particularly in times of crisis.

Putin and Zelensky (Images 10.2 and 10.3, respectively), as leaders of the warring nations, become the individuals most visible and representative of the battle to defend their respective group spirits. Each draws his energy and power not only from personal strength and charisma but also as carriers of the spirit of the group.

Image 10.2 Vladimir Putin

Image 10.3 Volodymyr Zelensky

Image 10.4 The Motherland Calls, Russian Statue Honoring the Heroes of the Battle of Stalingrad

To Putin's left in the collage is an image (Image 10.4) of the huge statue entitled *The Motherland Calls*. It can be thought of as symbolizing the Russian group spirt. *The Motherland Calls*, at a height of 85 meters (278 feet), sits in the center of a cluster of monuments named the *Heroes of the Battle of Stalingrad* in Volgograd, Russia. The statue portrays Nike, the goddess of victory, calling her sons and daughters to resist and defeat the enemy. *The Motherland Calls* takes on even greater symbolic, contemporary importance in carrying the spirit of Mother Russia as we learn about Putin's preoccupation with a Russian exile, Ilyan, who died in France. Ilyan was a fierce advocate of a mystical belief in Russia as a Holy Christian Motherland. Any means—including lying, manipulating, murdering—were justified in the restoration of a Holy Russia in Ilyan's view. Seen from that perspective, Putin has launched an invasion of Ukraine in the name of defending the sacred land of Russia from the increasing threat of godless Western Europe in the form of an encroaching NATO and the EU (European Union).

George Kennan, the architect of the West's post–World War II containment policy of the Soviet Union, warned about expanding NATO after the fall of the Berlin Wall and the collapse of the Soviet Union. Kennan was acutely aware that an expanding NATO represented a grave threat to Russian security in its memory of the Nazi invasion of Russia during World War II. Some say the economic threat of the EU in the form of Ukrainian economic growth and prosperity is an even greater threat to Putin's *kleptocracy*, in which a few enjoy the spoils of vast wealth while most of the country's population remains relatively underperforming in relation to the growth of the West.[5]

To Zelensky's right in the collage is an image (Image 10.5) of *The Independence Monument* in Ukraine. It is a victory column located on Maidan Nezalezhnosti (Independence Square) in Kyiv, commemorating the independence of Ukraine from Russia in 1991. In its celebration of the freedom of Ukraine, it is a perfect symbol of the "group spirit" for which the Ukrainian people are now fighting and dying. The figure atop the monument is Berehynia, a female spirit in Slavic mythology, who is regarded as a Slavic goddess, functioning as both "hearth mother and protectress of the home." Late-twentieth-century Ukrainian romantic nationalism centered on the matriarchal myth of Berehynia.[6]

Image 10.5 The *Independence Monument*, Statue of Berehynia, Celebrating Ukraine's Independence from Russia in 1991

Image 10.11 New Russian Orthodox Church Patriarch Kirill Conducts the Enthronement Service in the Christ the Savior Cathedral in Moscow on January 6, 2009 (UPI Photo/Alamy Stock Photo)

Image 10.12 Three Fallen Soldiers Are Mourned in Lviv, Ukraine (Finbarr O'Reilly/ *New York Times*)

Further down in the collage, the spirit of each group is further represented by their own version of the Eastern Orthodox Christian religion. The image on the left (Image 10.11) shows the installation of Kirill as patriarch of the Russian Orthodox

Church in 2009. Interestingly, Kirill, as patriarch, can be seen as representing both the spirit of the group and its archetypal defenses. The Russian Orthodox Church has become a political weapon of the state.

On the right is a church in Lviv, Ukraine (Image 10.12), where three Ukrainian soldiers are being mourned as fallen defenders of Ukraine against Russia.

Archetypal Defenses of the Group Spirit

Donald Kalsched postulated that, in response to severe trauma, an individual develops defenses of the personal spirit. I suggest that groups react in much the same way: When a group has been attacked at the core of its being and values—as the United States was on 9/11—or when a group has been corroded at the core of its being and values—as Islam has been for the past 500 years—archetypal defenses are mobilized to protect the vulnerable and injured group spirit. These archetypal defenses can be ferocious and inhuman.

The demonic defenses often direct their primitive aggression back onto the wounded spirit of the group, as evidenced in the self-mockery and self-denigration entrenched in the humor and self-perception of any number of oppressed minorities. But, just as often, these same defenses of the group spirit can turn their savage aggression out onto whomever or whatever appears to be a threat to the spirit, basic value, or identity of the group. I see this response as automatic, reflexive, and in some ways the most natural way for the group psyche to react. Those individuals identifying with the archetypal defenses of the group spirit can torture people in prison, behead people, and blow themselves and others up—without regard for their own personal well-being or the humanity of those who happen to be in their path. As defensive agents of a wounded group spirit, they are not constrained by normal human values or concerns. They are truly impersonal representatives of the group and its wounded spirit.

The ultimate, archetypal defense of the group spirit is the threat or actual use of nuclear weapons (Image 10.1). This looms over the whole conflict, either as a manipulative tactic or as a very real threat of the use of nuclear weapons in a conflict that escalates out of control.

Coiled serpents square off against one another at the center of the collage in Image 10.6. The most natural response to seeing coiled serpents in a defensive or aggressive posture in relation to one another is to think of evil—as in the serpent in the Garden of Eden. Their archetypal antagonism certainly can unleash the most evil and destructive forces known to humankind. However, they are also an expression of the natural posture that any living organism would take when its very existence is threatened with annihilation. This is not only true of individuals facing the threat of destruction but is also amplified exponentially when a group is, or perceives itself to be, under attack with the possibility of its very existence being eliminated. In this sense, the archetypal serpents squaring off against one another can be viewed as both the shadow (as Jung called it) and the normal response of any organism—individual or collective—when threatened

Image 10.1 Nuclear Blast

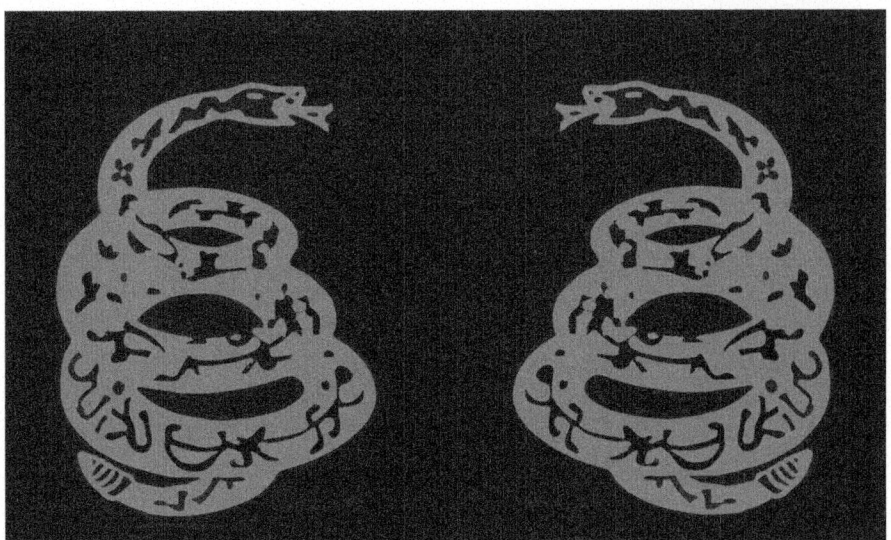

Image 10.6 Coiled Serpents as Archetypal Defenses of the Group Spirit

with annihilation. When archetypal defenses of the group spirit are mobilized, the casualties on both sides of the war defy imagination.

Non-human Casualties of the Axes of Destruction

Part of the destruction of war is non-human: buildings, tanks, infrastructure, ships, anything that gets in the way of the war machine. Image 10.7 shows the *Moskva*, flagship of Russia's Black Sea fleet, sinking after being hit by missiles from Ukraine. Both Ukraine and Russia suffer from the destructive havoc caused by war, although clearly, in this war, Ukraine's cities and infrastructure are bearing the brunt of the fury.

There are so many structures, including homes, hospitals, apartment housing, and every other kind of building, that have been destroyed in Ukraine, with Image 10.8 being only one example, that the cost in human life, dislocation, rebuilding, and time is inestimable.

Human Casualties of the Axes of Destruction

No one has a clear idea of how many Russian soldiers have lost their lives in the war with Ukraine, but the figure already appears to be far greater than fifteen thousand. It has been reported that Russia has already lost as many soldiers in a

Image 10.7 The Sinking of the Russian Ship *Moskva*

Image 10.8 Destruction of Ukrainian Homes

few months of fighting in Ukraine as it did in the nine-year war with Afghanistan. Image 10.9, of a lone, frozen Russian soldier near a tank, says more than numbers in the thousands.

This stark image of a Ukrainian civilian (Image 10.10) killed in Kyiv by Russian shelling brings the horror of war into human focus.

Second Axis: Where Different Levels of the Psyche Are Embodied in the Imagery—Archetypal, Cultural, and Individual

The second interwoven axis that the collage represents is the one formed by the different levels of the psyche as it manifests in the world: the archetypal, the cultural, and the individual or personal. These levels of the psyche often interpenetrate and overlap one another, but there are times that phenomena more clearly arise from one level or another. Simultaneously, the dynamic relationship between the spirit of the group and its archetypal defenses is in play at every level in which psyche appears.

Archetypal Embodiments of the Conflict

In the collage, there are two images (Image 10.1 and Image 10.6) that emerge from the deepest, archetypal level of the psyche.

Image 10.9 The Body of a Russian Soldier in Kharkiv, Ukraine (Tyler Hicks/*New York Times*)

Image 10.10 Ukrainian Citizen Killed by Shelling While Fleeing (kyiv.dsns.gov.ua)

Image 10.1 Nuclear Blast

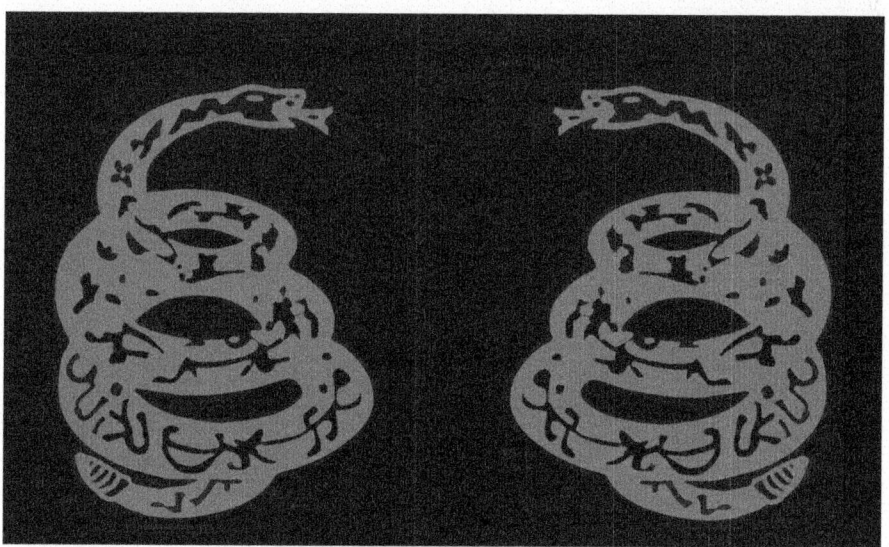

Image 10.6 Coiled Serpents as Archetypal Defenses of the Group Spirit

The atomic bomb (Image 10.1) emerges as an archetypal symbol of destructive power. This was apparent to Robert Oppenheimer as he witnessed the first test detonation of the bomb on July 16, 1945. A line from the Hindu sacred text, the Bhagavad Gita, came to his mind: "Now I am become Death, the destroyer of worlds."

The second image coming from the archetypal realm of the psyche is of the two snakes squaring off against each other (Image 10.6). They symbolize an instinctual reaction of life defending itself against the imminent threat of attack, injury, and possible death. This threat can come to an individual, to a group, or to the whole planet, as in in our current climate change crisis and the extinction anxiety that causes many of us to shudder.

Cultural Embodiments of the Conflict

In the collage, there are several images where the cultural level of the psyche is represented as embodying the conflict.

Images 10.11 and 10.12 depict two different Eastern Orthodox ceremonies—the installation of Patriarch Kirill of Russia in one and the funeral services of fallen Ukrainian soldiers in the other. The churches become symbolic carriers and expressions of the two cultures.

Images 10.13 and 10.14 communicate at another level of the cultural or group level of the psyche in what I term *cultural complexes*. These images depict landmark

Image 10.11 New Russian Orthodox Church Patriarch Kirill Conducts the Enthronement Service in the Christ the Savior Cathedral in Moscow on January 6, 2009 (UPI Photo/Alamy Stock Photo)

Image 10.12   Three Fallen Soldiers Are Mourned in Lviv, Ukraine (Finbarr O'Reilly/ New York Times)

Image 10.13   Siege of Leningrad by Nazis During World War II

Image 10.14 Bolshevik Occupation of Ukraine in 1918

events in the history of Ukraine and Russia. These events have become embedded in the collective memory and emotional life of the citizens of Ukraine and Russia. As collective memory, they have the tendency to reinforce a given view of history in terms of how people view contemporary events. This self-selecting reinforcement of memory is accompanied by heightened emotion that is easily triggered and takes on a life of its own as an autonomous cultural complex, always ready to be triggered and contribute to the meaning of events. Cultural complexes are carriers of deeply held beliefs, collective memory, and powerful emotion. Image 10.13 shows the 900-day siege of Leningrad (now St. Petersburg) by the Nazis, beginning in 1941. It is no accident that Putin refers to the Ukrainians as Nazis as he is evoking the terrible memory of the Russian suffering at the hands of the Germans, which is the trigger for a potent cultural complex. And the Ukrainians have their own cultural complex of having suffered at the hands of the Russians, as evoked by Image 10.14 of the 1918 siege of Kyiv by the Bolsheviks.

Individual Embodiments of the Conflict

Images 10.2 and 10.3 are clear examples of the multiple layers of psyche at which an image can communicate. Putin and Zelensky are both individuals who simultaneously speak for the group at the cultural level of the psyche and for the archetype as very different kinds of leadership and authority.

Image 10.2 Vladimir Putin

Image 10.3 Volodymyr Zelensky

Image 10.9 The Body of a Russian Soldier in Kharkiv, Ukraine (Tyler Hicks/*New York Times*)

Image 10.10 Ukrainian Citizen Killed by Shelling While Fleeing (kyiv.dsns.gov.ua)

Images 10.9 and 10.10 are more clearly speaking from the personal or individual level of the psyche. Perhaps as victims of the war, they symbolize more than the personal—but it is very much through the personal that these images bring home an experience of the horrible individual costs of war.

Third Axis: The Mythopoetic Imagination—*Gods and Demons Churning the Milk Ocean*

In working on this collage and its commentary, I consulted with various colleagues to see if these ideas and images spoke to them as having any meaning or relevance. The consultation turned into a set of lively, informal exchanges that became a way of continuing the creation of the collage. Here are some of the highlights of those communications. I started with my colleague John Beebe, because I felt that the images in the collage formed a kind of "spine" of destructive energies that pour forth when the archetypal defenses of the group spirit are activated. John has written extensively on "the spine of integrity" from a typological perspective in a most creative way, and I wondered what John thought about my using the word *spine* to describe this far more negative process. John was of the opinion that *spine* was not the right word because the spine is a living, flexible part of organisms. John wrote:

> What the collage you have created powerfully depicts is a not so much a spine as a posture of demonic opposition, as befits a country with its back up, like Russia today, using a massively totalitarian stance in lieu of a spine . . . I wouldn't call it spine because it doesn't contain the vulnerability and aliveness of a spinal cord within, but only has the outer mimetic shell persona of one. The totalitarian posture is shameless and ultimately soulless, more a façade than a breathing link between ego and Self, because as a defense of the Self it has not accepted limitation as a condition of individuation and the ability to recognize otherness and others as a value. So, I myself would use another word than *spine* for what erects and gives temporary stature to that defensively aggressive posture so perfectly conveyed by your collage: perhaps the *defensive stance of massed destructiveness*.

John's response led me to further consider an essential question about archetypal defenses of the group spirit—whether they could be different from one group to another. In other words, Russia and Ukraine are locked in a terrible struggle in which the archetypal defenses of the group spirit on both sides are now dominant players in this deadly war. Are these archetypal defenses the same on both sides, or are they different in any significant way? I asked John this additional critical question and found his response most suggestive:

> I think archetypal defenses of the group spirit are definitely involved, and I think those of the Ukrainians are different from those of the Russians. *It's possible to oppose with integrity, and to be daimonic rather than demonic* so that the very same archetypal positions can create an infusion of healthy spirit rather than an egoistic determination to conquer. The difference lies in the integrity with which the shadow is held.

In his book *Energies and Patterns in Psychological Type*, John lists the demonic/daimonic as an archetype in the unconscious of any self-organizing personality, and this could be the personality of a group as well as an individual. John goes on to say:

> The demonic/daimonic archetype structures and patterns the area of undermining and redemption. As shadow, it demonically undermines self and others, often to an evil degree; but when held and deployed with integrity, that is, holding ourselves responsible for our long-term effects on others, the same energy can become daimonic—uncannily angelic, an inspiriting energy that creates ever further opportunities to develop integrity . . . Integrity is often followed

by synchronicity. What I have chosen to call the Opposing Personality in all of us can become the voice of conscience in a group as well as individual ego, and that conscience can link with the even deeper daimon in us that wants us to consider the needs of the Other we have been defending ourselves against. *When the group resorting to archetypal defenses realizes the shadow of defensiveness with integrity, the demonic energy involved is itself transformed into the daimonic, an uncanny spirit that infuses the group with a different quality of energy which can take even a people under threat beyond self-righteous self-assertiveness.* At that point, actions informed by respect for others begin to emerge. The group self has arrived at a stage of concern that knows that other groups have selves as well.

When that awareness emerges, even an initially hostile engagement with the other may inspire a willing sensitivity to the needs of the whole, enabling the political process that follows to be transformative. Deep waters, but beautiful to contemplate.[7]

The upshot of my exchanges with John is that I did not use *spine* in my subtitle. I stayed with *axis/axes*. But it also helped make clearer to me the possibility that archetypal defenses of the group spirit can be related to in different ways by different groups of people. When the shadow aggressiveness of these defenses is held with integrity, a group might be able to take these destructive, undermining, and demonic energies and potentially transform them into something daimonic that can become "an occasion for the infusion of spirit." Renée Cunningham's book *Archetypal Nonviolence: Jung, King, and Culture through the Eyes of Selma* documents such a process.[8] All of this can end up sounding like nice but abstract theory when the war on the ground is so ugly and destructive, no matter who is demonic or daimonic. But it is helpful to imagine our way to a possible differentiation of these "archetypal defenses of the group spirit" based on how leaders and groups of people relate to the huge energies released when they are triggered. As John put it, "Integrity can infuse the archetypal defenses of the group with a spirit that takes the group beyond self-righteous self-assertion."

In response to John's pointing me in the direction of demonic/daimonic, I began to research the symbolic imagery in ARAS (Archives for Research into Archetypal Symbolism) related to the relationship between the demonic and daimonic. It did not take long to find a stunning Indian image that features the conflict between the daimonic and demonic in the image of the *Gods and Demons Churning the Milk Ocean*. The description of the image in ARAS states:

Two groups of figures are massed on opposite sides of a central axis, or axis mundi, consisting of a mountain resting on the back of a tortoise and bearing the figure of the god Vishnu. The axis mundi operates as a churning stick surrounded by sea, and wrapped around it, a serpent's long body serves as a cord that reaches to two opposing shores. On the left shore are the gods, all of whom wear crowns, while the demons are amassed on the right. People and animals appear to be coming out of the water, some of them aided by figures on either shore . . . The gods and the demons work together, churning the milk ocean in order to obtain the elixir of immortality.[9]

Can the struggle between opposing "archetypal defenses of the group spirit" be related to the "churning of the milk ocean" in which the battle between demonic and daimonic forces is wired into the basic structure of human existence? How is the effort to create the "elixir of immortality" part of this battle? Is the "elixir of immortality" for Putin's Russia symbolized by the *Motherland Russia* statue? Is the "elixir of immortality" for Zelensky's Ukraine symbolized by *The Independence Monument*? Gazing at the *Churning of the Milk Ocean* (Image 10.15) suggested to me a mythological underpinning to the Ukraine–Russia war. Does the Hindu vision offer us a glimpse of a common mythologem or mythopoetic insight into the seemingly unending conflicts between groups of people that are the hallmark of human history?

After all, the Hindu spiritual imagination's capacity to picture the nature of time and space and the unfolding of human affairs is extraordinary in the vastness and depth of its vision. It is quite likely that the Hindus have known something about the nature of war and the relationship between the demonic and daimonic long before the West was born. Eons ago, the Hindus' religious intuition anticipated something about the nature of the birth and destruction of galaxies and the cosmos

Image 10.15 Gods and Demons Churning the Milk Ocean (Bequeathed by Mrs. Grace S. Anderson in memory of her husband, John Anderson, MD, CEO, FRS)

Figure 10.2 This Landscape of "Mountains" and "Valleys" Speckled with Glittering Stars Is Actually the Edge of a Nearby, Young, Star-Forming Region Called NGC 3324 in the Carina Nebula. Captured in Infrared Light by NASA's New James Webb Space Telescope, This Image Reveals for the First Time Previously Invisible Areas of Star Birth.

that we are now witnessing scientifically in the first images from NASA's James Webb telescope (Figure 10.2).

The Webb telescope images almost make the first image of this collage—the human creation of the nuclear weapon—look puny, even though Robert Oppenheimer thought of a line from Hindu scripture on witnessing the first detonation of a nuclear weapon: "Now I become Death, the destroyer of worlds." But perhaps I am indulging in a mythopoetic flight that can easily serve as its own dissociative defense that takes us way too far from the horrific realities of the war on the ground in Ukraine. It offers us very little in terms of being able to confront and do something about the ruthless and barbaric destruction that is beyond comprehension or our capacity to emotionally take in the toll in suffering, loss, and death of our fellow human beings.

It can all get quite overwhelming and too heady, but, essentially, we are tracking archetypal serpent images as they appear in various forms. Can we imagine the transformation of demonic, destructive energies into something daimonic, creative, even spiritual at the level of the group psyche? *Can the Hindu kundalini model of serpentine energies located at the base of the spine in individuals be extended to the energies of large groups of humans in which war and the mobilization of archetypal energies of the group spirit erupt from the lowest-level chakras of group psyches?*

In tracking the archetypal serpentine energies, have I inadvertently created a collage that depicts a kundalini of war? Have I stumbled upon a kind of mythopoesis in which the collective psyche can be imagined as having its own way of expressing group kundalini-like energies? In the case of the war in Ukraine, those kundalini-like chakra energies of the group psyche have dwelled for the most part at the lowest level of chaotic destruction and aggression. We have seen a lot of the demonic and little of the daimonic, although many will point to the emerging spirit of the Ukrainian people and the renewal of the spirit of democratic freedom in the West as a hopeful sign of how the daimonic can offer an "infusion of healthy spirit rather than an egoistic determination to conquer."

Concluding Thoughts

Clearly, all of these questions and possibilities point to the fact that this is a very unfinished work in progress, an active imagination that began with a meditation on the energies and symbolic images of the archetypal defenses of the group psyche in the Ukraine–Russia war. The current incarnation of the collage and its commentary are intended to be open-ended, to serve the purpose of stimulating reflection and leading to more questions rather than easy answers. There are no underlying certainties or clear answers to the gaping, age-old human wounds opened once again by the current war in Ukraine.

And yet, how easy it is to be both drowned and carried away by these imponderables! As Jungians, we love to look for the possibility of transformation. Our core mantra of alchemical transformation is chanted even in the darkest moments when it seems as though our world is practicing the reverse alchemical art of turning gold into shit.

It would be easy for this conversation about demonic/daimonic to turn into its own circular argument, going round and round in the question of when and how and whether the demonic archetypal defenses of the group spirit might be related to in such a way that they become daimonic. But there seems to be little doubt that these defenses are real, that they are potent, and that they are raining down destruction on the people of Ukraine and the soldiers of Russia. Elucidating the reality of the archetypal defenses of the group spirit and their destructive potency is the central point of this chapter. I will let my colleague Betty Teng, with whom I have developed the podcast and then book *Mind of State: Conversations on the Psychological Conflicts Stirring US Politics & Society*, have the last word in this discussion about demonic/daimonic:

> Where does this all lead us? How does this alleviate suffering? Can we make sanitized theories and analogies about such baseness? I have a *polis or politics* part in me that asks these questions. But the *psyche* in me seeks space, a container, a means to hold paradoxes, as noxious as they might be. It could also be my Buddhist underpinnings: things rise in the world and so how do we accept them—even the horrors and the wanton suffering—as a part of reality, as they are? Your chapter seeks to bridge the gap between the two, between *polis* and *psyche*, as it applies to the Russia/Ukraine war.[10]

Once again, this is a very unfinished work in progress whose goal is to stimulate the *psyche* and the *polis* in each of us and to create enough mental space to reflect on many levels simultaneously. It is created in the spirit of Olga Tokarczuk who writes, in *Drive Your Plow over the Bones of the Dead*:

> It's a good thing that God, if he exists, and even if he doesn't, gives us a place where we can think in peace. Perhaps that's the whole point of prayer—to think to yourself in peace, to want nothing, to ask for nothing, but simply to sort out your own mind. That should be enough.[11]

Notes

1 C. G. Jung, "Wotan," in *The Collected Works of C. G. Jung*, vol. 10, eds. Herbert Read, Gerhard Adler, Michael Fordham, and William McGuire, trans. R. F. C. Hull (Princeton: Princeton University Press, 1968), § 395.

2 Donald Kalsched, *The Inner World of Trauma: Archetypal Defenses of the Personal Spirit* (London, Routledge, 1996).

3 Thomas Singer, "The Cultural Complex and Archetypal Defenses of the Collective Spirit: Baby Zeus, Elian Gonzales, Constantine's Sword, and Other Holy Wars," *The San Francisco Jung Institute Library Journal* 20, no. 4 (2002): 4–28; Thomas Singer, "Unconscious Forces Shaping International Conflicts: Archetypal Defenses of the Group Spirit from Revolutionary America to Confrontation in the Middle East," *The San Francisco Jung Institute Library Journal* 25, no. 4 (2006): 6–28.

4 Noam Chomsky, "Reaching beyond the Professions," in *The Dangerous Case of Donald Trump*, ed. Bandy Lee (New York: St. Martin's Press, 2017), p. 357.

5 For links related to the Motherland, Ilyin, Putin, and Russia, see Dimitry Kotenko, "Russian Cultural Complexes and the Shadow Aspects of European Civilization," YouTube, February 22, 2022, https://youtu.be/BOM0bUNmIbE; Timothy Snyder, "Ivan Ilyin, Putin's Philosopher of Russian Fascism," *The New York Review*, March 16, 2018, www.nybooks.com/daily/2018/03/16/ivan-ilyin-putins-philosopher-of-russian-fascism/; Alexander Dugin, "The Far-Right Mystical Writer Who Helped Shape Putin's View of Russia," *The Washington Post*, May 12, 2022, www.washingtonpost.com/outlook/2022/05/12/dugin-russia-ukraine-putin/; "Ezra Klein Interviews Timothy Snyder," *The Ezra Klein Show*. Podcast transcript, *The New York Times*, March 15, 2022, www.nytimes.com/2022/03/15/podcasts/transcript-ezra-klein-interviews-timothy-snyder.html

6 For a concise history of modern Ukraine in the context of the struggle for freedom and independence, I suggest two places to begin: Wikipedia, s.v. "History of Ukraine," November 8, 2023, 6:30 UTC, https://en.wikipedia.org/wiki/History_of_Ukraine; and Timothy Snyder, *The Road to Unfreedom. Russia, Europe, America* (New York: Vintage, 2018).

7 John Beebe, *Energies and Patterns in Psychological Type* (London: Routledge, 2016), p. 44; italics added.

8 Renée M. Cunningham, *Archetypal Nonviolence: Jung, King, and Culture through the Eyes of Selma* (London: Routledge, 2021).

9 Archive for Research in Archetypal Symbolism, ref #:7AR.076, https://aras.org

10 From a personal conversation with Betty Teng by email.

11 Olga Tokarczuk, *Drive Your Plow over the Bones of the Dead*, trans. Antonia Lloyd-Jones (New York: Penguin Random House, 2018).

Chapter 11

Archetypes in War

Jörg Rasche

I am writing these lines in June 2023, a day after the breaking of the big dam of Kakhovka near Kherson with its unforeseeable consequences. It is also the day when the trial of Oleg Orlov starts in Moscow. Orlov was one of the founders of Memorial, the organization that documented victims of Stalin's terror. These events belong together: The destruction of the limited resources of our world and the threat against a prominent and fearless advocate for human rights are both expressions of a kind of endgame, of a cataclysm of human rationality and values. In the last many years, I have tried not to fall into a complex of anger and depression, not to project my own cultural shadow aspects elsewhere (as Gert Sauer warns of in Chapter 2 of this book). But, in the last decade, my inner gyroscope of balance and my positive feeling for Gorbachev's vision of "Our Common European Home"[1] has been shaken. Instead, strong and archaic cultural complexes are activated all around us and in us, and this means for me that we must take care of our own psychic houses as well as those of our friends and enemies, as far as that is possible.

Kiev, the Russian Jerusalem

To start with what is close to my heart. I have been in Lviv (Lemberg) and Kiev (Kyiv) to give seminars and supervise in sandplay therapy and analytical psychology several times between 2012 and 2019. I learned to love this country with its kind and open-minded people, its wheat and sunflower fields, and its fabulous old churches with golden domes in the form of onion bulbs. But those impressions were also mixed with less visible but rising memories of not-so-distant traumatic history, in which my own country, Germany, had played a sinister role in World War II. After I visited Babyn Yar, the site where the occupying Nazis had killed more than 32,000 Jews in two days in 1941, I lost my voice for some days. I realized how deeply the traumatic history has shaped the inner world of generations here, and what was triggered again when Stalin's troops came back in 1943.

DOI: 10.4324/9781032695143-15

And, by an unconscious intuition, I quoted in a Kiev seminar in 2019 the poem by Alfred, Lord Tennyson:[2]

The Kraken

Below the thunders of the upper deep,
far, far beneath in the abysmal sea,
His ancient, dreamless, uninvaded sleep
The Kraken sleepeth: faintest sunlights flee
About his shadowy sides; above him swell
Huge sponges of millennial growth and height;
And far away into the sickly light,
From many a wondrous grot and secret cell
Unnumbered and enormous polypi
Winnow with giant arms the slumbering green.
There hath he lain for ages, and will lie
Battening upon huge sea worms in his sleep,
Until the latter fire shall heat the deep;
Then once by man and angels to be seen,
In roaring he shall rise and on the surface die.

I was not aware what the "unnumbered and enormous polypi" of the archaic monster, which would reappear at the end of the world, could be. There was something apocalyptic in the air. I knew that there had been war in the east of Ukraine since 2014, but I could not imagine the pending invasion by Russia in 2022.

I was perplexed by some paradoxical impressions. In the center of old Kiev, on high hills overlooking the wide River Dnieper, there are three monuments that are reminders of the traumatic and controversial history. There is the monument for the Red Army and its heroic struggle against Hitler and Germany in World War II. Just a short distance away from this black obelisk, there is another memorial for the estimated 3.5–7 million victims of the great Holodomor famine in 1931–1932, caused by the collectivization program and the genocide of the Kulaks (independent farmers) by the Stalin administration. So, the accomplishments and crimes of Stalinism are memorialized quite close to one another. Again, just some hundred meters away is the third site of the fantastic Cave Monastery, with many golden domes and hundreds of meters of underground tunnels and caves. There, the monks of former centuries are buried. When the graves were opened afterward, the dead bodies were found intact. The conclusion was that they must have been saints. Today, the caves are open to the public, and many citizens go down into the narrow caves with candles. They pray and cry! I had the visceral impression that this was the only authentic place to mourn the unbearable history and fate of this tormented country. But, again not far away, there is a fourth memorial site: Maidan Square, the site of the Orange Revolution in 2004 and the Maidan of Dignity and Honor in 2014.

The Cave Monastery, the Cathedral of St. Sophia in the old city center, and St. Michael Cathedral (reconstructed after its demolition by Stalinists who had wanted to build in its place the largest monument to Lenin ever) are sacred sites for all Russians. Kiev has been the offspring and center of the Russian Orthodox Church since 998. Here King Volodymyr and his people were baptized in the river and adopted the Byzantine or Eastern Orthodox version of Christianity, including its rituals and the veneration of ikons.

Whereas Moscow later claimed to be the *Third Rome* (after Rome in Italy and Constantinople in Byzantium), Kiev's older tradition is related to Byzantium and Jerusalem. The *Holy City* is understood as the site of God's incarnation. As the Holy City is God's abode, the worshipper venerates God's and the saint's real presence in the Orthodox Ikon. The magic of these traditions is palpable all over Ukraine, Russia, and other Orthodox cultures such as Bulgaria and Greece. Kiev as the *Russian Jerusalem* is especially significant for the Moscow tradition because of the centuries-old competition between the two regions and cities. Kiev is much older than Moscow and can legitimately claim itself as the birthplace of Russian culture, although those favoring Moscow have created an alternative mythology of origins. Most importantly, for the deep-rooted Russian cultural complex and identity, *Holy Kiev* can never become part of a pagan Western hemisphere.

Coming from similar depths of the collective or cultural unconscious, we find that Dmitry Kotenko (Chapter 7) interprets the war against Ukraine as a *reconquest of the graves* of the lost heroes from the Great Patriotic War (World War II). In fact, Putin often calls up memories of Nazi Germany's crimes in World War II. We do not know what is really going on in Putin's mind, but we can be sure that the destruction of Kiev's holy sites would cause deep offense to the Russian people.[3] It is worth noting that the fate of the original Jerusalem in Israel/Palestine and the eternal struggle about claims to the city show a comparable dynamic in the cultural complexes of Jews, Muslims, and Christians.

As others in this book have noted, nationalism is a very young development. Until the age of the Enlightenment and the French Revolution, each state was a kind of sacred institution with a king and queen at its top, sitting just beneath God's umbrella. In this sense, Russia too was a sacral (holy) institution until the revolutions of 1907 and 1918. The mentality of the people under Lenin, Stalin, and—still today—Putin shows similarity to the attitudes that existed under the tsars. For many living in Russia, Moscow is far away, as far away perhaps as God. But the Russian people still have the sacred ikons of his saints, and the living presence of the saints is felt in the ikons. And what comes down to citizens of the vast Russian land from Moscow still has to be accepted without question. The characters from the great Russian literature of Pushkin, Gogol, Dostoevsky, and Tolstoy struggled in the energy field of this complex of the holy authority residing in Moscow. There were, of course, exceptions to living within the acceptance of this cultural complex: Mikhail Bulgakov and Taras Shevchenko come to mind in their open opposition to the holy authority residing in Moscow.

Ecology and Economy

Elena Volodina writes in Chapter 4 of this volume about the mysterious Russian soul and its traces in history. She points to the magnificent literature of nineteenth-century Russia as a treasury of the various characters that have come to symbolize the Russian soul and its cultural complexes. But propaganda appeals to the simplistic thinking and powerful emotions of cultural complexes; it can exploit them in times of crisis. In fact, the very activation of cultural complexes in the collective psyche can be manipulated to provide a defensive, deflective smoke screen behind which other interests veil themselves.

During wartime, rarely we do find information about the real interests of the combatants and their leadership. *In fact, in times of war, truth is among the first victims, and the psychological attitude of preexisting cultural complexes becomes an important tool to be used to mobilize the collective psyche of nations and their allies.* Who is interested in activating and heating up such collective patterns of feeling, thinking, and acting out that can be used to energize large groups of people? Who needs to be motivated, and what are the unspoken goals in motivating them?

To answer such questions, inquiring about the change in current global economics is important. As Karl Marx said: "Das Sein bestimmt das Bewusstsein" (The social reality determines the consciousness). Today, our social reality is more and more about climate crisis and the existential pressure to change our sources and habits of fuel consumption. What does it take to reduce our need for fossil energy? And how can we reduce our need for fossil fuels when we are simultaneously experiencing a growing demand for energy to fuel our growing appetites? And who is going to feed China in the future? Fuel and food, oil and wheat seem to be essential elements in the growing rapprochement between Russia and China. China needs both, and Russia can provide ample oil from its own resources. Russia gives China oil and wheat (by the way, the Chinese eat more rice than wheat); China gives Russia a huge ally in building its axis against the United States and the West.

In this food/fuel hunger is a key to understanding the conflict on a *materialistic level*. Ukraine's farmers produce a large amount of the world's wheat. Ukraine is rich in fossil gas and oil, and that is a driving factor in the interests of the companies behind NATO on one side and Putin's circle and competitors on the other side. Many countries in today's desolate world ecology need the produce of Ukraine's agriculture. In the Donetsk region, there are also important layers of *rare earth minerals* that are needed for computers of every kind. Russian industry and its economy are in bad shape. After Gorbachev, very few investments have been made in Russia, and the selling of natural resources is now the basis of Putin's economy. In that arena, there is competition with US companies that have now managed to sell their own gas to Europe, much of which is produced via highly problematic *fracking technology* (out of slate containing sand) and delivered by ships overseas to liquefied natural gas (LNG) terminals. Regarding the rare minerals needed for digital technology, China is now Putin's business partner and has its own stake in the game. In times of ecological crisis, the use of fossil carbons is obsolete, and so Putin's exports will be more and more limited to countries that don't care about ecology. So Putin becomes a hostage of China. On the Western side, the climate crisis has become an argument for the West to stop the Nord Stream pipelines from Russia to Germany.

War as Raid

Historians have analyzed the war economy of Hitler's Third Reich, stating that the robbing and pillaging of Jewish property were essential to stabilize the insolvent German state in 1938.[4] They filled the state's cashboxes. The Holocaust would ensure that the robbed Jewish people would not return. This analysis neglects other dimensions of the murder of millions of Jews, but there is a parallel to the Ukraine war: Now, the finances of the Russian Federation are in a dire condition, mostly as a consequence of Yeltsin's liberal policies in favor of the oligarchs who robbed the Russian people as surely as the Nazis robbed the Jewish people. The state's (i.e., Putin's) income from the sale of fossil fuels is needed for the military industry and also to keep alive a minimum of the infrastructure required to sustain the vast country, from the Urals to Vladivostok. For these economic reasons, the war against Ukraine is a criminal raid. The official narrative of fighting "Nazis in Ukraine" is little more than a barefaced lie and camouflage. Triggered cultural complexes about the dreaded invasion of barbarians from the West help to keep the Russian people silent. Dmitry Kotenko's Chapter 7 about *transcorruption in which the West has been a shadowy colluder* reveals a mafia-style fusion of politics and economics.

Concerns about ecology do not play a role in Putin's Russia or in Putin's mind. In fact, the melting permafrost and the burning forests in Siberia are just the peak of a disaster, releasing unmeasurable quantities of carbon dioxide and methane. Putin nevertheless has chosen a way backward. Alexander Etkind[5] writes about Putin's rejection of climate change and any kind of modernization, and how it has brought the state and the entire society into a kind of *archaization*—a reactionary restoration of patriarchal, authoritarian, and Orthodox religious mentality and behavior.[6] Oleg Orlov has openly named Russia a totalitarian state and, for uttering these words, he has received a two-and-a-half-year prison sentence. In the big cities, this backward movement is not so obvious, but, in the vast rural territories, life seems to stand still.

Whereas in Europe churches are empty, in the Russian Federation (and also Ukraine), thousands of churches have been built over the past twenty years, and two hundred others are planned just for Moscow. All of them follow the same architectural pattern, a cross with a dome at its center. Inside, you find the *iconostasis*, the wall of ikons separating the nave from the sanctuary, and the usually closed room for the celebrating priest. The boom in erecting churches goes hand in hand with a transformation of the economy toward a *war economy*.

Another activated complex seems to be violence in general and the rising occurrence of chronic trauma in Russian society. Whereas, in Ukraine, a kind of a culture for memory and remembering has begun and is encouraged, the memory of the shadow side of Russian history not only is hidden but is, in fact, officially forbidden. You risk being sentenced for years if you say something critical about the Russian state. This produces a kind of schizophrenic mentality. The ever-present secret (or not secret) police, the frequent use of torture, the labor camps, and the arbitrary resettlements and evacuations have created an atmosphere of permanent insecurity, depression (alcoholism), and brutality.[7] A Ukrainian colleague told me: "In the good old days they caught you and you had a trial, but now they come in the night and shoot you secretly in the forest." The rate of brutality against women is very high.[8] The disillusioned conclusion of some Russian observers is that "from the people there will be no open protest." The saying is *One country, one President.* There are exceptions, but, according to the latest studies, more than 70 percent of Russians are in favor of Putin's war in Ukraine.

The split in the cultural complex, on the other side, enforces, as Russian friends told me, just the opposite attitude in private life: a cynical disinterest in what the government does outside of the Russian Federation. The cult of violence in the media is associated with a brutalization and criminalization of language, which is seen in the official media and official statements and with Putin himself. He is notorious for his primitive and pornographic style. Vice President Medvedev's vocabulary is even worse.

So what drives Putin, and what drives the West? Obviously, there are different models or patterns of thinking. Following the former imperialistic model of the Western capitalist states, today we have a global system of interconnectedness and exploitation of subordinate countries, under the hegemony of the United States. Zbigniew Brzezinski, the counselor of many US presidents, presented in 1997 his outlook on *The Grand Chessboard: American Primacy and Its Geopolitical Imperatives.*[9] The enlargement of NATO will push Russia back eastward into a non-European, (pseudo-)traditional mentality—exactly what Putin's re-archaization seems to show. "Russian heritage" will compensate for the loss of imperial power. The result is what Kotenko calls "transcorruption."

On the Russian side, Putin leads the country into a kind of medieval imperialism. His heroes are Tsar Peter the Great and Stalin—the complement of Hitler. The nuclear bomb is the joker in his dangerous game. The Western powers behave in a complementary manner. Militarization of society goes on as well, and, in the West also, old cultural complexes are reactivated. Putin is seen as a reincarnation of the monster of the ugly and brutal Russian as imagined in the Cold War—a narrative from Nazi times but also a memory of the rapes carried out by Russian soldiers in 1945 Germany. It looks as though, both in Russia and in the West, we are on a one-way dead-end street. It is in the logic of complementary cultural complexes: Russia, losing its European orientation, is driving eastward. Europe will miss it.

The Slavic Symbol of the Onion Bulb

Archetypes are neither good nor bad. They are potential unconscious patterns for reaction and for interpreting the world. But some are especially constellated in particular surroundings and times. One of those quite particular but rarely mentioned surroundings is local climate. Today, we learn more about its influence on our lives, our moods, our conscious and unconscious strategies. Climate change has already had a deep impact on our minds and it will demand many more changes and adaptations in our behavior than in the past.

There are traumatized cultures that have always had to struggle against difficult climatic conditions. In the north of Russia, for example, the climate is much harsher than in the south. The long, very cold winter and the short, but hot summer shape the cultural attitudes of the people in quite different ways than the mild temperate climate in Western Europe and the south. The Mediterranean climate in Odessa or on the Crimea peninsula differs substantially from the demanding struggle to survive in the north and makes the Black Sea a kind of positive dreamland. It is as if the archetype of the good, nourishing mother is more easily experienced in the south.

There is a widespread symbol of the survival of nature in cold environments: the *bulb of an onion*. It is a very old, pre-Christian symbol that dates back to ancient Asian caves and Byzantine churches. It became a typical element of Eastern Orthodox Christian architecture, in Ukraine as well as in Russia. The onion is also essential in the Slavic kitchen. It has magic powers, for example, as the bulb of garlic (*Allium sativum*). On top of religious buildings, everywhere, golden onions raise their shining shapes to the sky. The golden domes connect Earth with Heaven, symbolizing the divine promise to support life on Earth in harsh times, and also the hope and faith of the people. The onion (*Allium cepa*) contains and stores vitamins

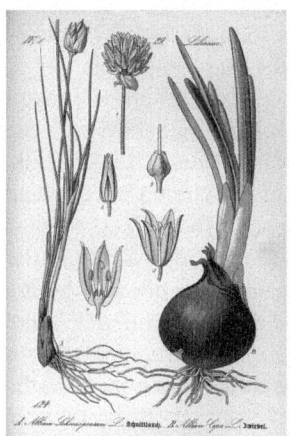

Figure 11.1 The Onion (*Allium cepa*) and St. Sophia's Cathedral, Kyiv, Ukraine (Onion: from Professor Dr. Otto Wilhelm Thomé, *Flora von Deutschland, Österreich und der Schweiz* [Gera, Germany, 1885]; Cathedral: Photo by Rbrechko, CC BY-SA 4.0 DEED)

and carbohydrates; the plant survives the winter under the frozen earth. In spring, a shoot comes out of the maternal bulb and builds a new plant.

Seen symbolically, the onion is something like the *Self*—the trunk equals the *ego-Self relationship* (in Neumann's term, the *ego-Self axis)*, and the flower the *ego*. Keeping this symbol in mind helps me a little to contemplate our current catastrophe. The Russian Orthodox Church and its representatives are quite reactionary and support Putin's deconstruction of Russia, leading it back to antidemocratic and quasi-medieval conditions, but the old Slavic symbol of the onion bulb reminds us that, one day, the winter will be over.

War, Manipulation, and Collective Schizophrenia

The crimes and cruelties committed by Putin's soldiers are beyond imagination. They have predecessors in the Second Chechen War, in Georgia, in Azerbaijan, and, over the last century, all over the socialist empire (Dmytro Zaleskyi lists Ukraine's history of suffering in Chapter 6). Millions of refugees carry the burden of generations of trauma and uprooting. Svetlana Alexievich and others have collected the mental marks and traces of a still-ongoing pandemonium in interviews. Even in comparison with Vietnam in the 1970s or the Iraq War in 2003, the dreadful war crimes of the Russian army and its associated warlord troops are comparable only with the sadism and cold-blooded acts of Nazi Germany in World War II in Poland, the Baltic states, Ukraine, and Russia.

I have already named the collective anesthesia and amnesia in Russia and the mix of manipulation by the media and the prescribed silence that dictates Russian public and private responses to the war in Ukraine. They are essential for Putin's power. The question remains how this extreme state of madness could develop in a once respected, civilized European country on its way to modernity. The parallel I see is in the German psychosis in Nazi times. But the Russian population, in general, doesn't seem to be fanatical in supporting Putin's war. There is a sense of a deep, ongoing depression and a lethargy that may well be connected with the disillusionment regarding the hopes for bettering their lives after Stalin's death, after the thaw under Khrushchev, after perestroika, and after extreme poverty and the establishment of the predatory oligarchy under Yeltsin. Maybe the people gave up. Many excellent artists and writers left the country. This looks a bit similar to the decline of the late GDR or East Germany in its last two decades before 1989. The former enthusiasm gave way to cynicism, and the heroic official *Homo Sovieticus* became, as Alexijewitsch calls it, a "beaten man" who struggles only for his individual survival. Natalia Pavlikova gives evidence of the loss of faith in the collectivist ideal of the failed Soviet Union in Chapter 9.

There are also, as ever, extreme ultranationalist groups supporting Putin's war, but I hope they are not representative of the deeper mentality of most in the Russian Federation. Besides a generational conflict, we see the state's massive and monopolist indoctrination. I find it extremely difficult to view the photos of tortured people and totally destroyed cities in the Donbas region or the flood disaster on the River Dnieper following the destruction of the Kakhovka Dam and, in the same time frame, to see the businesslike behavior of the Russian president and his foreign minister on TV, or to hear the fanatic, bottomless curses of his followers such as Medvedev, Prigozhin, and Kadyrov. It looks like a schizophrenic illness has overtaken an entire civilized nation. All this reminds me of the darkest times in German history.

So my own cultural complex regarding Russia is activated, too. I always regarded Russian culture as an important part of my European world. Growing up in western Germany I visited Moscow and Leningrad in 1967, the height of the Cold War, when I was seventeen. I was curious to see what was going on in the other side of the world. I even learned a bit of Russian language to read Pushkin and Mayakovsky. I loved the socialist idea that a world without wars and famine could be possible. I saw the abandoned churches in Moscow and also hoped that one day the old, bleached frescoes and ikons there would be restored.

When I studied Slavistics at the Free University Berlin one semester, I read about Stalin's crimes and the gulag system and realized that a real socialism would never be possible without democracy and human rights. This New Ethic—which, following Erich Neumann, requires the willingness to look at your individual and cultural shadow aspects—stimulated my engagement in the 68ers student movement we had in West Germany. On the eastern side of the Berlin Wall (erected in 1961) was the strange world of the totalitarian state with its ideology for a better world. The split in the collective mentality can also be seen in the unified Germany of today. Among people from the former East Germany (the socialist GDR), we often find a basic sympathy for Russia, the "Big Brother," an understanding of its fear of being attacked by the West, and only minor disappointment or indifference about the Russian aggression against Ukraine. I suppose that there are still remnants of the brainwashing system of the so-called socialist state. In the former West Germany, people are more critical and upset about Putin's war. Most official media follow the line of military support for Ukraine and defending democracy with arms at the borders. This has caused the basic convictions and assumptions of the peace movement to come into question. The slogan "No war again" is now interpreted as support for Putin's aggression. And to talk about the dangers of NATO's expansion and the gigantic profits of the industrial-military-digital complex is now taboo.

Somehow, we all seem to be infected by polarizing moods at the same time. In some ways, we are just as paralyzed as the people under Putin's regime. I often feel confused, as if I am being trapped by controversial statements about reality, without hope in the face of general ecological disaster. This is also because of the manipulative bubble of information from which we get our information and opinions, which makes collective cultural complexes so dangerous. Every animal, including the human animal, goes crazy when caught in a trap without hope for an exit.

War as a Reality

The expansion of NATO provided the actual field for violence, and Putin brought the war to Ukraine. Russia will not be the same for a long time. The mysterious Russian soul (Volodina in Chapter 4) has lost its magic, possibly forever, as has the beautiful Russian revival after perestroika.[10] In our Jungian discussions in Germany in the 1970s, we had long talks about the archetypal dimensions of war and the need for pacifism. Hans Dieckmann, Horst-Eberhard Richter, and Jan Galtung[11] were pioneers in these discussions during the time of the Cold War, the Cuban missile crisis, and the My Lai massacre in Vietnam. We talked about changing *Feindbilder* (images of the enemy) and the dehumanization and de-individualization of the "enemy" as well of people wearing a uniform. Germany did not participate in the Iraq War for good reasons: The German slogan was "Nie wieder Krieg"— Never Again War. Gandhi was the hero of nonviolent resistance. Today, Eugen Drewermann[12] and David Steindl-Rast[13] represent a radical, Christian-based pacifism. The conclusion they reach is that, in times of ecological collapse, any war is obsolete. The reality of the Russian aggression and its archaic brutality reminds us, nevertheless, that we didn't learn the lessons of the two world wars.

Maybe a conclusion might be: To defend our world and democracy with arms seems to be necessary, unfortunately, but it will be not sufficient. War is never a solution. Mutual anxiety and threats lead to spirals of defense mechanisms, hatred, and violence. We have to listen to the other, to try to feel with him, to share his concerns and problems, to try to understand what is going on in the collective unconscious—and to unveil dangerous and criminal strategies behind the triggering of collective projections. Unleashed cultural complexes are dangerous. It is absolutely necessary not to lose an inner balance, an inner gyroscope, and to care for the relationship between ego and Self at the individual and collective level. So I return to the symbol of the onion bulb in the Slavic tradition. Don't give up hope and don't forget gratefulness for our life, even during the long winter of our soul's journeys.

I am deeply grateful to all who contributed to this volume, even in dangerous circumstances. I hope to see you all after the end of this war.

Notes

1 Wikipedia, s.v. "Common European Home," last updated August 11, 2023, 23:41 UTC, https://en.wikipedia.org/wiki/Common_European_Home. The most famous use of the term *Common European Home*, arose when Gorbachev presented his concept of "our common European home" or the "all-European house" during a visit to Czechoslovakia in April 1987. In his main address in Prague he declared: "We assign an overriding significance to the European course of our foreign policy. . . . We are resolutely against the division of the continent into military blocs facing each other, against the accumulation of military arsenals in Europe, against everything that is the source of the threat of war. In the spirit of the new thinking we introduced the idea of the 'all-European house' . . . [which] signifies, above all, the acknowledgment of a certain integral whole, although the states in question belong to different social systems and are members of opposing

military-political blocs standing against each other. This term includes both current problems and real possibilities for their solution."

2 Alfred, Lord Tennyson, "The Kraken," https://poets.org/poem/kraken

3 Some say that Ukraine is mentally divided into Western- and Russian-oriented parts. The integrity of the Ukraine state means to hold these parts together.

4 For example, see Götz Aly, *Hitlers Volksstaat. Raub, Rassenkrieg und Nationaler Sozialismus* [Hitler's beneficiaries: Plunder, racial war, and the Nazi welfare state] (Frankfurt am Main: S. Fischer, 2005).

5 Alexander Etkind, *Russia against Modernity* (Cambridge, UK: Polity, 2023).

6 This re-archaization is what Brzezinski had in mind when he wrote that Putin's state, when losing its European orientation, will move mentally eastward. Zbigniew Brzezinski, *The Grand Chessboard: American Primacy and Its Geopolitical Imperatives* (New York: Basic Books, 1997). See also Natalia Pavlikova's essay (Chapter 9) in this book.

7 See Tina Gershäuser, Boris Schumatzki, and Vladimir Esipov (2023), "Interviews in *Russia under Putin—Woher kommt die Gewalt?" Deutsche Welle*, April 4, 2023; Svetlana Alexijewitsch, *Secondhand-Zeit* [Second-hand time] (Berlin: Hanser Berlin, 2013).

8 Gershäuser, Schumatzki, and Esipov, "Interviews in *Russia under Putin.*"

9 Zbigniew Brzezinski, *The Grand Chessboard.*

10 Christiane Bauermeister, *Der Gute Russentisch* (Berlin: Transit Verlag, 2021). Bauermeister provides an excellent panorama of the free development of arts and literature after perestroika, until Putin's coming to power.

11 Hans Dieckmann was a Jungian analyst in Berlin and president of the IAAP (International Association of Analytic Psychology) from 1985 to 1988; see Hans Dieckmann, "Gedanken über den Begriff des Feindbildes," in *Weltzerstörung, Selbstzerstörung* (World destruction—self-destruction), eds. Hans Dieckmann and Ann Springer (Berlin: Walter, 1988), pp. 127–141. Horst-Eberhard Richter was Dieckmann's complementary Freudian peace activist; see Horst-Eberhard Richter, *Zur Psychologie des Friedens* (Hamburg: Rowohlt, 1984). Jan Galtung was a pioneer in peace and reconciliation studies; see Johan Galtung, *Strukturelle Gewalt. Beiträge zur Friedens- und Konfliktforschung* (Hamburg: Rowohlt, 1982).

12 Eugen Drewermann, *Reden gegen den Krieg* (Düsseldorf: Patmos, 2002).

13 Eugen Drewermann is a radical Christianity-based pacifist. Brother David Steindl-Rast is a Benedictine monk and activist for interreligious dialogue. He is the founder of www.gratefulness.org. The C. G. Jung Association Berlin invited both for presentations. I am deeply grateful for their inspiration. See also David Steindl-Rast, *A Listening Heart. The Art of Contemplative Living* (New York: Crossroad, 1983).

Index

active witnesses (readers as) xx
alchemical nigredo 114, 133
Alexievich, Svetlana 55–56, 61, 184
Anna Karenina complex 66, 69
ARAS 172
archetypal defenses of the group spirit in Russia and Ukraine (collage): first axis (spirit and archetypal defenses intersect) 156–164; second axis (different levels of the psyche embodied) 163–170; third axis (mythopoetic imagination) 170–175; Axes of Destruction in 154–156; overview 151–154, *152*
archetypes: core 14, 17–18; and cultural complexes 2–6; demonic/daimonic 171–175; Great Father 110, 139–141; Great Mother 108–110, 138–141; hero 99; Mother 108–110; triggering of 1–2, 151
Arne, T. 81
autonomy: of cultural complexes 4; as "island mind" value 18–19
"axis of evil" 154

"babushka with the flag" 101–102, *101*, *102*
Babyn Yar 177
Baker, J. 48–49
Bandera, S. 86
Beachy Head *15*, *32*
Beauvois, D. 82, 84
Beebe, J. 170–172
Bellos, Linda 31
Berdyaev, N. 107
Berehynia 158
Berkenbusch, I. 38–39
Berlin Wall (fall of) 1
Bion, W. 77–78, 81, 103

Black Square 113, 114
Blake, William 24
Bodrow, S. W. 47
Bolshevik occupation of Ukraine *168*
Borodyanka locker *102*, 103
boundlessness complex 107–110, 115, 116
Brexit: arguments deployed against Europe 79; events of 78–79; "global Britain" narrative 81; impacts of 78; as "over-withdrawing" compensation 33; populist grievances and 80–81; related to profound narcissistic wound 74–75; voting patterns 81
"Brexit Way, The" *80*
Britain: economic changes 78; Eurosceptic voices in 79; hereditary class in 28; history and myth relationship 24–26; immigration from former Warsaw Pact states 79–80; invasions of 16; "kingdoms" in 24–26; membership of the European Economic Community (EEC) 79; mythic image of an island 15–18; new creation myth as symbol 31–34; post-war narrative 29–31; relationship with Ukraine 82; selective remembering of history 26–29
British, The (TV program) 30
Britons as an island race 16–20
Brodsky, J. 63
Brooke, Rupert 24
Brzezinski, Z. 182
burial sites, destruction of ancient 143–144
Burns, Robert 24, 25

Cameron, D. 80
Campbell, J. 22, 120, 121
Canada Memorial 33–34, *34*

WORTHY